Math Everywhere
ONTARIO EDITION

(4)

SENIOR MATH EVERYWHERE AUTHORS
Peter Rasokas, Barry Scully, Jan Scully, Bryan Szumlas

MATH EVERYWHERE K–8 AUTHOR TEAM

Brendene Barkley	Linda Miller
Luisa Busato	Emma Mills Mumford
Geoff Cainen	Carla Pieterson
Tara Cook	Pamela Quigg
Garey Edgar	Maureen Rousseau
Donna Green	Robert Stoddart
Liz Holder	Lori Wiens
James King	Barbara E. Worth

CONSULTANTS

ASSESSMENT CONSULTANTS Kelly Lantink, Kevin Akins
EDITORIAL CONSULTANT Mary Jean Tyczynski
MATHEMATICS DEVELOPMENT CONSULTANTS Mary Ellen Diamond, Kathleen Nolan
MATHEMATICS LITERACY CONSULTANT Cathy Marks Krpan
TECHNOLOGY CONSULTANTS Marilyn Legault, Doug McKnight

Elementary Education Advisory Board

CURRICULUM ADVISOR Les Asselstine
LITERACY ADVISOR David Booth
STAFF DEVELOPMENT ADVISOR Rod Peturson

Harcourt Canada

Orlando Austin New York San Diego Toronto London

National Library of Canada Cataloguing in Publication Data
Main entry under title:
    Math everywhere 4
ISBN 0-7747-1538-3
    1. Mathematics. I. Rasokas, Peter, 1949–

QA107.M34498 2002   510   C2002-901042-X

Editorial Project Manager: Ian Nussbaum
Developmental Editors: Sasha Patton, Joanne Close, Carol J. Fordyce, Erynn Prousky
Production Editor: Amelia Eng
Production Coordinator: Cheri Westra
Production Assistant: Agnes Mlynarz
Permissions Editor and Photo Research: Karen Becker
Art Direction and Design: Sonya V. Thursby/Opus House Incorporated
Composition: Sonya V. Thursby/Opus House Incorporated, Susan Purtell
Printing and Binding: Friesens
Cover Image: Alcazar Castle, Spain © Garry Adams/Maxx Images
    Alcazar Castle in Segovia, Spain was built in the eleventh century.

∞ Printed in Canada on acid-free paper.
1 2 3 4 5   07 06 05 04 03

Welcome to *Math Everywhere!*

Did you know math is all around you? Math is in your classroom, it's in your home, and it's in your city or town.

Math has also been used throughout history and can be used to plan the future.

At the beginning of this year, in **Start-Up Math**, you will review what you already know about math and prepare for the school year.

In **Unit 1, Math Across Canada**, you will learn about numbers, patterns, shapes, and measurement as you travel across our country.

In **Unit 2, Medieval Math**, you will learn about shapes and measurement, and about numbers and patterns as you travel back in time to visit medieval castles and feasts.

In **Unit 3, Math in Our Dynamic World**, you will learn about numbers, data, patterns, and measurement as they relate to the animal kingdom.

At the end of the year, in **Celebrating Math**, use what you have learned about math this year to plan a sports event.

At the end of each chapter, you will review what you have learned and show your understanding of math by doing a wrap-up activity.

You will play games, solve riddles, and solve problems while learning all about math!

You will see yellow shapes in some parts of the book:
- tells you that you will be solving a problem.
- lets you know that your answers will show what you understand about math.
- shows questions that will let you apply what you know about math.
- tells you that you will communicate what you know about math.

We hope you enjoy using this book and that you have fun learning that math **is** everywhere.

Contents

Chapter 2
Math in Western Canada   65

This chapter focuses on *Number Sense and
Numeration*. This chapter also touches upon
Patterning and Algebra, *Geometry and Spatial Sense*,
Measurement, and *Data Management and Probability*.

Chapter 3
Math Across the North

This chapter focuses on *Number Sense and Numeration* and *Patterning and Algebra*. This chapter also touches upon *Measurement* and *Data Management and Probability*.

Unit Two

Medieval Math

Chapter 6
Math for a Medieval Festival   228

This chapter focuses on *Measurement*.
This chapter also touches upon *Number Sense
and Numeration*, *Patterning and Algebra*,
and *Data Management and Probability*.

Unit Three

Math in Our Dynamic World

Chapter 7
Plant and Animal Math   269

This chapter focuses on *Number Sense and
Numeration* and *Data Management and Probability*.
This chapter also touches upon *Patterning and Algebra*,
Geometry and Spatial Sense, and *Measurement*.

Chapter 8
Habitat Math 311

This chapter focuses on *Number Sense and Numeration* and *Data Management and Probability*. This chapter also touches upon *Measurement*.

Chapter 9
Measuring People's Impact 354

This chapter focuses on *Data Management and Probability*. This chapter also touches upon *Measurement*.

Celebrating Math

Celebrating Math lets you know what you have learned about math while celebrating the end of the year.

Start-Up Math

Welcome to *Math Everywhere*! Today you are starting a new year of learning. Starting something new can be exciting. During the next few days you will use what you already know to complete several mathematics lessons. The Start-Up lessons are designed to prepare you for the lessons and the math concepts in *Math Everywhere 4*. Before you start the year, read the problem on the chalkboard in this picture. With a partner, come up with as many questions as you can. Share your questions with the class. Have fun!

Lesson 1

My Thoughts About Math

Get Started

"Get Started" gives you a few quick activities to prepare you for the math lesson.

1. What do you think of when you think of math? In your journal, write down all the ideas, pictures, and words that come to mind.

2. In a group or as a class, brainstorm as many math words as you can.

Build Your Understanding

Reflect on Math

The title gives you a clue about what you will be learning.

In your journal, respond to the following questions:

1. What is math?

2. Where is math used?

3. How do you use math in your everyday life?

4. What do you hope to learn in math this year?

5. Set a math goal by completing the following sentence:
   By the end of ____ (month) I will be able to ____ because ____ .

What Did You Learn?

The "What Did You Learn?" sections are designed for you to think about what you have learned in the lesson.

1. Share your journal thoughts with a classmate.

2. Record in your journal how your thoughts about math compared to the thoughts of your classmate.

Practice

The "Practice" section includes many different types of activities that you can do to practise or review what you have learned, or to challenge yourself further.

1. Make a title page for mathematics. Your title page can show what you know about mathematics.

2. Use your journal thoughts to write a song or poem about mathematics.

3. Design a math cartoon.

DENNIS THE MENACE

"MAKE UP YOUR MIND. FIRST YOU TELL ME 3 PLUS 3 IS SIX, AND NOW YOU SAY 4 PLUS 2 IS SIX!"

4. Create a game that requires math skills.

5. Write a math problem for another classmate to solve.

6. a) Below is a list with dollar values for each letter of the alphabet. Work in a group. Calculate the dollar value of each person's name in your group.

   A = $0.01   B = $0.02   C = $0.03
   D = $0.04   E = $0.05   F = $0.06
   G = $0.07   H = $0.08   I = $0.09
   J = $0.10   K = $0.11   L = $0.12
   M = $0.13   N = $0.14   O = $0.15
   P = $0.16   Q = $0.17   R = $0.18
   S = $0.19   T = $0.20   U = $0.21
   V = $0.22   W = $0.23   X = $0.24
   Y = $0.25   Z = $0.26

   b) Arrange the dollar amounts that your group created from the least to the greatest.

7. a) What is the most expensive word you can make using the list above?
   b) What is the least expensive word you can make?
   c) Share your words with a partner.

Extension

8. Using the pattern above, make a list of words that equals $1.00.

Looking at Numbers

Get Started

You Will Need
• old magazines and newspapers
• construction paper

1. Where are numbers found? Find numbers in magazines and newspapers. Cut and paste them onto a piece of construction paper to make a number collage.

2. Find something in the classroom that you can hold in your hand. In your notebook, write down everything about the object that is related to math, for example, size and shape.

Build Your Understanding

Find and Construct Numbers

Imagine that a group of classmates put together the following list about numbers:

Numbers can be odd like 1, 13, and 127.

Numbers can be even like 8, 58, and 274.

Numbers can be found in stories like 101 Dalmatians.

Numbers are used to tell the temperature like 24°C.

Numbers are found on calculators, telephones, and computers.

Numbers are not letters.

1. What is an even number? What is an odd number? Where do you see these numbers around you? What other stories have you read that have numbers?

2. You Will Need
   • base-ten blocks
   a) Use base-ten blocks to show each of the numbers found in the list above.

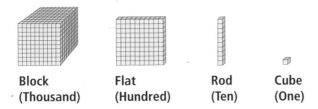

Block
(Thousand)

Flat
(Hundred)

Rod
(Ten)

Cube
(One)

b) Draw a place-value chart in your notebook like the one below and record the numbers that you make. An example has been done for you.

Number	Thousands (Block)	Hundreds (Flat)	Tens (Rod)	Ones (Cube)
304		3	0	4

c) Can you represent the number 304 in a different way than how it is shown in the place-value chart? Share your answer with a partner.

What Did You Learn?

1. With a classmate, make up your own list about numbers and post it in your classroom.

2. Use the base-ten blocks to make numbers for a classmate to calculate.

Practice

1. In your notebook, rewrite the list about numbers from this lesson's activity, but use words instead of the numbers (for example, use "one" instead of "1").

2. On a blank place-value chart show numbers by drawing pictures of the cubes (ones), rods (tens), flats (hundreds), and blocks (thousands) in each column, instead of recording the numerals.

Lesson 3

Solving Number Problems

Get Started

Complete an addition calculation grid. Describe any patterns that you see.

+	1	2	3	4	5	6	7	8	9
1									
2		4							
3						9			
4									
5									
6				10					
7									
8									
9									

Build Your Understanding

Calculate and Problem Solve

1. Use your knowledge of addition, subtraction, multiplication, division, and problem solving to answer the following questions. Show your work in pictures, numbers, and words.

   a) It snowed 18 cm on Monday. On Tuesday it snowed 5 cm more than on Monday. How much snow fell on Tuesday? How much snow fell over the two days?

   b) On Wednesday, it snowed half as much as it did on Monday. How much snow fell over the three-day period?

> **Vocabulary**
>
> **centimetre:** (cm) A unit of length
>   100 cm = 1 m
> **dozen:** A group of 12

2. Klaus wrote in his math book
343 – 212 = ■.
What is the correct answer? Explain how you came to this result. Here is another question:
781 – 403 = ■. Show your work.

3. Draw a picture to show how two dozen dimes could be shared equally among four people. Make a math sentence or equation for this problem.

4. You Will Need
• blocks or counters

What does 4 x 2 mean? Use blocks or counters to help you. Write a word problem for this question.

Tip

To help you answer a question, consider making a chart of the information you know.

What Did You Learn?

1. Record and then explain to a classmate the steps you use to solve math problems.

2. With your classmates, make a poster showing problem-solving approaches.

3. Make a list of the problem-solving strategies you use or know.

Practice

1. Make up several math problems that each have the answer 12. Try to have at least one problem that requires addition, one that requires subtraction, one that requires multiplication, and one that requires division. Try to make problems that you think will be different from the ones that other students might create.

2. Make up a number pattern that involves either addition or subtraction. Explain your pattern.
For example, 3, 6, 9, 12, 15, ■.

3. Look back in this lesson to the addition grid. Then design and complete your own multiplication grid.

Lesson 4

Measuring and Recording Length

Get Started

You Will Need
• metric ruler

1. Use a metric ruler to measure the lengths of three objects in your classroom. In your journal, record the names of the objects and their measurements.

2. What was the longest object you measured? What was the shortest object you measured?

Build Your Understanding

Make a Record

You Will Need
• paper clips
• metric ruler

1. **a)** Use a metric ruler and paper clips to produce a paper-clip chain that is approximately 10 cm long.

   b) Without measuring, make a list of objects that you think are about as long as your paper-clip chain. Use your chain to check if your estimations were correct.

   c) Rearrange your list of objects so they are in order from largest to smallest.

2. **a)** What size is your shoe? Remove your right shoe and measure the bottom of it with a ruler.

   b) What unit of measurement did you use? Why?

   c) Does the unit of measurement you chose match the size written on your shoe? Explain why or why not.

3. Survey either the boys or girls in your class and complete the tally chart below. An example has been done for you.

Shoe Size	Number of People
Example: Girls Size 3	⊞⊞ |||

Vocabulary

metre: (m) A unit of length
1 m = 100 cm
survey: A method of gathering information by asking questions and recording people's answers

4. What conclusions can you make by looking at your survey?

What Did You Learn?

1. How did your estimations compare to the actual measurements of your objects in Build Your Understanding question 1?

2. How do you decide what unit of measurement to use when measuring an object? Give examples to support your answer.

3. Explain to a classmate what you know about surveying.

Practice

1. Repeat Build Your Understanding question 1, this time using a metre stick and a paper-clip chain that is approximately 1 m long.

2. Design and construct your own survey to share with the class.
   a) What questions will you ask?
   b) What will the choices be?
   c) How will you record the information?

3. Make a list in your notebook of the strategies you used in Build Your Understanding to find out information and solve problems.

Problems to Solve

Here are some fun problems for you to solve. You will be given a helpful problem-solving strategy to use in each problem. Later in the year, when you learn about more strategies, you will get the chance to choose the strategies you want to use.

Problem 1

Organizing Numbers

STRATEGY: ACT IT OUT

Playing a role or acting out a problem helps you to see the problem so you can figure out a solution.

OBJECTIVE:

Demonstrate an understanding of arrays

Problem-Solving Steps

There are four steps you can follow to help you solve a math problem. You will be reminded of these steps throughout the year:

1. **Understand the problem:** Rewrite the problem in your own words. If you can, draw a picture of the problem. List or highlight important numbers or words.

2. **Pick a strategy:** For example, "Act It Out," "Draw a Picture," "Use Objects," and "Guess and Check."

3. **Solve the problem:** Use a strategy to solve the problem. Describe all steps using math words and/or symbols. Try a different strategy if you need to. Organize the results using a diagram, model, chart, table, or graph.

4. **Share and reflect:** Did the strategy you picked work? Would a different strategy also work? Does your solution make sense? Could there be more than one answer to the problem? How did other people in your class solve the problem?

Problem

Imagine that your classroom is divided into rows of desks. There is the same number of desks in each row. How would you assign students to desks? Where would the students in your class sit? Use the "Act It Out" strategy to help you.

Reflection

1. How many desks would there be in your classroom? How does this number compare to the number of students in your class?

2. What information is missing that would help you solve the problem?

3. Is there more than one answer to this problem? Explain.

4. Was the "Act It Out" strategy a good strategy to use for this problem? Explain.

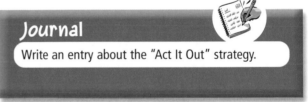

Journal

Write an entry about the "Act It Out" strategy.

Extension

Your school is holding an assembly in the gymnasium for 144 students. Some of the students have volunteered to help set up the chairs. If all rows have the same number of chairs, how might you set up the chairs? How many rows of chairs will you need, and how many chairs will be in each row? How many different ways could you set up the chairs? Show your work in pictures, numbers, and words.

Problem 2

Using Coordinate Systems

STRATEGY: DRAW A PICTURE OR DIAGRAM

You can draw simple pictures or diagrams to help you figure out the solution to a problem. With pictures or diagrams, you can see how the parts of the problem work together.

OBJECTIVE:

Demonstrate an understanding of coordinate systems

Problem

You Will Need
• ruler

Central Elementary School is located at the intersection of Fifth Street and Fourth Avenue. Each morning Grace walks three blocks north and four blocks east to get to school.

Tip

Problem-Solving Steps
1. Understand the problem   2. Pick a strategy
3. Solve the problem   4. Share and reflect

Where does Grace live? Use the "Draw a Picture or Diagram" strategy to help you solve this problem.

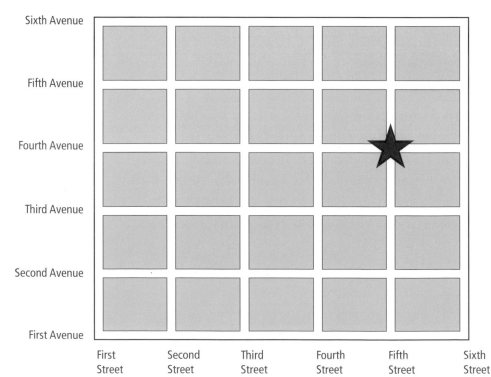

School

Reflection

1. What are you investigating?

2. What information did you need to know to solve this problem?

3. What additional information could help you solve this problem?

4. Was the "Draw a Picture or Diagram" strategy helpful in solving this problem? Explain.

5. How could you improve your picture?

Extension

1. Place a store and hospital on your map. Describe how a person would get from the school to the hospital and from the school to the store. Create more problems like these. Give them to a classmate to answer.

2. Describe how far away you live from your school?
   Use the "Draw a Picture or Diagram" strategy to help you solve this problem.

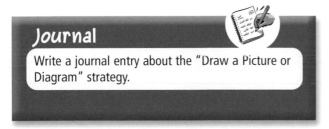

Journal

Write a journal entry about the "Draw a Picture or Diagram" strategy.

Problem 3

Working With Numbers

STRATEGY: USE OBJECTS

Using objects can help you organize information so you can see the solution. You can use simple objects, such as counters or play money.

OBJECTIVES:

Solve a problem involving whole numbers

Problem

You Will Need
• different coloured counters

Robin was getting party bags ready to give out to eight of her friends at her birthday party next week. She bought 32 stickers, 8 erasers, 24 pieces of candy, and 16 pencils. Each party bag will be the same. How many of each item will Robin put in each party bag? Use the "Use Objects" strategy to answer this problem. Show all of your work in pictures, numbers, and words.

Tip

Problem-Solving Steps
1. Understand the problem
2. Pick a strategy
3. Solve the problem
4. Share and reflect

Reflection

1. What information in the problem was very important? Why?

2. What objects helped you solve this problem? How?

3. Is the "Use Objects" strategy a good strategy to help solve this problem? Explain why or why not.

4. Is there a different strategy you could use to solve this problem? Explain.

Extension

1. List items that you might put in a party bag. Decide how many of each item will be in one bag. How many friends will be at your party? How many of each item will you need in order to make a party bag for every friend? Show your work in pictures, numbers, and words.

2. Make up a cost for every different item in the party bag you created. How much will one party bag cost? How much money will all the party bags cost in total? Share your answers with a classmate.

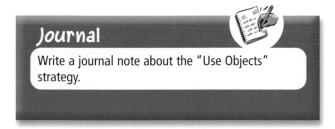

Journal

Write a journal note about the "Use Objects" strategy.

Problem 4

Estimating and Calculating Money Amounts

STRATEGY: GUESS AND CHECK

To use the "Guess and Check" strategy, you make guesses and then check to see if your answers are correct. You can use the "Guess and Check" strategy for large numbers or for many pieces of information. The "Guess and Check" strategy can lead you to other strategies.

OBJECTIVES:

Estimate and calculate money to $50.00

Problem

You Will Need
• play money

Carlo and Dana raised a total of $45.00 for the school fundraiser. Carlo raised two times more money than Dana. How much money did each student raise? Use the "Guess and Check" strategy to solve this problem. Show all of your work.

Tip

Problem-Solving Steps
1. Understand the problem
2. Pick a strategy
3. Solve the problem
4. Share and reflect

Reflection

1. Restate the problem in your own words.

2. How close was your first guess to the actual answer?

3. How many guesses did it take for you to arrive at the actual answer?

4. How did you change your guess each time to get closer to the actual answer?

5. Was the "Guess and Check" strategy helpful in solving this problem? Explain.

Extension

What other combinations of bills and coins could Carlo and Dana have brought to school?

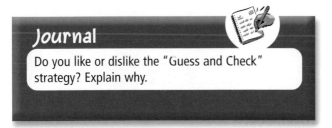

Journal

Do you like or dislike the "Guess and Check" strategy? Explain why.

Unit 1
Math Across Canada

Math is all around us. It is in the number of shapes and measurements of each building we enter and in many of the things we do and see. In Unit 1, you will travel across Canada, exploring math in different cities and places of interest.

In Chapter 1, you will explore numbers, distances, and shapes throughout Eastern and Central Canada. At the end of the chapter you will create a poster about what you learned on that part of the voyage.

In Chapter 2, you will be in Western Canada, measuring rivers, exploring shapes, and working with schedules from Manitoba to British Columbia. At the end of this chapter, you will design a game using the math skills you have learned.

In Chapter 3, you will explore Canada's vast North, encountering math at every turn. At the end of the chapter you will create a math travel brochure about the places you have visited using the math skills and concepts you have learned.

Bon voyage!

Math in Eastern Canada

The first part of your math journey takes you from Atlantic Canada to Ontario. During your travels you will

- count and record numbers
- build and measure towers
- add and subtract four-digit numbers
- multiply and divide by 3 and 4
- estimate and measure distances
- add and subtract money up to $10.00

At the end of this chapter, you will use the math skills you have learned to create a poster about your math journey.

Answer these questions to get you ready for your adventure:

1. Find where you live on this map. How far away do you live from Ottawa, the nation's capital?
2. How far do you live from St. John's, the first stop on the journey?
3. How can you figure out the distance?

Have fun!

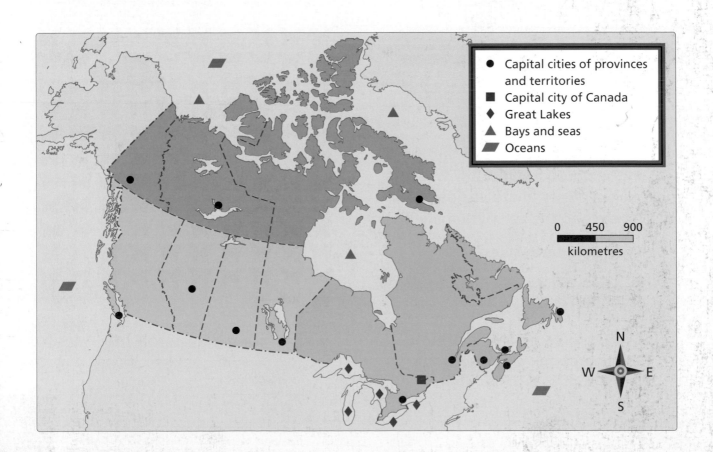

Lesson 1

Exploring Place Value to Hundreds

TRAVEL LOG

PLAN:
Your first math experience will be counting butterflies at the botanical garden in St. John's.

DESTINATION:
St. John's, Newfoundland and Labrador

DESCRIPTION:
- St. John's, Newfoundland and Labrador is the most eastern city in Canada.
- The Memorial University of Newfoundland Botanical Garden in St. John's has a beautiful cottage garden with a number of plants that attract butterflies.

Memorial University of Newfoundland Botanical Garden, St. John's

Get Started

You Will Need
- base-ten blocks

1. Estimate the number of butterflies in the photograph. (How will you make your estimate as close as possible to the actual number?)

2. Count the butterflies.

3. Use base-ten blocks to illustrate the number of butterflies.

4. Copy this place-value chart into your notebook and record the number of butterflies on it:

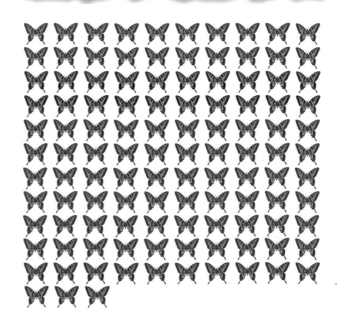

Number	Sketch of Base-Ten Blocks	Hundreds (flats)	Tens (rods)	Ones (cubes)

5. How many hundreds (flats) did you need, how many tens (rods), and how many ones (cubes)?

6. Use base-ten blocks to show the numbers for the three groups of butterflies shown on the right. Record and sketch the numbers on your place-value chart.

7. Read your numbers out loud with a classmate. Explain how you recorded the numbers on the chart.

8. Can you make the numbers in your place-value chart using different base-ten blocks? Share your results with a partner.

Number	Sketch of Base-Ten Blocks	Hundreds (flats)	Tens (rods)	Ones (cubes)
184				
285				
437				

Technology

You can use a paint/draw computer program to create a place-value chart. Use different symbols to show the ones, tens, and hundreds.

Build Your Understanding

Count and Record Numbers

You Will Need
- base-ten blocks to represent butterflies
- place-value chart

Imagine that you and your classmates are counting butterflies at the botanical garden in St. John's. Get into groups of three to four students.

1. Choose a number of hundreds, tens, and ones that make a number less than 1000. Put the blocks on the table. These blocks represent the butterflies that your group found.

2. Move from table to table estimating how many butterflies each group has. Record your guesses on a separate piece of paper.

3. Return to your table and record the number of base-ten blocks accurately on your place-value chart.

4. Take your chart and move from table to table counting the butterflies. Record the numbers on your group's chart.

5. Use base-ten blocks to make the numbers in your chart in different ways. Sketch the different ways on a separate piece of paper.

What Did You Learn?

1. How many butterflies did your group have in hundreds, tens, and ones? Explain how you counted the butterflies.

2. Explain what you did when a place value had more than nine blocks.

3. Who had the most butterflies? Who had the least? How do you know?

4. Explain how you overcame challenges while counting and recording numbers.

Practice

Write each of the following numbers in words. For example: 256 is two hundred fifty-six.

1. 685　　**2.** 847　　**3.** 390

Write the numeral for each:

4. four hundred fifty-one

5. eight hundred six

Write each of the following numbers in expanded form.
For example: 983 = 900 + 80 + 3

6. 139　　**7.** 230　　**8.** 458

9. 702　　**10.** 985

Sketch each of the following numbers using base-ten blocks.
For example: 613 is

11. 294　　**12.** 774　　**13.** 909

 Write each of the following numbers in standard form.
For example: 200 + 50 + 6 = 256
　　　　　　 800 + 1 = 801

14. 600 + 40 + 2 = ▪

15. 200 + 10 + 7 = ▪

16. 300 + 9 = ▪

17. 900 + 80 = ▪

18. 400 + 4 = ▪

Complete:

19. 584 = ▪ + 80 + 4

20. ▪ = 900 + 40 + 3

21. 208 = 200 + ▪

22. Explain what one thousand looks like. Use numbers, pictures, and words.

Lesson 2

Exploring Place Value to Thousands

TRAVEL LOG

PLAN:
You will make towers of blocks. Your towers will show large numbers in the thousands.

DESTINATION:
Halifax, Nova Scotia

DESCRIPTION:
• Years ago captains needed the light from lighthouse towers like this one to land their boats safely.
• These boats carried people, supplies, fish, and even treasures.

Peggy's Cove, Nova Scotia

Get Started

You Will Need
• base-ten blocks

The illustration shows 1627 in two ways. Is it easier to count the blocks in illustration A or B? Explain your answer to a classmate.

How is recording a number on the place-value chart like stacking blocks in a tower?

Number	Thousands (blocks)	Hundreds (flats)	Tens (rods)	Ones (cubes)
1627	1	6	2	7
1627				

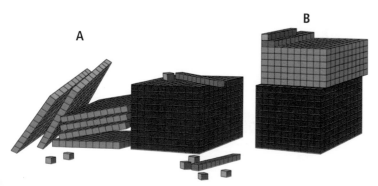

A

B

1. With one or two classmates, make a tower of base-ten blocks to show a number greater than 1000.

2. Ask another group of students to estimate how many blocks are in your tower.

3. Ask the group to count the base-ten blocks. How many thousands, hundreds, tens, and ones does your tower have?

4. Compare your tower to another group's tower. Which tower shows a larger number? How do you know?

5. Record the number of blocks in each tower on a place-value chart.

6. Do you think the height of a tower is related to the size of the number it shows? Share your answer with a classmate.

Build Your Understanding

Compare Numbers

You Will Need
• base-ten blocks
• place-value chart

Build the following towers with base-ten blocks. Record each number on a place-value chart, like the sample below:

Number	Thousands	Hundreds	Tens	Ones
967		9	6	7
1207				
1270				
720				
1072				

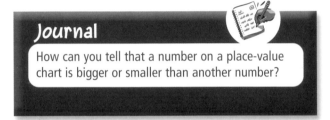

Journal

How can you tell that a number on a place-value chart is bigger or smaller than another number?

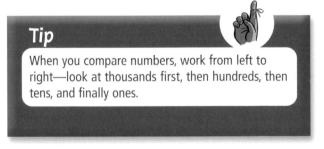

Tip

When you compare numbers, work from left to right—look at thousands first, then hundreds, then tens, and finally ones.

What Did You Learn?

1. How do you know your towers show the right numbers?

2. Which tower is the tallest?

3. Which tower is the shortest?

4. Can any of the towers be made with only tens? How do you know?

5. Can any of the towers be made with only hundreds? Why or why not?

6. a) Order the towers from smallest to largest based on the number they represent.

   b) How can you tell you have ordered the towers correctly?

Practice

Compare using < or >:

1. $1420.00 ▢ $1245.00

2. $19.00 ▢ $190.00

3. $503.00 ▢ $790.00

4. $2040.00 ▢ $2400.00

5. $1107.00 ▢ $1170.00

6. $1910.00 ▢ $990.00

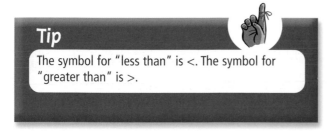

Tip

The symbol for "less than" is <. The symbol for "greater than" is >.

Record these numbers on a place-value chart:

7. 245

8. 1234

9. 648

10. 852

11. 1148

12. 750

Extension

13. Make a tower. How many different towers can you make with the same number value?

Math Problems to Solve

These students are comparing how much money they have raised in one year for a special class trip:

Use this chart to answer the following questions:

Student	Money Raised
Andrea	$503.00
Bart	$1420.00
Dana	$1245.00
Evan	$99.00
Ali	$190.00
Grace	$600.00
Henna	$19.00
Ian	$1800.00

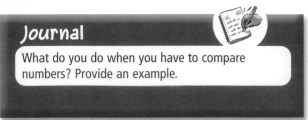

Journal

What do you do when you have to compare numbers? Provide an example.

14. What is the largest amount of money? smallest amount?

15. How many students can collect their money in $10.00 bills? How do you know?

16. How many students can collect their money in $100.00 bills? How do you know?

17. Which students have collected more than $1000.00?

18. Which students have collected less than $500.00?

19. Use $100.00, $20.00, $10.00, and $5.00 bills, and $2.00 and $1.00 coins to name

    a) two ways Evan could pay his money

    b) one way Grace could pay using only $20.00 bills and coins

    c) all the ways Henna could pay her money.

20. Record the students in order from the least to the greatest amount of money they raised. Explain how you decided on your order.

21. Record how many multiples of $10.00 can be found between the amounts of money raised by Dana and Bart.

22. Record how many multiples of $100.00 can be found between the amounts of money raised by Grace and Ian.

Lesson 3

Adding and Subtracting Whole Numbers

TRAVEL LOG

PLAN:
You will work with dates of buildings in Saint John and buildings around the world. You will add and subtract these numbers to calculate time intervals.

DESTINATION:
Saint John, New Brunswick

DESCRIPTION:
- Saint John is the oldest city in Canada. It became a city in 1783.
- In 1877, the Great Saint John Fire destroyed most of the city. Many buildings had to be rebuilt.

Loyalist House, Saint John, New Brunswick

Get Started

You Will Need
- place-value chart

Vocabulary

difference: The answer to a subtraction problem
sum: The answer to an addition problem

Workers built Loyalist House from 1817–1820. Today, many people visit it to see how people lived in the early nineteenth century.

1. a) Mentally calculate how long it took to build Loyalist House. With a partner, compare strategies you used to answer this question.

There are many ways we can do this:

1817 + ■ = 1820

or 17 + ■ = 20 (since 1817 and 1820 both start with 18)

or 1820 – 1817 = ■

or 20 – 17 = ■

b) When we add or subtract three-digit or four-digit numbers, it is like adding or subtracting two-digit numbers.

Add these sets of numbers. You may use counters or base-ten blocks:

$$\begin{array}{r} 25 \\ + 13 \\ \hline \end{array} \qquad \begin{array}{r} 48 \\ + 23 \\ \hline \end{array} \qquad \begin{array}{r} 97 \\ + 85 \\ \hline \end{array}$$

c) What did you do when the ones digits or the tens digits added up to a number greater than 9?

$$\begin{array}{r} 48 \\ + 23 \\ \hline \end{array}$$

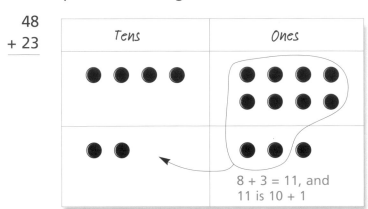

8 + 3 = 11, and
11 is 10 + 1

You do this regrouping when you add any column on a place-value chart.

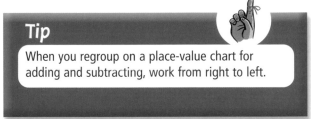

Tip

When you regroup on a place-value chart for adding and subtracting, work from right to left.

2. Estimate then add these numbers:

$$\begin{array}{r} 245 \\ + 476 \\ \hline \end{array} \qquad \begin{array}{r} 1798 \\ + 7432 \\ \hline \end{array}$$

3. Describe to a classmate what you did to add the numbers.

Some people add from the left. They regroup as they move to the right:	Other people add from the right. They regroup as they move to the left (like a place-value chart):	When you mentally calculate 683 + 739, you might think like this:
$$\begin{array}{r} 683 \\ + 739 \\ \hline 1300 \\ 110 \\ 12 \\ \hline 1422 \end{array}$$ This way is useful for mental calculations and estimations.	$$\begin{array}{r} {}^{1\,1} \\ 683 \\ + 739 \\ \hline 1422 \end{array}$$ Which way works best for you?	683 is close to 700 and 739 is also close to 700. 700 + 700 = 1400. 683 is 17 less than 700, but 739 is 39 more than 700. The difference between 39 and 17 is 22. The answer is 1400 + 22 = 1422. How would you do this question?

4. Estimate then subtract these pairs of numbers. You may use counters on a place-value chart.

$$
\begin{array}{r} 64 \\ -\ 25 \\ \hline \end{array}
\qquad
\begin{array}{r} 123 \\ -\ 67 \\ \hline \end{array}
$$

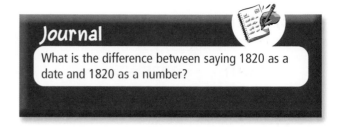

How do you regroup when you subtract 123?

$$
\begin{array}{r} \\ -\ 67 \\ \hline \end{array}
$$

One way to regroup is by using a place-value chart.

Each chart shows 123.
This chart shows 123: 1 hundred, 2 tens, and 3 ones.

Hundreds	Tens	Ones
●	● ●	● ● ●

You can't subtract 7 ones from 3 ones.

Hundreds	Tens	Ones
●	● ◯ Trade 1 of the tens for 10 ones.	● ● ● ● ● ● ● ● ● ● ● ● ●

You can subtract 7 ones from 13 ones. But you can't subtract 6 tens from 1 ten. Use your place-value chart to regroup again.

Hundreds	Tens	Ones
◯ Trade 1 hundred for 10 tens.	● ● ● ● ● ● ● ● ● ● ●	● ● ● ● ● ● ● ● ● ● ● ● ●

Now you are ready to subtract 6 tens and 7 ones. 0 hundreds, 11 tens, and 13 ones is another way to write 123.

5. a) Subtract these pairs of numbers.

```
  701        2425
- 484      - 1639
```

b) Describe to a classmate what you did to subtract the numbers.

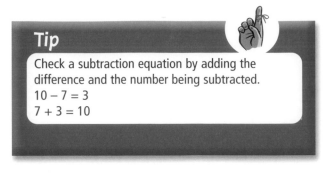

Tip

Check a subtraction equation by adding the difference and the number being subtracted.
$10 - 7 = 3$
$7 + 3 = 10$

Build Your Understanding

Add and Subtract

You Will Need
- base-ten blocks
- place-value chart

Vocabulary

decade: 10 years
century: 100 years
The year 1967 is in the twentieth century.
millennium: 1000 years

Many buildings in Europe and Asia are older than buildings in Saint John. Use the chart on page 31 to find out the difference in their ages. Use base-ten blocks or a place-value chart to help you.

1. What is the difference in age between:
   a) Loyalist House and the Colosseum?
   b) the Taj Mahal and Chambord?

2. Put the buildings in order from oldest to newest. How do you know your order is correct?

3. Which two buildings were constructed 752 years apart?

4. Which buildings were built in the second millennium? the first millennium?

5. Which building was built in the sixteenth century? How do you know?

6. How many decades passed between the times Chambord and the Taj Mahal were built?

7. Find two dates that total 2695.

Name of Place, City, Country
Date Constructed (A.D.)

| Loyalist House, Saint John, Canada 1817 | Taj Mahal, Agra, India 1630 | Westminster Abbey, London, England 1065 | Chambord, Loire Region, France 1519 | Colosseum, Rome, Italy 72 |

What Did You Learn?

1. How did you subtract the dates of the buildings?

2. Which calculation was the hardest? the easiest? Why?

3. What millennium are we in now?

Practice

Mentally add these numbers:

1. 41 + 30 = ▧   **2.** 68 + 32 = ▧

3. 15 + 28 = ▧   **4.** 34 + 66 = ▧

Explain what strategy you used.

| **5.** 430
+ 790 | **6.** 653
+ 849 | **7.** 2896
+ 1711 |
| **8.** 8932
+ 5908 | **9.** 1999
+ 999 | **10.** 5007
+ 9339 |

Check by subtracting one of the numbers being added from the sum. Show your work.

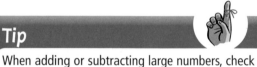

Tip

When adding or subtracting large numbers, check your calculations by estimating to the nearest 100. For subtraction equations you can also check your answers by adding the difference to the number you subtracted.

Subtract these numbers:

11. 578
－ 362

12. 725
－ 640

13. 1977
－ 1088

14. 5934
－ 460

15. 4203
－ 2376

16. 7000
－ 3021

Check by adding. Show your work.

Add or subtract. Show your calculations:

17. 638 + ▢ = 1420

18. ▢ + 478 = 2670

19. 4008 − ▢ = 3389

To what century do these dates belong?

20. 1688   **21.** 2001   **22.** 964

Extension

Estimate to the nearest 100 and add these numbers:

23. 450
+ 210

24. 782
+ 177

25. 246
+ 329

Estimate to the nearest 1000 and subtract these numbers:

26. 8460
－ 798

27. 6843
－ 5211

28. 4500
－ 3699

Show What You Know

Review: Lessons 1 to 3, Place Value

1. Explain what the number 1702 means using numbers, pictures, and words.

2. You have 1007 marbles and your friend has 1070 marbles. Your friend thinks that he has more marbles than you do. How can you explain who has more?

3. You have $63.00. Your friend says that it's about $70.00. Do you agree? Explain using numbers, pictures, and words.

4. Which numbers can you use to make each problem correct? You may only repeat a number once in each problem.

a) ▢▢6
+ ▢▢▢
    950

b) ▢2▢
+ ▢▢▢
    950

c) ▢▢▢
+ ▢▢▢
    950

d) ▢5▢
－ ▢▢
    950

e) ▢▢2
－ ▢▢
     96

f) ▢▢▢
－ ▢▢
     96

Lesson 4

Multiplying by 3

TRAVEL LOG

PLAN:
You will help students track the number of ice-cream scoops they eat by multiplying by 3.

DESTINATION:
Cavendish, Prince Edward Island

DESCRIPTION:
• People all over the world know this town—and the house called Green Gables—because Lucy Maud Montgomery used it as the setting for her book, Anne of Green Gables.

Green Gables House, Cavendish, Prince Edward Island

Get Started

Multiplication is a fast way to add groups of the same number of items.

For example:

2 hands (2 groups) of 5 fingers make 10 fingers.

5 + 5 = 10 = 2 x 5 = 10

or
5 rows of 2 stamps make 10 stamps.

2 + 2 + 2 + 2 + 2 = 10

 2

 + 2

 + 2

 + 2

 + 2

= 5 x 2 = 10

You Will Need
• a hundreds chart
• a yellow crayon

1. On a hundreds chart, colour the number 3 yellow. Count by three and colour the number you land on yellow. Continue counting by three and colouring every third number yellow.

2. What pattern do you see on the hundreds chart?

3. Try counting by 3 without looking at the hundreds chart. (Remember the patterns you noticed.)

Build Your Understanding

Multiply by 3

You Will Need
• counters

Our travellers have just visited Green Gables. They are treating themselves to three-scoop ice-cream cones.

Help them track how many scoops of ice cream they eat. Record and calculate your multiplication sentence for each question.

1. a) How many scoops of ice cream will be served after 3 students get their three-scoop ice-cream cones?

   b) after 4 students get their cones?

   c) after 8 students get their cones?

2. a) 6 more students from another bus have joined the group. How many scoops of ice cream will be served after 10 students get their cones?

   b) after 11 students get their cones?

   c) after 14 students get their cones? Show how you would multiply to get the number of scoops.

3. Another bus pulls up to the ice-cream stand. There are 26 more students who want three-scoop ice-cream cones. Show how you would multiply to find out the total number of scoops that would be served to these students.

What Did You Learn?

Look at the sentences you recorded in Build Your Understanding to answer these questions.

1. Find and record the patterns in the following products:

   a) 3 x 3 and 9 x 3   b) 4 x 3, 8 x 3, 12 x 3   c) 4 x 3 and 3 x 4.

2. Explain how you multiplied 15 x 3 and 26 x 3.

3. Why do we multiply numbers instead of adding them?

Practice

Mentally multiply these numbers:

1. 5 x 3 = ■   **2.** 7 x 3 = ■   **3.** 9 x 3 = ■

4. 2 x 3 = ■   **5.** 6 x 3 = ■   **6.** 3 x 3 = ■

7. 4 x 3 = ■   **8.** 8 x 3 = ■   **9.** 3 x 7 = ■

10. 3 x 6 = ■   **11.** 3 x 5 = ■   **12.** 3 x 9 = ■

Find the missing numbers:

13. ■ x 3 = 24   **14.** ■ x 2 = 6   **15.** ■ x 3 = 18

16. ■ x 3 = 27   **17.** 3 x ■ = 12   **18.** 3 x ■ = 15

19. Explain the difference between question 2 and question 9.

Multiply these factors:

20. 11 x 3 = ■   **21.** 15 x 3 = ■   **22.** 20 x 3 = ■

23. 24 x 3 = ■   **24.** 12 x 3 = ■   **25.** 21 x 3 = ■

26. 3 x 16 = ■   **27.** 3 x 10 = ■   **28.** 3 x 22 = ■

Math Problems to Solve

29. Andrea, Ali, and Carlo want to buy bake-sale tickets to raise money for the local library. 1 ticket costs $1.00 or 3 tickets cost $2.00. Andrea spends $4.00 on tickets. Ali spends $8.00. Carlo spends $5.00. How many tickets did they buy in all? Show your work.

30. In Juan's classroom there are 8 groups of 3 students. In Maria's classroom there are 3 groups of 8 students. Draw a picture to show what each of their classrooms might look like. Record and calculate a multiplication sentence for each classroom.

Lesson 5

Dividing by 3

TRAVEL LOG

PLAN:
You will divide by three to find out how many turns students took on the Carnaval slide.

DESTINATION:
Québec City, Québec

DESCRIPTION:
- This is where the French settlers made their home in 1608.
- Each February, Québec City hosts Carnaval, a big celebration with many outdoor activities.

Carnaval, Québec City, Québec

Get Started

In Lesson 4, you discovered that you could find a product quickly when you multiplied the two factors.

What if you know the product and only one factor? How do you find the other factor?

Sri, Bart, and Dana buy a package of mints at a store. There are 24 mints in the package. How can they divide the mints so they each get the same number?

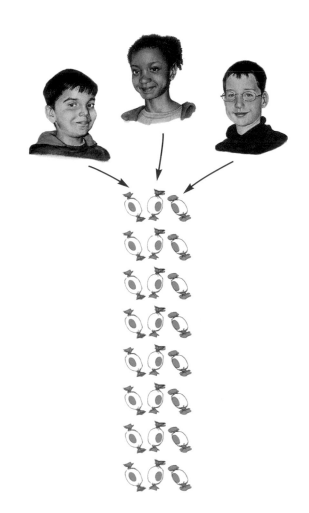

We see from the illustration that
24 − 3 − 3 − 3 − 3 − 3 − 3 − 3 − 3 = 0.
We can also say that 24 ÷ 3 = 8.
Division is a fast way to subtract just like multiplication is a fast way to add.

1. Create a multiplication sentence using these numbers: 24, 3, 8.

2. Choose a multiplication sentence from Lesson 4. Write a division sentence for it. Draw a picture for each sentence.

3. What have you learned about the relationship between multiplication and division?

Tip

Check a division equation by multiplying. Multiply the divisor by the quotient to get the dividend. For example, to check $12 \div 2 = 6$, multiply 2 (divisor) by 6 (quotient) to get 12 (dividend).

Build Your Understanding

Divide by 3

You Will Need
- counters
- drawing to represent the three slides

Even though it is not *Carnaval*, your tour guide has arranged for your group to take turns on the three big slides. One person goes down each slide at the same time. Dana counts how many people come down every five minutes.

Complete a chart like this one.

Five-minute intervals	Number of people down all three slides	Estimated number of people down one slide	Calculated number of people down one slide
first five minutes	21	Between 5 and 10	$21 \div 3 = 7$
second five minutes	27		
third five minutes	30		
fourth five minutes	36		
fifth five minutes	39		
sixth five minutes	24		
seventh five minutes	42		

1. Estimate how many people came down each slide every five minutes. Discuss how you made your estimates.

2. Make a model using counters and a drawing of the three slides.

3. Use your model to help you calculate how many people came down each slide.

When a number becomes too big to divide mentally by a one-digit number, try dividing the tens by the one-digit number then dividing the ones by the one-digit number:

$36 \div 3 = ?$

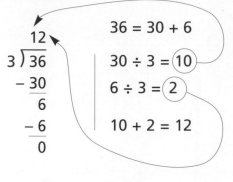

$36 = 30 + 6$

$30 \div 3 = 10$

$6 \div 3 = 2$

$10 + 2 = 12$

Vocabulary

dividend: The number to be divided
divisor: The number by which another is divided
quotient: The result when one number is divided by another

$12 \div 6 = 2$

12 is the dividend. 6 is the divisor. 2 is the quotient.

Tip

Check a multiplication equation by dividing. For example, $6 \times 2 = 12$. Remember that 6 and 2 are factors and 12 is the product. Now divide the product (12) by one of the factors (2). Your answer is 6!

What Did You Learn?

1. How did you make your predictions? How accurate were they?

2. a) What was the total number of times students went down all three slides?

   b) How many times did the students come down each slide? Show two ways to calculate this.

3. How does multiplication help you check a division sentence?

Practice

Mentally divide these sets of numbers:

1. $18 \div 3 = \blacksquare$ **2.** $12 \div 3 = \blacksquare$ **3.** $21 \div 3 = \blacksquare$

4. $6 \div 3 = \blacksquare$ **5.** $9 \div 3 = \blacksquare$ **6.** $6 \div 2 = \blacksquare$

7. $18 \div 3 = \blacksquare$ **8.** $30 \div 3 = \blacksquare$ **9.** $3 \div 3 = \blacksquare$

Find the missing numbers:

10. $\blacksquare \div 3 = 9$ **11.** $15 \div \blacksquare = 5$ **12.** $21 \div \blacksquare = 7$

13. $\blacksquare \div 3 = 2$ **14.** $18 \div \blacksquare = 6$ **15.** $\blacksquare \div 3 = 1$

16. $\blacksquare \div 3 = 8$ **17.** $12 \div \blacksquare = 4$ **18.** $\blacksquare \div 3 = 11$

19. How did you find the missing numbers in questions 10 to 18? What strategy did you use?

20. Explain the difference between question 4 and question 6. Use numbers, pictures, and words.

Practise dividing larger numbers. Show your work.

21. $3)\overline{42}$ **22.** $3)\overline{39}$ **23.** $3)\overline{45}$ **24.** $3)\overline{51}$

25. $3)\overline{66}$ **26.** $3)\overline{72}$ **27.** $3)\overline{84}$ **28.** $3)\overline{63}$

Math Problems to Solve

For each problem show your work using pictures, numbers, and words.

29. After a fun day, the guide wants to give a juice box to each person on the bus. There are 48 people on the bus. The juice boxes come in packs of three boxes. How many packs does the guide need so that everyone gets a juice box?

30. The guide wants to get the juice boxes ready for the next group. There will be 50 students and 10 teachers. How many packs does the guide need so that everyone gets a juice box?

Multiplying by 4

TRAVEL LOG

PLAN:

As you travel out of Québec City, you will count cars and calculate the number of wheels they have by multiplying by four.

DESTINATION:

The Trans-Canada Highway

DESCRIPTION:

• The Trans-Canada Highway stretches from coast to coast.

Trans-Canada Highway between Québec City and Montréal

Get Started

Bart counted 14 blue cars. How can we calculate how many wheels are on these cars? (Multiplication is a fast way to add.)

When multiplying a two-digit number by a one-digit number, multiply the ones first, and then multiply the tens:

```
   14              24               32
  x 4             x 4              x 4
  ───             ───              ───
   16 (4 x 4)      16 (4 x 4)        8 (4 x 2)
+ 40 (4 x 10)   + 80 (4 x 20)   + 120 (4 x 30)
  ───             ───              ───
   56              96               128
```

When multiplying a three-digit number by a one-digit number, multiply the ones column, then multiply the tens column, and then multiply the hundreds column:

```
   136                278
  x 4                x 4
  ───                ───
   24 (4 x 6)         32 (4 x 8)
  120 (4 x 30)       280 (4 x 70)
+ 400 (4 x 100)   + 800 (4 x 200)
  ───                ───
   544               1112
```

The traditional method carries the tens to the tens column and carries the hundreds to the hundreds column:

```
  1 2              2
  136             205
 x 4             x 4
 ───             ───
  544             820
```

Build Your Understanding

Multiply by 4

Some students are counting cars and motorcycles on the highway.

1. Calculate the total number of wheels for each group of vehicles. Complete a chart like the one to the right.

2. Add some more vehicles to the chart and complete each row.

Tip

Check the number of wheels for each vehicle in your chart by dividing the product by one of the factors.

Vehicle	Number Seen on Highway	Number of Wheels per Vehicle	Total Number of Wheels
	16	4	16 x 4 64
	27		
	35		
	21		
	4		

What Did You Learn?

1. How did you calculate the total number of wheels for each group of vehicles?

2. Which calculation was the least challenging? Why?

3. Which calculation was the most challenging? Why?

Practice

Mentally multiply these numbers:

1. 6 x 4 = ▩   **2.** 3 x 4 = ▩

3. 5 x 4 = ▩   **4.** 2 x 4 = ▩

5. 7 x 4 = ▩   **6.** 4 x 4 = ▩

Find the missing numbers:

7. ▩ x 4 = 16   **8.** 7 x ▩ = 28

9. 4 x ▩ = 24   **10.** ▩ x 4 = 36

Multiply these sets of numbers:

11. 10 x 4 = ▩   **12.** 17 x 4 = ▩

13. 20 x 4 = ▩   **14.** 25 x 4 = ▩

15. 30 x 4 = ▩   **16.** 36 x 4 = ▩

17. 40 x 4 = ▩   **18.** 42 x 4 = ▩

19. 50 x 4 = ▩   **20.** 51 x 4 = ▩

21. 60
        x 4

22. 70
        x 4

Math Problems to Solve

23. Ian and Julie live on a farm. Ian is sitting on the grass. He sees cows and chickens and starts counting their legs. Julie is sitting on the fence. She also decides to count all the cows and chickens. Ian tells Julie that he counted 46 legs. Julie tells him she counted 14 cows and chickens. How many chickens did Ian and Julie count? How many cows did they count? Use numbers, pictures, and words to show your work.

24. Create a problem that requires multiplication of a two-digit number by 4. Give it to a classmate to solve.

Two-Digit Multiplication Game

You Will Need
- numbered cards from 1 to 7 or playing cards using aces and numbered cards from 2 to 7. (The aces will represent the number one.)
- a calculator to check answers
- two players (Player A and Player B)
- timer or stopwatch
- scoring sheet

How to Play

1. One player shuffles and deals the cards.

2. Each player puts a card down at the same time. Together, the two cards represent a two-digit number. Player A's card represents the tens digit. Player B's card represents the ones digit.

3. Player A must multiply the two-digit number on the cards by 4 correctly within 30 seconds. If correct, that player gets 5 points. If incorrect, the player gets no points.

4. Each player puts another card down at the same time, and Player B takes his or her turn.

5. Total your points after each player takes 5 turns.

Try the game again and shorten the time period to 20 s.

Lesson 7

Dividing by 4

TRAVEL LOG

PLAN:
You will divide large numbers of tourists into groups of four for dinner at a restaurant in Montréal.

DESTINATION:
Montréal, Québec

DESCRIPTION:
• Montréal is one of Canada's largest cities. It is located on the St. Lawrence River.
• Most people in Montréal speak French.
• This city is well known for its hockey team, theatre, artists, and great restaurants.

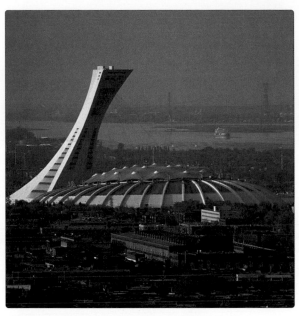

Olympic Stadium, Montréal, Québec

Get Started

At the restaurant, each table seats 4 people. If 15 students want to sit together, one table will have fewer than four students. How do we know this?

There are 48 people on the bus. How many tables will they need? How can you calculate this?

Vertical Division

Vertical division is the traditional method of division:

$$4\overline{)68}$$
$$\begin{array}{r} 17 \\ 4\overline{)68} \\ -40 \\ \hline 28 \\ -28 \\ \hline 0 \end{array}$$

Step 1
How many groups of 4 are there in the first digit of the dividend? ($6 \div 4 = 1$ group of 4)

Step 2
Place the quotient 1 over the 6.

Step 3
Multiply the quotient 1 by 4 and place the answer beneath the 6. ($4 \times 1 = 4$)

Step 4
Add zeroes for blank spaces and subtract 40 from 68.

Step 5
How many groups of 4 are there in 28? ($28 \div 4 = 7$)
Write the quotient 7 over the 8.

Step 6
Subtract 28 from 28. No remainder.

Dividing by Distribution

$$\begin{array}{c} 10 + 5 + 2 = 17 \\ 4\overline{)40 + 20 + 8} \end{array}$$

Step 1
Rename the 68 into numbers that add up to 68, but are multiples of the divisor. Try to use large multiples so the question is not too long
$68 = 40 + 20 + 8$ is better than
$68 = 20 + 20 + 20 + 4 + 4$

Step 2
Divide each new number by 4.
($40 \div 4 = 10$)
($20 \div 4 = 5$)
($8 \div 4 = 2$)

Step 3
Add the quotients.

Here are two examples:

$$4\overline{)96} \qquad\qquad 4\overline{)38}$$
$$4\overline{)80 + 16} \qquad\quad 4\overline{)20 + 18}$$
$$\begin{array}{c} 20 + 4 = 24 \\ 4\overline{)80 + 16} \end{array} \qquad 4\overline{)20 + 16\ (+2)}$$
$$\qquad\qquad\qquad\qquad \begin{array}{c} 5 + 4\ (+2\ \text{remainder}) \\ 4\overline{)20 + 16\ (+2)} \end{array}$$

Vocabulary

remainder: The amount left over when one number is divided by another. For example, for 20 counters divided into 3 groups, there would be 2 counters left over.

Build Your Understanding

Division Without a Remainder

The tour-bus group enters the restaurant in Montréal. The restaurant manager tells the students that five different groups of people will be eating at the restaurant this evening.

1. Use vertical division to calculate how many tables will be needed for each group of people. Remember that each table seats four people.

2. Copy the chart in your notebook and complete it.

3. Check each calculation by multiplying the quotient with the divisor.

Group	Number of People	Number of Tables (seating a maximum of 4 at each table)
1	56	
2	48	
3	64	
4	96	
5	84	

What Did You Learn?

1. Which method of division do you prefer—vertical division, dividing by distribution, or using counters? Why?

2. What made the vertical method easy or hard to use?

3. List the steps that you followed to divide by distribution.

4. How does dividing by distribution help you to divide large numbers?

Mentally divide these numbers:

1. 16 ÷ 4 = ■   **2.** 28 ÷ 4 = ■   **3.** 12 ÷ 4 = ■   **4.** 4 ÷ 4 = ■

5. 20 ÷ 4 = ■   **6.** 24 ÷ 3 = ■   **7.** 12 ÷ 3 = ■   **8.** 15 ÷ 3 = ■

Solve each question:

9. ■ ÷ 4 = 3   **10.** ■ ÷ 4 = 2   **11.** ■ ÷ 4 = 6   **12.** 28 ÷ ■ = 7

13. 4)‾44   **14.** 4)‾64   **15.** 4)‾92   **16.** 4)‾52

Extend the pattern and explain the rule.
Here is one example.

2, 4, 6, ■, ■, ■ …

Rule: Add 2.

17. 4, 8, 12, ■, 20, ■, ■, ■   **18.** 4, 8, 16, ■, ■   **19.** 96, 48, 24, ■, ■

Math Problems to Solve

20. Four students receive a bag of mints. They want to divide the mints so they each have the same number of candies. It's a big bag, so they each take a portion to count. Carlo counts 22, Evan counts 31, Dana counts 19, and Sri counts 24. How many mints will they each get? Show two ways you can calculate this using pictures, numbers, and words.

21. Create a problem that requires division of a two-digit number by 4. Give it to a classmate to solve.

Extension

22. Music and math have much in common. Math plays an important role in music. Investigate and explain why. Who could you ask in your school for more information?

Show What You Know

1. Complete:

  a) $7 \times 3 = \blacksquare$ **b)** $4 \times 6 = \blacksquare$ **c)** $5 \times 8 = \blacksquare$ **d)** $9 \times 2 = \blacksquare$

  e) $8 \times 3 = \blacksquare$ **f)** $4 \times 7 = \blacksquare$ **g)** $\blacksquare \times \blacksquare = 15$ **h)** $\blacksquare \div 3 = \blacksquare$

  i) $\blacksquare \times \blacksquare = 24$ **j)** $\blacksquare \div 4 = \blacksquare$ **k)** $\blacksquare \times \blacksquare = 24$ **l)** $\blacksquare \div 5 = \blacksquare$

2.
  a) $\begin{array}{r} 36 \\ \times\ 4 \\ \hline \end{array}$ **b)** $\begin{array}{r} 80 \\ \times\ 3 \\ \hline \end{array}$ **c)** $\begin{array}{r} 28 \\ \times\ 4 \\ \hline \end{array}$

  d) $\begin{array}{r} 40 \\ \times\ 5 \\ \hline \end{array}$ **e)** $\begin{array}{r} 62 \\ \times\ 5 \\ \hline \end{array}$ **f)** $\begin{array}{r} 53 \\ \times\ 3 \\ \hline \end{array}$

3. **a)** $45 \div 5 = \blacksquare$ **b)** $28 \div 4 = \blacksquare$ **c)** $36 \div 4 = \blacksquare$

  d) $21 \div 3 = \blacksquare$ **e)** $6 \div 3 = \blacksquare$ **f)** $30 \div 5 = \blacksquare$

4. **a)** $4 \overline{)48}$ **b)** $3 \overline{)63}$ **c)** $2 \overline{)72}$ **d)** $5 \overline{)95}$

5. How would you explain multiplication to someone who doesn't know how to multiply?

6. How would you explain division to someone who doesn't know how to divide?

7. Where would you or your family use multiplication outside of school?

8. Where would you or your family use division outside of school?

9. What is the difference between 8×4 and 4×8? Use numbers, pictures, and words to explain your answer.

10. What does $24 \div 4$ look like? Use pictures to show your answer.

11. Describe how you would multiply 29×3.

12. Describe how you would calculate $60 \div 4$.

Lesson 8

Multiplying by 100

TRAVEL LOG

PLAN:
You will calculate the distance between cities and how long it takes to travel from city to city in Eastern Canada.

DESTINATION:
Eastern Canada

DESCRIPTION:
• Canada is the second-largest country in the world. (Russia is the largest country in the world.) Since Canada is such a large country, it can take a long time to travel from place to place.

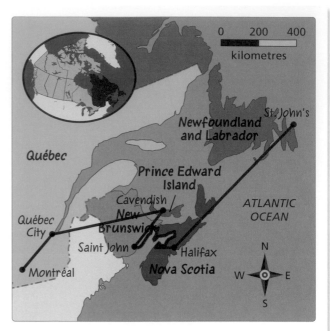

Get Started

On many Canadian highways, the speed limit is 100 km/h. If you had to travel 200 km, how long would it take if you drove at the speed limit?

200 km ÷ 100 km/h = 2 h

If it takes 4 h to go from one town to another by highway, then you know that there is a distance of 400 km between the two towns, if you are travelling at a rate of 100 km/h.

100 km/h x 4 h = 400 km

Tip

kilometres = km
hours = h
kilometres per hour = km/h
minutes = min

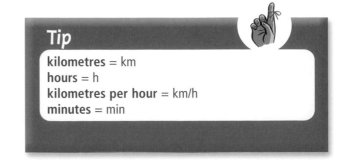

Make a timeline to show the distance you could drive
on a highway in 4 h.

1. Extend the timeline. How far could you go in 6 h?

2. How far could you go in 0.5 h?

3. Imagine that you are in a car that travels 7 km/10 min.
How far would you travel in   **a)** 20 min?   **b)** 0.5 h?   **c)** 1 h?

4. Draw a timeline for question 3 to show how far you could travel.

Build Your Understanding

Multiply by 100 and Estimate Distance

Calculate the distances between the cities in the chart. Show your
calculations two ways—on a timeline and in a multiplication or division sentence.

Cities	Hours to Travel by Car With No Stops at 100 km/h	Approximate Distance Apart (km)
Halifax to Saint John	4 h 15 min	
Saint John to Cavendish	3 h	
Cavendish to Québec City	8 h	
Québec City to Montréal	2 h 30 min	

1. How many highway kilometres (approximately) are there between

   a) Halifax, Nova Scotia and Saint John, New Brunswick?

   b) Québec City, Québec and Montréal, Québec?

   c) Saint John, New Brunswick and Cavendish, Prince Edward Island?

   d) Cavendish, Prince Edward Island and Montréal, Québec?

   e) Saint John, New Brunswick and Québec City, Québec?

   f) Halifax, Nova Scotia and Montréal, Québec?

What Did You Learn?

1. How did the number of hours help you to find the distances
between cities?

2. How did you calculate the answer to question 1(a) in Build
Your Understanding?

Practice

Mentally multiply these sets of numbers:

1. 8 x 10 = ◼   **2.** 8 x 100 = ◼

3. 5 x 100 = ◼   **4.** 2 x 10 = ◼

5. 59 x 10 = ◼   **6.** 13 x 100 = ◼

7. 28 x 10 = ◼   **8.** 9 x 10 = ◼

9. 4 x 100 = ◼   **10.** 7 x 10 = ◼

Journal

Look at your answers to the practice questions. Now imagine that a friend has trouble answering them. Write rules that would help your friend to multiply by 10 and 100.

Math Problems to Solve

11. You and your family visited several towns. You want to calculate how far you travelled. Here are the times it takes to travel from one town to another, travelling at the speed of 100 km/h:

home to town A — 2 h

town A to town B — 4 h

town B to town C — 5 h

How far did you travel to go to town C and home again? Show your calculations on a timeline and in a multiplication or division sentence.

Extension

12. Use the chart in Build Your Understanding to answer the following question: If you left Halifax at 1:00 P.M., what time would you arrive in Saint John, New Brunswick?

Lesson 9

Adding and Subtracting Money to $10.00

TRAVEL LOG

PLAN:
You will buy several different items from the gift shop with $10.00, then you will calculate the change.

DESTINATION:
Ottawa, Ontario

DESCRIPTION:
- Ottawa is the capital of Canada.
- You can visit the Parliament Buildings and House of Commons where the Prime Minister and other politicians work.
- Every year, thousands of people visit the capital. Many buy souvenirs to remind them of their visit.

Parliament Buildings, Ottawa, Ontario

Get Started

1. How can your knowledge of addition and subtraction help you to make change from a $10.00 bill for three items?

2. Add the numbers below:

    395   459   70

3. Subtract the sum from 1000.

4. Repeat questions 2 and 3, but change the numbers to dollar amounts.

5. Which way was easier to do? Why?

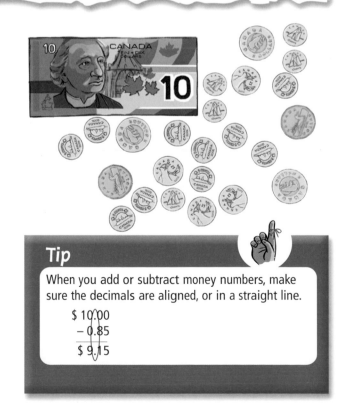

Tip

When you add or subtract money numbers, make sure the decimals are aligned, or in a straight line.

$$\begin{array}{r} \$\,10.00 \\ -\ 0.85 \\ \hline \$\,9.15 \end{array}$$

Build Your Understanding

Add and Subtract Money

You are in a gift shop in Ottawa. You want to buy as many items as you can with $10.00.

Here are some of the items in the gift shop.
All prices include taxes.

1. What is the maximum number of items you can buy with $10.00? What would these items be?

2. After buying your items, how much change would you receive from the cashier? How do you know?

3. Which coins would you get back in change? What are some other ways you could get your change back?

1. How did you decide which items you were going to buy that would add up to less than $10.00? With a partner, compare strategies you used to answer these questions.

2. How did you check to see that you chose the most items possible?

Practice

1. Work out the change from $10.00 after buying each of the following items separately. Here is an example to get you started:

   Pack of pencils: $2.75

   $10.00
   − 2.75
   ———
   $7.25

   Change: $5.00 bill, a $2.00 coin, and a quarter

2. key chain $3.65

3. writing pad $4.10

4. map $3.50

5. For questions 2 to 4, record another way you could make the change.

A Math Problem to Solve

6. Grace buys 5 stamps at $0.48 each and 5 postcards for $0.75 each. Predict whether she will have enough money left over from $10.00 to buy a $4.00 pen. Find out if your prediction is correct. Show your work using numbers, pictures, and words.

Journal

How can you figure out the change from $10.00 quickly in your head when you buy an item for $4.50?

Lesson 10

Problem-Solving Calculations

TRAVEL LOG

PLAN:
You will calculate how many windows are in a skyscraper.

DESTINATION:
Toronto, Ontario

DESCRIPTION:
• Toronto's skyline includes many skyscrapers, including First Canadian Place, Canada's tallest skyscraper, and the Royal Bank Plaza.

First Canadian Place, Toronto, Ontario

Get Started

You Will Need
• calculator or base-ten blocks or linking cubes

Some of Toronto's skyscrapers are rectangular prisms, like First Canadian Place. It is 290 m high and has 72 storeys. Imagine that there are 17 windows per side on each floor. All four sides have the same number of windows.

Vocabulary

rectangular prism: A three-dimensional shape in which all six faces are rectangles. A square prism is a rectangular prism with two square faces.

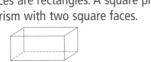

Use base-ten blocks or linking cubes to create one floor of windows. Remember that there are 17 windows per side and 4 sides.

1. How many windows are there in one storey? two storeys? three storeys?

2. Use your calculator to find out how many windows would be in a 72-storey building.

3. How can you check your answer?

Build Your Understanding

Calculate

You Will Need
• calculator

A window company is installing windows in a skyscraper.
Here are the facts:

• The building is 30 storeys tall.

• There are four sides to the building. All sides will have windows.

• On each storey, there will be 14 windows on each side.

Use your calculator to find the total number of windows that will
be installed.

Toronto skyline

What Did You Learn?

Explain in numbers, pictures, and words how you calculated the
total number of windows in the skyscraper.

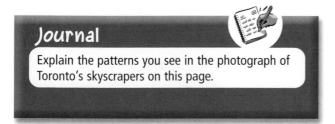

Journal

Explain the patterns you see in the photograph of
Toronto's skyscrapers on this page.

Practice

Use your calculator to record a multiplication sentence for the number of windows on each skyscraper below. All the buildings have 4 sides with the same number of windows per side.

1. a 15-storey building with 22 windows per side.

2. a 45-storey building with 30 windows per side.

3. a 54-storey building with 42 windows per side.

Find the correct path to Ontario Place in Toronto by correctly answering the following math questions in order.

4. 148 x 3 **5.** 2164 + 3865 **6.** 68 ÷ 4

7. 4)‾52‾ **8.** 4302 – 2418 **9.** 816 x 4

Remember to record your path. Show your work.

Journal

Explain how you approached each multiplication sentence to find the path to Ontario Place.

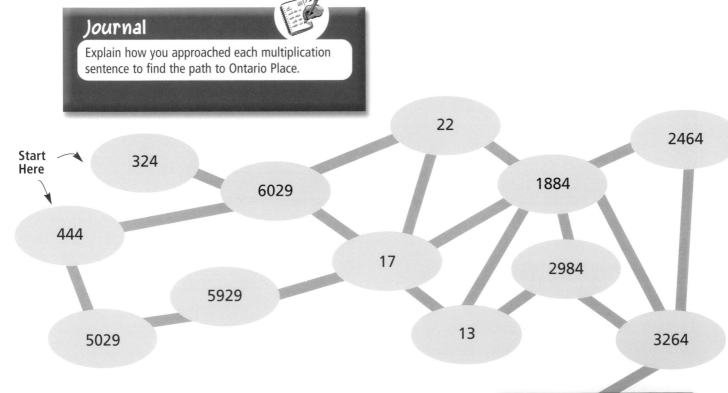

Start Here

324

6029

444

22

2464

1884

17

2984

5929

13

5029

3264

A Math Problem to Solve

10. There are 128 windows in a building. Each side has the same number of windows. How many windows would be on each side and on each storey? How many storeys could the building have?

Lesson 11

Multiplying and Dividing by 5

TRAVEL LOG

PLAN:
You will review multiplication and division by 5. You will also use your calculation skills in a game.

DESTINATION:
Sudbury, Ontario

DESCRIPTION:
- Sudbury, Ontario is home to Science North where you can take part in many activities and games that make learning about our world fun.
- Sudbury is known for its rich nickel mines.

Science North, Sudbury, Ontario

Big Nickel Monument, Sudbury, Ontario

Get Started

1	2	3	4	5	6	7	8	9	10
11	12	13	14	15	16	17	18	19	20
21	22	23	24	25	26	27	28	29	30
31	32	33	34	35	36	37	38	39	40
41	42	43	44	45	46	47	48	49	50
51	52	53	54	55	56	57	58	59	60
61	62	63	64	65	66	67	68	69	70
71	72	73	74	75	76	77	78	79	80
81	82	83	84	85	86	87	88	89	90
91	92	93	94	95	96	97	98	99	100

What patterns do you see on the hundreds chart? Practise multiplying by 5 and then dividing by 5. Try going down columns, and then across rows.

Divide and multiply the following.

Here are examples to get you started.

$$
\begin{array}{r}
17 \\
5\overline{)85} \\
-5 \\
\hline
35 \\
-35 \\
\hline
0
\end{array}
\qquad
\begin{array}{r}
82 \\
\times 5 \\
\hline
10 \ (5 \times 2) \\
+400 \ (5 \times 80) \\
\hline
410
\end{array}
$$

1. $5\overline{)75}$ **2.** $5\overline{)60}$ **3.** $\begin{array}{r}19\\ \times 5\end{array}$ **4.** $\begin{array}{r}13\\ \times 5\end{array}$

Lesson 11: Multiplying and Dividing by 5

57

Build Your Understanding

Game: Fickle Nickels (Multiply by 5)

You Will Need
- 2 number cubes
- paper and pencil
- calculator
- 2 to 4 players

Journal

What did you like about the game you played in class? What didn't you like? Why?

Object
Be the first player to reach 500 points.

How to Play

1. Each player rolls one number cube. The player with the highest number goes first.

2. At each turn, a player rolls both cubes.

3. The player adds the numbers on the cubes, then multiplies the number by 5.

4. The player then says the total, and adds it to the score sheet.

5. If a player rolls the same number on both cubes (a double), the player multiplies the number by 10, then divides by 5.

For example, if a player rolled double threes, the player would multiply 3 by 10, then divide by 5. The answer would be 6. This number is subtracted from the player's score.

6. A player does not receive any points for multiplying incorrectly.

7. The first player to reach 500 points wins the game.

What Did You Learn?

1. Was this a fair game? How do you know?
2. What did you find most difficult about playing the game? What did you do to make it less difficult?
3. Explain the strategies you used to play the game.

Practice

Multiply:

1. ■ x ■ = 25   **2.** 4 x 5 = ■   **3.** ■ x 5 = 35

4. 6 x 5 = ■   **5.** 2 x 5 = ■   **6.** ■ x 5 = 5

7. 3 x ■ = 15   **8.** 30 x 5 = ■   **9.** 50 x 5 = ■

10. 25 x 5 = ■   **11.** 42 x 5 = ■   **12.** 73 x 5 = ■

Divide:

13. 35 ÷ 5 = ■   **14.** 15 ÷ 3 = ■   **15.** 40 ÷ 5 = ■

16. 45 ÷ 5 = ■   **17.** 5 ÷ 5 = ■   **18.** 75 ÷ 5 = ■

19. 85 ÷ 5 = ■   **20.** 60 ÷ 5 = ■

Math Problems to Solve

21. The grade 4 students are getting $5.00 each to spend on a school trip. There are 65 grade 4 students. What is the total amount of money needed for all of the students? Use numbers, pictures, and words to show your work.

22. While on the trip, the guide wants to split the 65 students (and the 10 adult helpers) into equal groups. How many students and adults will be in each group? Use numbers, pictures, and words to show your work.

Extension

23. Work in a group to design your own game based on Fickle Nickels. Design a rules sheet like the one on page 58 and give it to another group. After they have played your game discuss it with them. Is there anything about your game you would change?

Chapter
1

Chapter Review

1. Write each of the following numbers in expanded form:
   a) 67   **b)** 336   **c)** 1805   **d)** 4029

2. Write each of the following numbers in words:
   a) 58   **b)** 482   **c)** 6701

3. Write the numeral for each:
   a) three hundred twenty-six
   b) seven thousand one hundred five
   c) Sketch questions 3 (a) and (b) using base-ten blocks.

4. Study the following estimates for subtraction:

$$873 \rightarrow 900 \qquad 848 \rightarrow 850$$
$$-754 \rightarrow -800 \qquad -813 \rightarrow -810$$
$$\overline{\qquad 100 \qquad} \qquad \overline{\qquad 40 \qquad}$$

   a) Explain why the first example was estimated to the nearest hundreds and why in the second example it was best to estimate to the nearest tens.

   b) Which estimation would be closer to the actual answer?

   c) Calculate the actual answer.

5. Put the following numbers in order from greatest to smallest:
   a) 829, 928, 899   **b)** 1707, 707, 1077

6. Add or subtract:

a) 36	**b)** 485	**c)** 1553	**d)** 81	**e)** 600	**f)** 1603
+ 28	+ 59	+ 1918	− 27	− 342	− 716

7. Name the century and the millennium that the following numbers belong to:
   a) 1577   **b)** 687   **c)** 2010   **d)** 2399

8. Show two ways you can group this array of counters to create two multiplication sentences.

9. Multiply the following:

a) 3 x 7 = ▨   **b)** 4 x 2 = ▨   **c)** 6 x 3 = ▨   **d)** 5 x 4 = ▨

e) 16   **f)** 24   **g)** 51
    x 4   x 3   x 4

h) Show two ways you can check if your multiplication calculation is correct in question 9 (g).

10. Divide

a) 4)24   **b)** 18 ÷ 3 = ▨   **c)** 4)16   **d)** 3)9

e) 48 ÷ ▨ = 12   **f)** 3)69   **g)** 72 ÷ 3 = ▨   **h)** 4)50

i) What can you do to check if your division calculations are correct?

11. Complete the pattern. State the rule.

a) 1, 3, 5, ___, ___, ____   **b)**   1, 4, 9, ___, ___, ___

c) Make your own pattern and state the rule.
    Trade with a partner.

12. a) How many kilometres will you travel in four hours if the car is going 45 km/h and you don't make any stops?

b) Draw a timeline to show how far you will drive.

13. Imagine you are in a car that travels 5 km/10 min. How far would you travel in

a) 20 min?   **b)** 0.5 h?   **c)** 2 h?

14. Multiply the following:

a) 8 x 10 = ▪ **b)** 176 x 10 = ▪ **c)** 4 x 100 = ▪ **d)** 93 x 100 = ▪

e) In your notebook, explain a shortcut when multiplying by 10 and 100.

15. a) Stephanie bought a tennis racket for $5.25 and a pack of cards for $2.49. She gave the cashier a ten-dollar bill and received six coins in return. What coins could Stephanie have received? Show all your work.

b) What other coins could Stephanie have received? Record at least 2 other ways.

16. What observations can you make about products of numbers multiplied by 5? Use examples to explain your answer.

17. Explain in your notebook how you estimate, and give an example.

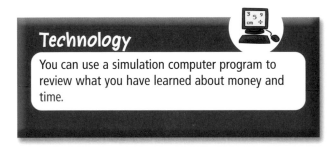

Technology

You can use a simulation computer program to review what you have learned about money and time.

Chapter 1

Chapter Wrap-Up

You Will Need
- your journal
- poster paper
- markers
- crayons
- glue
- scissors
- construction paper

Congratulations on reaching the end of the first part of your journey!

Throughout Chapter 1 you have encountered many math skills and concepts along the way from St. John's to Toronto, including

- counting and recording numbers
- comparing numbers
- adding and subtracting 4-digit numbers
- multiplying and dividing by 3, 4, and 5
- estimating and calculating distances
- adding and subtracting money

You have also learned many fascinating facts about our country.

Work in a small group to apply your math skills and share what you have learned about math—and about Eastern Canada—with younger students.

With your group, list the mathematics you have used in this chapter. List some things you have learned about Eastern Canada. Together, decide what you want to put on your poster. Keep these ideas in mind as you plan and create your poster:

- Your poster must focus on more than one of the skills you studied in this chapter.
- The poster must have a title.
- There must be at least one graph and one chart.
- Your audience is students younger than you.
- All group members must take part in the poster.

Good luck with your project, and have fun creating your math poster. You may have a chance to present your poster to a younger class.

Technology

You can use a paint/draw computer program to create an electronic version of this poster.

Tip

Do a rough plan of your poster. This way you can make sure all of your group's ideas are included and fit. The final copy of your poster should be neat and colourful.

Math in Western Canada

In this chapter, you will travel through the provinces of Western Canada. As you travel, you will

- measure using decimal numbers
- examine and describe two-dimensional shapes
- multiply two-digit numbers
- solve questions about time
- conduct a survey

At the end of the chapter, you will invent a game where you can apply many of your new math skills.

Answer these questions to help you prepare for the second leg of your journey:

1. Estimate the length, width, and height of your desk. Then measure it with a ruler to check your estimate. Estimate and measure other objects in your classroom.

2. What shapes do you see in your classroom? Draw the shapes you see in your notebook and label them. Share your shapes with a partner.

You are now ready to continue on your journey. Good luck!

Winnipeg, Manitoba

Wheatfields in the Prairies

Dinosaur fossils such as those of the T-Rex have been found in the Badlands of Alberta.

Exploring Units of Measurement

TRAVEL LOG

PLAN:
You will measure the length of some of the rivers in Manitoba and use several units of measurement. You will also learn how to convert units of measurement.

DESTINATION:
Manitoba

DESCRIPTION:
Your bus heads west to Manitoba, a province of many rivers.

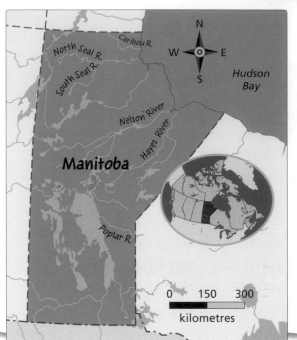

Get Started

1. In your notebook, record the unit, millimetres (mm), centimetres (cm), metres (m), kilometres (km) you would use to measure these items:

Vocabulary

millimetre (mm): A unit of length. 1000 mm = 1 m
centimetre (cm): A unit of length. 100 cm = 1 m
decimetre (dm): A unit of length. 10 dm = 1 m
metre (m): A unit of length. 1 m = 100 cm
decametre (dam): A unit of length. 1 dam = 10 m
hectometre (hm): A unit of length. 1 hm = 100 m
kilometre (km): A unit of length. 1 km = 1000 m
trundle wheel: A small wheel used to measure distances that are too long for a tape measure or that aren't straight

A
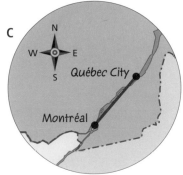

B

C
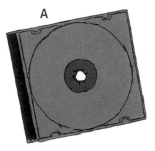
Québec City
Montréal

D

E

2. In your notebook, measure and record the length of these items in both millimetres and centimetres.

A

B

C

D

E _____

Use your measurements to answer these questions:

3. If a line is 2 mm longer than 1 cm, how can you write its length in centimetres?

4. How do you record a measurement of 1 cm 2 mm in millimetres?

5. What is another way of writing 4 cm 6 mm in centimetres?

Build Your Understanding

Estimate and Measure Length

You Will Need
- string
- ruler
- pencil

1. Form groups of two or three.
Look at the map on page 66.

2. What does the bar at the bottom right tell you about distances on the map? How can we use this to find the actual length of the rivers?

3. Discuss how you can measure the rivers using a string, ruler, and pencil.

4. Use the string to measure the rivers.

5. Copy and complete the chart on page 68. The first river has been done for you.

> **Tip**
>
> To convert cm to mm, simply multiply the given number by 10. This moves the decimal one place to the right.
> Example: 5.0 cm x 10 = 50 mm or 5.0 cm = 50 mm
> To convert mm to cm, simply divide the given number by 10. This moves the decimal one place to the left.
> Example: 70.0 mm ÷ 10 = 7.00 cm or 70.0 mm = 7.00 cm.
>
> 1 mm = 0.1 cm   10 mm = 1 cm
> 100 cm = 1 m   1000 mm = 1 m
> 1000 m = 1 km
> The scale on the map means 1 cm = 150 km.

Name of Major Manitoba River	Length in mm	Length in cm	Length in cm Rounded to the Nearest Ones Digit	Length in km According to the Map's Scale
Caribou River	13 mm	1.3 cm	1 cm	150 km
Nelson River				
North Seal River				
South Seal River				
Hayes River				
Poplar River				

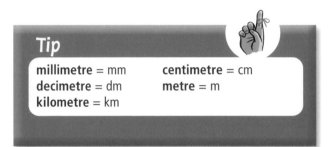

Tip

millimetre = mm   centimetre = cm
decimetre = dm   metre = m
kilometre = km

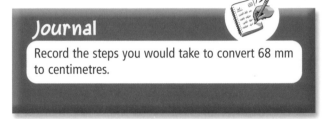

Journal

Record the steps you would take to convert 68 mm to centimetres.

What Did You Learn?

1. Describe how your group decided to measure the rivers.

2. What is the relationship between millimetre measurements and centimetre measurements? Use examples to support your answer.

3. How did you figure out the actual length of each river in kilometres, according to the map's scale?

4. What is the total length of the rivers you measured? Show your calculations.

5. Why do you think a scale is an important feature on a map?

Practice

Name the measurement unit you would use to measure these items. Explain your choices.

1.

2.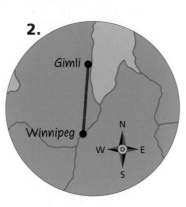

3.

4.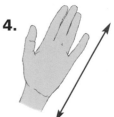

Convert these measurements.

5. 2 cm = ■ mm

6. 90 mm = ■ cm

7. 46 mm = ■ cm

8. ■ cm = 53 mm

9. 8.7 cm = ■ mm

10. 2 m = ■ cm = ■ mm

11. ■ m = 400 cm = ■ mm

12. ■ cm = 3000 mm = ■ m

A Math Problem to Solve

13. Ali is investigating how many paper clips she can pick up using a magnet.

a) She attaches the first paper clip onto the magnet.

b) The second paper clip attaches at one end to the first paper clip.

c) She continues until the magnet can no longer attract any more paper clips.

Ali knows that each paper clip is 32 mm in length. She has a chain of three paper clips hanging from her magnet.

What is the approximate length of the chain of paper clips in centimetres? Show your work by using pictures, numbers, and words.

Technology

You can use a problem-solving computer program to learn about some new problem-solving strategies. Keep track of the ones you used.

Lesson 2

Estimating and Measuring Length

TRAVEL LOG

PLAN:
You will work in groups to estimate and chart body measurements.

DESTINATION:
Winnipeg, Manitoba

DESCRIPTION:
- *Winnipeg is the capital city of Manitoba.*
- *It is known for its many elm trees. In fact, the city has more than 250 000 elm trees.*
- *Elm trees can grow to be as tall as 25 m!*

Elm trees at the Manitoba Provincial Legislative Building in Winnipeg

Get Started

Some elm trees can grow as much as 38 cm a year. Imagine that you were 125 cm tall last year. You grew 2.2 cm during the year.

1. How tall are you now?

2. How did you calculate your new height?

3. Now imagine that a classmate asks you how tall you are. How would you say your height?

4. Estimate your height in centimetres. Then, with a partner, measure each other using centimetres. Was your estimate close? Discuss with your partner how you would convert your height into millimetres.

Build Your Understanding

Measurement

You Will Need
* measuring tape
  (with centimetre and millimetre
  markings)

	Student 1			
	Estimate		Actual	
	cm	mm	cm	mm
Arm Span				

1. Work in a group of four to make the
   following body measurements: arm
   span (shoulder to wrist), wrist to elbow,
   foot lengths, pinky finger length.

2. Before you begin, estimate each body
   part in centimetres and millimetres.
   Record your estimates on a chart like
   the one shown.

Technology

You can use a computer to design and complete
the chart above.

3. Now measure each body part. Record your
   measurements on your chart. Measure in centimetres
   and then convert the measurement to millimetres.

What Did You Learn?

1. Discuss as a group what patterns you see in your data.

2. Use pictures, numbers, and words to describe all the
   patterns you have discovered.

Practice

1. Take your chart home and have your family complete it.
   Report any interesting findings that you discovered.

2. If you increased your measurements by five times and
   converted them to metres, how big would you be?
   Show your work.

Lesson 3

Exploring Two-Dimensional Shapes

TRAVEL LOG

PLAN:
You will learn to recognize and describe various two-dimensional (2-D) shapes in a tangram. What 2-D shapes do you see in the picture of Buffalo Days?.

DESTINATION:
Regina, Saskatchewan

DESCRIPTION:
• Regina is the capital of Saskatchewan.
• Each summer, this capital city has a celebration called Buffalo Days where people enjoy parades, square dancing, and rodeos.

Buffalo Days celebrations in Regina

Get Started

Use a tangram or follow your teacher's instructions to cut paper into the shape of a tangram.

1. Describe each tangram piece by the name of its shape, number of sides, and type of angles (for example, right angle).

2. How many different four-sided figures can you construct using two or more tangram pieces? Each side must touch the full side of another piece. Record your results.

Vocabulary

angle: The figure formed by two line segments or rays that share the same endpoint

right angle: An angle of 90°

obtuse angle: An angle that has a measure greater than a right angle (between 90° and 180°)

acute angle: An angle that has a measure less than a right angle (less than 90°)

tangram: A puzzle created from a square cut into five triangles, a square, and a parallelogram

parallelogram: A shape that has four sides with opposite sides that are parallel

Build Your Understanding

Construct Two-Dimensional Shapes

You Will Need
• tangram pieces

Work with a partner for this activity.
Take turns completing the following steps:

1. Make a shape with three or more tangram pieces. One side of each piece must touch another side of a tangram piece. Do not show your partner your work.

2. Keep your shape covered. Describe it to your partner.

3. Your partner also has a tangram. She or he uses your description to make the same shape. Your partner can ask you a maximum of three questions.

4. When you are finished, compare your two shapes.

5. Record the shape you made and the tangram pieces you used to make your shape.

6. Change roles.

What Did You Learn?

1. Was your partner able to make the same shape? Why or why not?

2. What shape was hardest to describe? What shape was easiest to describe?

3. Describe how the activity changed after you switched roles.

4. Think about your descriptions. Explain which role you preferred. What would you change the next time you did this activity? Why?

5. What mathematical words helped you to describe your shapes?

Practice

You Will Need
• tangram pieces

Work with a partner to complete these activities:

1. Use a chart like the one below. Complete the chart with your partner using your tangram pieces. The first one has been done for you.

2. Create two smaller squares with the tangram pieces. On a piece of paper, trace the pieces within the squares.

3. Create a rectangle with the tangram pieces. Trace the pieces within the rectangle.

4. There are three different triangles in the tangram. Explain how they are similar and how they are different.

Name of Shape	Number of Sides	Number of Right Angles, Acute Angles, Obtuse Angles	Number of Equal Sides
1. triangle 1	3	1 right angle; 2 acute angles	2
2.			
3.			
4.			
5.			
6.			
7.			

Booklink

Grandfather Tang's Story: A Tale Told With Tangrams by Ann Tompert and Robert A. Parker (Crown Publishing: New York, USA, 1990). This story about shape-changing fairies is illustrated using only tangrams. You can use tangrams to tell your own stories, too.

Journal

Why is it important to know the names and descriptions of shapes and how to make them?

Lesson 4

Classifying Polygons

TRAVEL LOG

PLAN:

You will learn about the properties of different polygons. You will play a game using polygons. Think of strategies that could help you win. When you are finished, think of ways to improve the game.

DESTINATION:

The Prairie Provinces (Manitoba, Saskatchewan, Alberta)

DESCRIPTION:

As your bus makes its way through the prairies, you notice that the land is very flat like two-dimensional shapes. Crops stretch in the distance as far as you can see. Sometimes, though, you can see a building in the distance.

Grain elevators on the Prairies

Get Started

You Will Need
• pattern blocks

As a large group, answer and discuss these questions about polygons to get ready for the game.

1. Name and draw polygons from a three-sided figure to an eight-sided figure.

2. What makes a figure a regular polygon?

3. Which pattern blocks are regular polygons? How do you know?

4. Which pattern blocks are not regular polygons? How do you know?

Vocabulary

polygon: A shape that has at least three straight sides

regular polygon: A polygon with all sides and angles equal

irregular polygon: A polygon with sides of different lengths without a pattern

quadrilateral: A polygon that has four straight sides

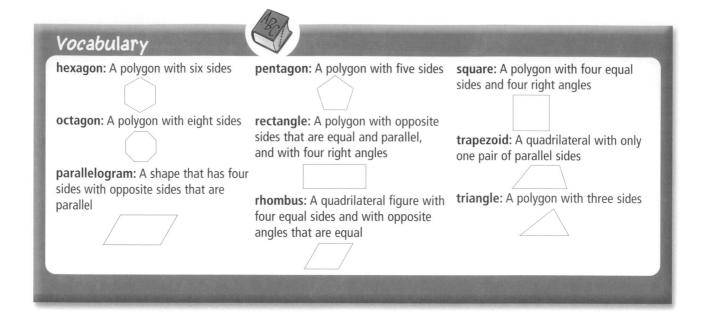

Vocabulary

hexagon: A polygon with six sides

octagon: A polygon with eight sides

parallelogram: A shape that has four sides with opposite sides that are parallel

pentagon: A polygon with five sides

rectangle: A polygon with opposite sides that are equal and parallel, and with four right angles

rhombus: A quadrilateral figure with four equal sides and with opposite angles that are equal

square: A polygon with four equal sides and four right angles

trapezoid: A quadrilateral with only one pair of parallel sides

triangle: A polygon with three sides

Build Your Understanding

Play With Polygons

You Will Need
- spinner face with eight divisions (two rhombuses, two triangles, and four shapes of your choice. Use pattern blocks to trace the shapes.)
- paper
- pattern blocks
- large hexagon pattern block
- paper clip
- pencil

Make a Spinner

1. Cut out a circle from a piece of paper. Design the circle like the one below, and use pattern blocks to trace the shapes.

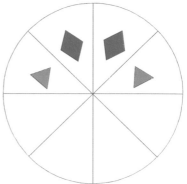

2. Hold the paper clip down with a pencil at the centre of the circle. Spin the paper clip with your finger.

Now you can use this spinner to play the following game with a partner!

How to Play

Play this game with a partner.

1. The spinner has eight spots, and four spots are free. Use pattern blocks to trace four shapes of your choice.

2. Each player spins the spinner. The player who lands on the block with the most sides is Player 1. Player 1 spins the spinner.

3. Depending on where the spinner lands, Player 1 must place one or two of the chosen blocks inside the large hexagon. The first piece must be placed on the side of the large hexagon. Any other piece must be attached to a side of a pattern block already inside the hexagon.

4. Player 2 spins the spinner. She or he must place one or two of the polygons named on the spinner beside any pattern block inside the hexagon.

5. If the hexagon is almost filled and a player spins a larger polygon that cannot fit, that player loses a turn.

6. Take turns until the hexagon is completely filled. The player who places the last possible piece in the large hexagon is the winner!

Variation
With your partner change one of the polygons on the spinner.

What Did You Learn?

1. What polygons did you choose? Why?

2. What polygons did you choose for a second game? Why?

3. When could you tell who was going to win? How did you know?

4. While you were playing, what strategies did you use? Explain.

5. Describe what you noticed about how the polygons fit into the hexagon.

6. How would you play the game differently next time?

1. a) In your notebook, make a chart like the one below. For each polygon, draw a diagram and fill in the number of sides and angles.

Name of Polygon	Diagram	Number of Sides	Number of Angles
triangle			
		5	
			7
hexagon			
		4	
			6

b) How could you complete some of the rows in your chart differently?

c) Add 3 more rows to your chart using different polygons.

2. Describe the relationship between these shapes:

a) trapezoid and hexagon

b) triangle and hexagon

c) rhombus and hexagon

Journal

Record your thoughts about the game. Describe how you could improve it. How would you test your improvements?

Record why you agree or disagree with this statement: "The game 'Play With Polygons' is based on skill."

Booklink

The Greedy Triangle by Marilyn Burns. Part of the Brainy Day Books Series. (Scholastic: New York, USA, 1995). An unhappy triangle decides to change his shape, only to find out that in the end, being a triangle wasn't so bad after all!

Show What You Know

Review: Lessons 1 to 4, Measurement and Polygons

1. Measure objects in your classroom and copy and complete this chart:

Item	Unit of Measure	Estimate	Actual
	mm		
		10 mm	
	cm		
		30 cm	
	m		
	m		

2. Convert these measurements.

   a) 5 cm = ■ mm   **b)** 70 mm = ■ cm

   c) 9.2 cm = ■ mm   **d)** 27 mm = ■ cm

   e) ■ m = 800 cm = ■ mm

   f) ■ cm = 2500 mm = ■ m

3. Use tangram pieces to make a shape or picture. Describe it to a classmate to see if they can make your shape or picture.

4. a) Identify objects in your classroom that have the following shapes. Then list the properties of each polygon.

Shape Name	Object	Sketch the Shape	Properties
Rectangle			
Square			
Triangle			
Trapezoid			

   b) What shapes are found most often in your classroom? Why do you think that this shape is used most often?

5. How would you explain to a friend what a rhombus is?

Lesson 5

Multiplying by 6

TRAVEL LOG

PLAN:
You will investigate how to organize athletes into groups of six for an opening ceremony.

DESTINATION:
Calgary, Alberta

DESCRIPTION:
Home of the Calgary Stampede, Calgary also hosted the Winter Olympics in 1988.

Calgary Stampede

1988 Calgary Winter Olympics

Get Started

Use a hundreds chart like the one on the right. Colour the multiples of 6 yellow, the multiples of 3 blue, and the multiples of 2 red. What patterns do you see? Discuss your observations with a group.

Technology
You can use a paint/draw computer program to show multiples of six using symbols.

1	2	3	4	5	6	7	8	9	10
11	12	13	14	15	16	17	18	19	20
21	22	23	24	25	26	27	28	29	30
31	32	33	34	35	36	37	38	39	40
41	42	43	44	45	46	47	48	49	50
51	52	53	54	55	56	57	58	59	60
61	62	63	64	65	66	67	68	69	70
71	72	73	74	75	76	77	78	79	80
81	82	83	84	85	86	87	88	89	90
91	92	93	94	95	96	97	98	99	100

Build Your Understanding

Multiply by 6

Put yourself back in time. You are working at Calgary's Winter Olympics. Your job is to help organize the athletes for the opening ceremonies into groups of six.

1. Create a chart into your notebook like the one below, and fill in the blanks:

Country	Groups of 6	Total
A	6 groups of 6	
B	7 groups of 6	
C	8 groups of 6	
D	9 groups of 6	

2. The first four countries to enter the stadium have their athletes organized in groups of 6. Calculate the total for each country.

3. In your notebook, write a multiplication sentence for each country in your chart.

What Did You Learn?

1. What do you notice if you divide the totals in the chart by 6?

2. Explain how multiples of 3 and multiples of 6 are related.

Practice

Mentally complete the following:

1. 6 x 6 = ■   **2.** 7 x 6 = ■   **3.** 6 x 5 = ■

4. 9 x 6 = ■   **5.** ■ x 6 = 48   **6.** ■ x ■ = 36

7. 6 x 8 = ■   **8.** 4 x 6 = ■   **9.** ■ x ■ = 12

10. Explain how you figured out the missing numbers in questions 6 and 9.

11. What is the difference between 7 x 4 = 28 and 4 x 7 = 28? Use pictures, numbers, and words to explain your answer.

Answer these questions:

12. 26
      x 6

13. 18
      x 6

14. 37
      x 6

15. 29
      x 6

16. 20
      x 6

17. 19
      x 6

18. 12
      x 6

19. 25
      x 6

20. Count by sixes using a hundred chart. Record all of the numbers that are multiples of 6 (for example, 6, 12, 18, 24).

21. What happens when you multiply by 6 and divide the product by 6? How are multiplication and division connected?

Math Problems to Solve

22. Carlo made a display of his model cars using 2 bookcases. He notices that he has 4 cars per shelf. One bookcase has 6 shelves and the other bookcase has 4 shelves.

Show two ways that Carlo can calculate how many model cars he has without counting them. Show your work in pictures, words, and numbers.

23. Sonia and Pedro each made some paper snowflakes to decorate a winter bulletin board. Each snowflake has 6 points. Sonia and Pedro counted all the points on their snowflakes. Sonia counted 60 points and Pedro counted 72 points. How many snowflakes did each make? Use pictures, numbers, and words.

Lesson 6

Dividing by 6

TRAVEL LOG

PLAN:
You will divide two-digit numbers by 6 and deal with remainders to divide items purchased at the mall.

DESTINATION:
Edmonton, Alberta

DESCRIPTION:
- Edmonton is the capital of Alberta.
- It is home to the West Edmonton Mall, the largest shopping centre in Canada.

West Edmonton Mall, Edmonton, Alberta

Get Started

The students to the right want to fairly divide 40 amusement park tickets among themselves.

1. How many tickets will each student get?

2. Will there be tickets left over? How do you know?

3. What would happen if only Grace and Bart were to divide the tickets?

4. What would happen if 2 more students wanted to join Grace, Andrea, and Bart and divide the tickets?

5. What strategies did you use to solve questions 1 through 4? Share your strategies with the class.

Vocabulary

remainder: The amount left over when one number is divided by another. For example, for 20 counters divided into 3 groups, there would be 2 counters left over.

remainder

Build Your Understanding

Dividing by 6 With Remainders

You Will Need
• counters

The students below visit the West Edmonton Mall. They buy 2 bags of jellybeans. The first bag contains 25 jellybeans that will be shared equally among half the students.

  1. How many jellybeans will each student get? Use counters to help you.

The second bag contains 29 jellybeans that will be shared equally among the remaining students.

  2. How many jellybeans will each student get?

  3. Explain your answers in pictures, numbers, and words.

All of the students decide to put both bags of jellybeans together and share them equally.

  4. How many jellybeans will each student get?

  5. Explain your answers in pictures, numbers, and words.

What Did You Learn?

1. How did the counters help you to find the answers to the questions?

2. What calculation can you do to prove that your division calculations are correct? Use examples to support your answer.

Practice

Mentally complete these equations.

1. 6 x 2 = ■   **2.** 12 ÷ 6 = ■   **3.** 24 ÷ 6 = ■

4. 4 x 6 = ■   **5.** 18 ÷ 3 = ■   **6.** 30 ÷ 6 = ■

7. 42 ÷ 6 = ■   **8.** 36 ÷ 6 = ■

Divide these equations.

9. 14 ÷ 6 = ■   **10.** 31 ÷ 6 = ■   **11.** 28 ÷ 6 = ■

12. 47 ÷ 6 = ■   **13.** 10 ÷ 6 = ■   **14.** 96 ÷ 6 = ■

15. 52 ÷ 6 = ■   **16.** 67 ÷ 6 = ■

A Math Problem to Solve

17. Christine found 2 quarters in the West Edmonton Mall. She decided to share her good fortune with 5 friends. What coins should she get in exchange so that she can divide the money equally? Show your work in pictures, numbers, and words.

Extension

18. A package of 25 jellybeans costs $2.00. A package of 34 jellybeans costs $3.00.

Which bag represents the best buy? Explain the reason for your choice.

Journal

Record what happens when you use a calculator to check a division question that has a remainder.

Lesson 7

Multiplying by 7

TRAVEL LOG

PLAN:
You will multiply one-digit and two-digit numbers by 7. Later you will calculate the age of bear cubs living in the Rocky Mountains.

DESTINATION:
The Rocky Mountains

DESCRIPTION:
Along the way between Alberta and British Columbia, you travel through the Rocky Mountains.

Rocky Mountains

Get Started

1. Work with a partner. Create two arrays of 7 using counters. Your first array should use one-digit numbers. Your second array should use two-digit numbers. Look at the examples to help you.

2. Write two multiplication facts for each array.

3. When you are finished, explain how your arrays relate to one another.

4. Use a hundreds chart to review and record multiples of 7. Try counting by 7s without looking at the hundreds chart. Practise with a partner.

Array 1

Array 2

Vocabulary

array: A grouping of numbers in rows and columns

Build Your Understanding

Multiply by 7

In the Rocky Mountains, there are 3 bear cubs who have cousins 7 times their ages.

Bear cub A is 4 months old. Bear cub B is 7 months old. Bear cub C is 13 months old.

How many months old is

1. the cousin of bear cub A?
2. the cousin of bear cub B?
3. the cousin of bear cub C?
   Show your work.

4. Find the age in years and months of each bear cub's cousin. You will need to convert the months to years.
5. If someone were seven times your age, what would be the age of that person?
6. What is the age of one of the adults in your home? What would be the age of something, such as a tree, that is seven times older than the adult?

What Did You Learn?

1. Describe the strategy you used to calculate the ages of the bear cubs' cousins.

2. What was the most difficult calculation to do in the problem? Explain how you calculated it.

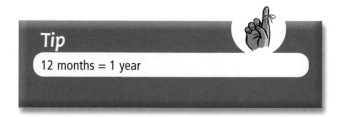

Tip

12 months = 1 year

Practice

Mentally multiply the following:

1. 4 x 7 = ▇   **2.** 2 x 7 = ▇   **3.** 6 x 7 = ▇

4. 5 x 7 = ▇   **5.** 7 x 7 = ▇   **6.** ▇ x 7 = 21

7. 7 x ▇ = 35   **8.** 28 = 7 x ▇

9.   10
      x 7

10.   18
       x 7

11.   34
       x 7

12.   23
       x 7

13.   47
       x 7

14.   81
       x 7

A Math Problem to Solve

15. The sales tax in some provinces is seven percent (7%). For each dollar you spend, you pay $0.07 extra.

For example, if you buy an item that costs $2.00, then you must pay 14¢ ($0.14) in tax.

How would you calculate the tax on an item that cost $4.00? $6.00? $20.00? $35.00?

What would be the total cost of each item?

Display your work in a chart.

Vocabulary

percent (%): A number out of 100. For example, 5% means 5 out of 100.

Cost of Item	Tax to be Paid	Total Cost
$2.00	$0.14	$2.14
$4.00		

Show What You Know

Review: Lessons 5 to 7, Multiplying and Dividing to 7

1. Create a set of flash cards with multiplication and division. Practise with a partner.

2. How would you explain to someone how to multiply 7 x 6 or 9 x 6 or 7 x 8? Use pictures, numbers, and words.

3. Your friend can only remember the facts up to 4 x 6. Using those facts, how could your friend calculate the answer to 8 x 6?

Lesson 8

Dividing by 7

TRAVEL LOG

PLAN:
You will study posters on tripods and how they can relate to dividing by 7.

DESTINATION:
Vancouver, British Columbia

DESCRIPTION:
• Vancouver is Canada's third largest city.
• Stanley Park is a famous landmark in Vancouver and is very popular with tourists. While walking through the park, you notice a display of posters for sale.

Totem poles in Stanley Park, Vancouver, British Columbia

Get Started

Each poster is on a tripod. Since a tripod has 3 legs, there would be 3 legs for each poster. How many legs would there be for 7 posters?

Vocabulary

tripod: A three-legged stand

Poster	Tripod Legs
7	21
14	42
21	147

Look at the chart above.

1. Describe the pattern in your notebook using pictures, numbers, or words.

2. Can you predict how many legs there would be for 28, 35, 42, and 49 posters? Explain how you made your predictions.

Lesson 8: Dividing by 7   89

Build Your Understanding

Buy Posters and Divide by 7

You Will Need
• chart

1. A group of four students decide to buy some of the posters. They each want to buy as many posters as they can with the money they have. All posters cost $7.00 each. Make a chart like the one shown to calculate how many posters each student can buy. The first one is done for you.

2. A different group of 5 students decide to buy some posters too. They have $70.00 altogether. How many posters can they buy? How many posters will each student in the group get if they are shared equally?

   Explain your answers in pictures, numbers and words.

Student	Money	Cost of 1 Poster	Total Number of Posters
A	$14.00		
B	$42.00		
C	$35.00		
D	$21.00		

What Did You Learn?

1. What do you notice about the amounts of money all the students had?

2. Are you able to mentally divide into each price? By what number?

3. How can you check to make sure your answers are correct?

Practice

Mentally calculate the following:

1. $14 \div 7 = \blacksquare$ **2.** $28 \div 7 = \blacksquare$ **3.** $49 \div 7 = \blacksquare$

4. $35 \div 7 = \blacksquare$ **5.** $21 \div 7 = \blacksquare$ **6.** $\blacksquare \div 7 = \blacksquare$

7. $21 \div \blacksquare = 3$ **8.** $8 \div 4 = \blacksquare$

Practise dividing with a remainder:

9. $7 \overline{)\, 23}$ **10.** $7 \overline{)\, 45}$ **11.** $7 \overline{)\, 55}$

12. $3 \overline{)\, 17}$ **13.** $5 \overline{)\, 29}$ **14.** $4 \overline{)\, 30}$

15. $7 \overline{)\, 87}$ **16.** $7 \overline{)\, 94}$

Write the next three numbers in each pattern:

17. 2, 4, 6, 8, $\blacksquare$, $\blacksquare$, $\blacksquare$ **18.** 35, 30, 25, $\blacksquare$, $\blacksquare$, $\blacksquare$

19. 49, 42, 35, $\blacksquare$, $\blacksquare$, $\blacksquare$ **20.** 7, 14, 28, $\blacksquare$, $\blacksquare$, $\blacksquare$

A Math Problem to Solve

21. A group of students are helping out their community by picking up garbage. Their goal is to collect 56 bags of garbage by the end of 4 weeks. How many bags will they need to collect each day to reach their goal? Show your work in pictures, numbers, and words.

Tip

1 week = 7 days

Technology

You can use a paint/draw computer program to create multiplication and division flash cards for 6 and 7. Print out the cards and cut them out to practise your multiplication and division.

Lesson 9

Estimating and Calculating Time

TRAVEL LOG

PLAN:
You will work with times on an analog clock.

DESTINATION:
The ferry from Victoria to Vancouver

DESCRIPTION:
- If you want to travel to Victoria, the capital of British Columbia, from Vancouver, you will probably take a ferry.
- These boats are so large people can take their cars on them. For example, the <u>Spirit</u> ferry can carry 2000 passengers and 470 cars.

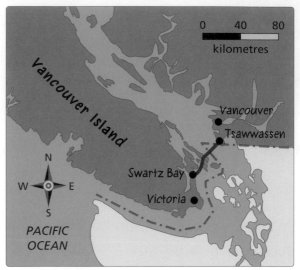

The red line on this map shows the ferry route from Tsawwassen to Swartz Bay.

Get Started

For each activity shown below, record whether the time is A.M. or P.M. (Use the vocabulary box on the next page to help you.) Discuss the reasons for your answers with a group.

Estimate and Calculate Time

You and your family are going to spend a day in Victoria. You board the ferry at Tsawwassen (near Vancouver) at 8:00 A.M. At Swartz Bay (near Victoria), a ferry leaves at the same time to travel to Tsawwassen. Ferries leave both ports every hour from 7:00 A.M. to 10:00 P.M. A one-way trip takes approximately 1 h 35 min.

> ### Vocabulary
> **A.M.:** Before noon (from 12:00 A.M. [midnight] to 11:59 A.M.)
> **P.M.:** After noon (from 12:00 P.M. [noon] to 11: 59 P.M.)

Ferry Schedule

From Tsawwassen to Swartz Bay

7:00 A.M.

8:00 A.M.

9:00 A.M.

You Will Need
• analog clock with moving hands

Answer these questions using A.M. and P.M. times:

1. You are going by tour bus to Victoria. The vehicle needs to be at the ferry station at least a half hour before the ferry leaves at 8:00 A.M. The bus arrives in the parking lot 40 min before the departure time. What time is it?

2. The ferry ride is 1 h 35 min long. What time do you arrive in Swartz Bay?

3. The bus arrives in Victoria at 9:55 A.M. The bus tours the city for 1 h 10 min and stops at Craigdarroch Castle. What time is it?

4. After an hour at the castle, you have lunch, which lasts 45 min. What time is it when you finish lunch?

5. After lunch, you and your family have three and a half hours to walk around the city of Victoria. What time do you need to be back at the bus?

6. How much time do you have before your tour goes for high tea at the Empress Hotel at 5:00 P.M.?

7. After high tea, which ferry ride do you think the group should take to return to Vancouver? Why?

What Did You Learn?

1. Compare your answers as part of a large group.

2. How did you calculate the times? With a partner, compare strategies you used to answer these questions.

Practice

In your notebook, briefly describe what you might do at these times:

1. 12:00 A.M.   **2.** 6:00 P.M.   **3.** 9:15 A.M. (Tuesday)

Write the times from the following sentences using numbers and A.M. or P.M. For example, twenty minutes after seven o'clock in the evening = 7:20 P.M.

4. In many schools, classes start at five minutes to nine o'clock.

5. Does school end at a quarter past three o'clock or half past three o'clock?

6. I will arrive at noon, just before lunch.

   Write the following times the way you would say them in a conversation:

7. 11:20 A.M.   **8.** 8:45 P.M.   **9.** 4:00 P.M.

A Math Problem to Solve

10. At 5:05 P.M. Carol orders pizza for dinner. The restaurant says that they will be there in 30 to 45 min. What is the earliest time the pizza can arrive? What is the latest time the pizza can arrive? Explain how you got your answers.

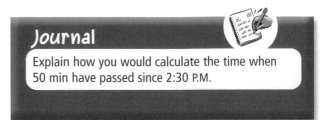

Journal

Explain how you would calculate the time when 50 min have passed since 2:30 P.M.

Lesson 10

Creating and Conducting a Survey

TRAVEL LOG

PLAN:

You will conduct a survey to find your classmates' opinions about one part of the trip.

DESTINATION:
Western Canada

DESCRIPTION:
- You have travelled to many interesting places in Western Canada.
- Look at the map to remind yourself of places you have visited.

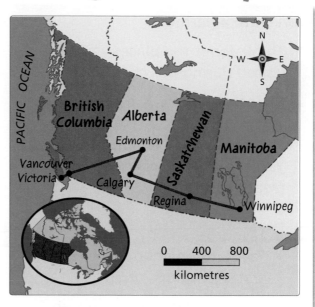

Get Started

You Will Need
- children's magazines

Look at some children's magazines. Many magazines survey children about what they like and don't like. Find a survey or use the one to the right. The question the survey authors ask is clear and short. How do the authors record the results of the survey? You will use this information when you design and conduct your own survey.

Look at the bar graph.

1. Think of three questions you could write about the graph for other students to answer.

2. Give your questions to a classmate to answer.

What Is Your Favourite Food?	
Food	Number of People
ice cream	15
pizza	25
hot dogs	10
french fries	20

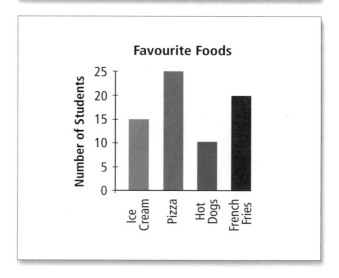

Lesson 10: Creating and Conducting a Survey   95

Create and Conduct a Survey

Work with a partner.

1. Think about the places you have visited during this chapter.

2. Choose one part of the trip. This will be the topic of your survey. Here are some examples of topics. You can use one of these topics or create your own.
   - favourite city
   - favourite activity
   - favourite method of transportation

3. Turn your topic into a question. Reread it to make sure it is clear and short.

4. Think about the survey in Get Started. How did the authors show results of their survey? Decide how you will show your results.

5. Predict the possible results of your survey based on your experiences. Record your predictions.

6. Conduct your survey. Get at least 20 responses.

7. Record the data that you gathered in your notebook. Examine your results and predictions.

8. How could you display your data?

Vocabulary

bar graph: A graph that uses parallel bars to show the relationship between quantities
data: Facts or figures about a topic. In a survey, data is information taken from people's responses to a questionnaire.
graph: A diagram that shows relationships between data. Many surveys show their results in a graph.

Tip

A fast way to record responses is to make a tally mark. For example, you can make a chart with these headings: Eastern Canada, Western Canada, Northern Canada. Draw a line to separate the headings. For each vote, draw one tally mark. When you get to five draw a line through the first four tally marks.

Calgary	Edmonton	Alberta
ⵌ	|||	ⵌ

What Did You Learn?

1. Share your results with your classmates. If other pairs of students chose the same topic that you did, how similar were your results? Explain the differences.

2. What question did you want answered in your survey? What did you find out?

3. Look at other students' surveys. Identify parts of their surveys that you would use if you were to do another survey. Give reasons why you would make these changes.

4. Discuss this activity with your partner. What did you find easiest to do? What did you find hardest to do? Give reasons why it was helpful to work with a partner for this activity.

5. What different ways did your classmates come up with to display and organize the data?

Practice

1. Look at surveys in magazines and newspapers. Record how your survey was similar or different.

2. Conduct another survey on a topic of your choice. Share your results with your classmates.

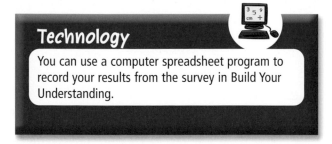

Technology

You can use a computer spreadsheet program to record your results from the survey in Build Your Understanding.

Lesson 11

Investigating Probability Using Multiplication

TRAVEL LOG

PLAN:
You will play a multiplication game. You will investigate how fair this game is and make changes to improve it.

Get Started

What are the chances of you rolling a product of 5 with two number cubes? Roll two number cubes (each with 1 to 6 counters) 15 times. Multiply the two numbers for each roll. Use tally marks to keep track of each roll on a chart like this one. Predict what product will turn up the most. You may use a calculator to help you.

	Number on Cubes																	
Roll	1	2	3	4	5	6	8	9	10	12	15	16	18	20	24	25	30	36
1																		
2																		
3																		
4																		
5																		

After you have made 15 throws, work as a class to record the data on a graph. Use your graph to answer these questions.

1. Which number was rolled the most? Which number was rolled the least?

2. Explain why one number is rolled more than another.

Build Your Understanding

Create a Calculation Game

You Will Need
- spinner (see page 76 for instructions on how to make one)

How to Play

1. Create a spinner. Divide the spinner into eight equal sections as illustrated, and write in the number expressions.

2. One player becomes Player A. The other player becomes Player B.

3. Take turns spinning.

4. Player A gets 2 points every time the spinner lands on a question whose product is an even number and 1 point if the product is an odd number.

   Player B gets 2 points every time the spinner lands on a question whose product is an odd number and 1 point if the product is an even number.

5. Predict who will win the game.

6. Play the game until each player has had 8 turns.

7. Record your scores. Create a score card like the one on page 100 to help you.

8. The player with the most points after 8 turns wins the game.

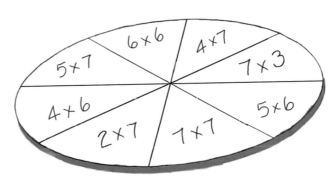

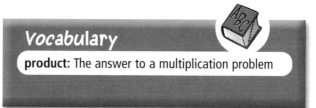

Vocabulary

product: The answer to a multiplication problem

Turn	Result	Score Player A	Player B
Example:	7 x 7 = 49 (odd)	1	
	5 x 7 = 35 (odd)		2
Turn 1			
Turn 2			
Turn 3			
Turn 4			
Turn 5			
Turn 6			
Turn 7			
Turn 8			
	Total Scores		

What Did You Learn?

1. How did your prediction of who would win the game compare to the results?

2. Would you describe this as a game of skill or a game of chance? Give reasons for your answer.

3. What makes the game fair or unfair?

Practice

Work with a partner to create your own probability game. How would you improve the calculation game? How would you make sure your game is fun? Exchange your game with another pair.

Chapter

2

NUMBER SENSE AND NUMERATION
MEASUREMENT
GEOMETRY AND SPATIAL SENSE
PATTERNING AND ALGEBRA
DATA MANAGEMENT AND PROBABILITY

Chapter Review

1. Estimate the length of each of the following lines, then measure the actual lengths with a ruler in both centimetres and millimetres. Copy and complete the chart below:

Line	Estimated Length	Actual Length in cm	Actual Length in mm
_____			
_____			

2. On a map, the distance between Toronto and Montréal is 6 cm. If the scale of the map is 1 cm to 100 km, how far is Montréal from Toronto in kilometres? Show your work using pictures, numbers and words.

3. Copy and complete the following:

a) 2 cm = ■ mm

b) 4 m = ■ cm = ■ mm

c) 5000 m = ■ km

d) 41 mm = ■ cm

e) 7 m = ■ cm

f) 6.3 m = ■ cm

4. Answer these riddles:

a) All my sides are equal in length and my angles are right angles. What am I?

b) I have one more side than a pentagon and all my angles are larger than right angles. What am I?

5. Make up your own polygon riddle like those in question 4. Give it to a partner to solve.

6. a) Name and describe the shapes in the tangram shown below.

b) How many small triangles fit in the largest triangle of a tangram? Show your answer in pictures, numbers, and words.

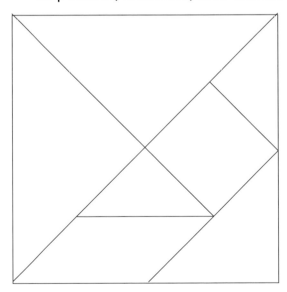

7. a) Copy the pattern below into your notebook. Continue the pattern with the next set of trapezoids and rhombuses.

   b) Explain the pattern in numbers and words.

8. a) The chart below shows how many customers Sri counted entering a grocery store each hour. Explain the pattern rule.

Hours	People Entering Store
10 A.M.	1
11 A.M.	3
12 P.M.	6
1 P.M.	10

   b) Explain the vertical and horizontal patterns in the table below. Are they consistent throughout the table?

410	420	430	440
510	520	530	540
610	620	630	640
710	720	730	740

   c) Create your own pattern on a number grid, and state the rule that you used.

9. Complete the following:
  a) 6 x 7 = ■   **b)** 3 x 6 = ■
  c) 5 x 7 = ■   **d)** 4 x 7 = ■
  e) 2 x 6 = ■   **f)** ■ x 7 = 14
  g) ■ x 6 = 24

  h) 17   **i)** 23   **j)** 52
      x 7   x 7   x 6

  k) Show how you would check your product for question 9 (j).

10. Divide the following:

  a) 6 ⟌ 30   **b)** 7 ⟌ 28

  c) 7 ⟌ 21   **d)** 6 ⟌ 42

  e) 7 ⟌ 35   **f)** 6 ⟌ 15

  g) 7 ⟌ 48   **h)** 6 ⟌ 39

  i) Show how you would check your quotient for question 10 (g).

11. In your notebook, write the time shown on the clocks below using A.M. or P.M.

12. If a plane left Vancouver at 12:35 P.M. and took 1 h 20 min to arrive in Calgary, what time did the plane land in Calgary?

13. Carlo did a survey with his class to see what colour of eyes everyone had. His tally results are below.

 a) Create a graph for this data and explain the results.

 b) Explain which eye-colour group has the most people? Which one has the least people?

Blue Eyes	Brown Eyes	Green Eyes	Violet Eyes	Dark Eyes
̶H̶H̶ |||	̶H̶H̶ ̶H̶H̶ |||	|||			||||

14. a) With a partner, conduct the same survey as Carlo did in question 13. How many students will you need to survey? Predict which eye-colour groups will have the most people and the least people.

 b) Display your data and explain the results.

 c) Compare your data to Carlo's.

15. a) In a group, create your own calculation game like the one on page 99. Write in eight multiplication or division expressions of your own. Decide if you are going to use the same rules and scoring system as the game on page 99. Predict who will win the game.

 b) Play your game. Was it fair or unfair? How would you improve your game?

Chapter 2

Chapter Wrap-Up ○▲■⬠

You will need
• your journal
• materials for creating a game

As part of a small group, you and your partners will create a game in which you will use the math skills you learned in Chapter 2. Before you do that, take some time to review what you have learned about math.

1. In groups, brainstorm math concepts or skills you studied in this chapter. Make notes in your journal.

2. a) Form small groups.

b) Brainstorm ideas for games. Let everyone speak freely. You may want to look at games you have played in this textbook so far for ideas.

c) Choose one or two students to record ideas.

d) Review your list of ideas. Decide on one idea that your group would like to develop as a game.

Here are some questions to think about:

- How many people can play?
- What math skills will be practised? You may want to look at the list of math skills you made to show your friend.
- Will players use prediction to help them play?
- What other strategies will players use?

- What materials will people need to play?
- Is your game based on skill or chance?
- How will you score your game?
- How will people know the rules?
- How will you decide who has won?
- What materials will you need to make your game?

3. Gather the things you need to create and play your game. As a group, test your game.

4. **a)** Once you have tested your game, gather in a group and review the game. Decide what you need to change to improve your game.

   b) Once you have added your improvements, test your game again.

   c) When you are happy with your game, you are ready to present it to others.

   d) Write the rules for your game on a piece of paper. With your teacher's help, plan a Math-a-thon game day for your class.

5. Play games created by other groups. With your group members, discuss how your game was similar to or different from other games.

6. Imagine that you work for a marketing company. Your job is to advertise your game to other people your age. Using newspapers, radio, television, or the Internet, create an advertisement for your game.

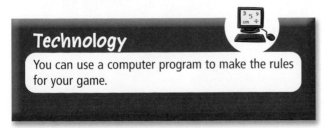

Technology

You can use a computer program to make the rules for your game.

Math Across the North

In this chapter, you will travel across Northern Canada—the Yukon, Northwest Territories, and Nunavut. Along the way you will

- work with place value to 10 000
- multiply and divide facts to 81
- divide two-digit numbers by a one-digit number
- multiply three-digit numbers by a one-digit number
- analyze number patterns
- practise graphing
- measure distances

At the end of this chapter, you will create a travel brochure using the math skills you have learned.

Answer these questions to help you prepare for the third stage of your trip:

1. What does 1000 look like? Use pictures, numbers, and words to describe 1000. What types of things come in thousands or are measured in thousands? Write your thoughts in your journal.
2. What month is your birthday in? As a class, survey the birthdays of your classmates and make a chart.

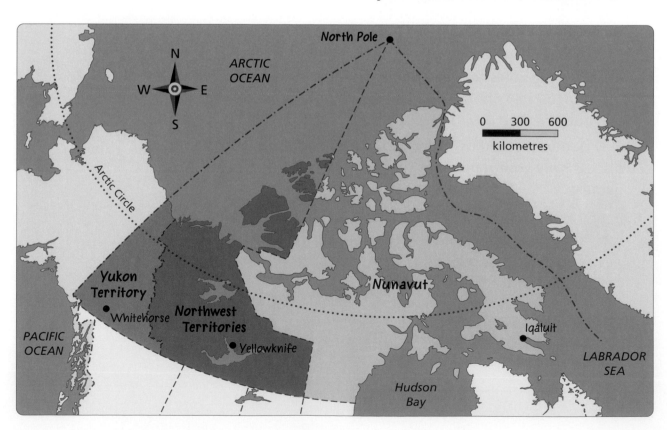

Lesson 1

Place Value to 10 000

TRAVEL LOG

PLAN:
You will compare and add numbers up to 10 000.

DESTINATION:
Canadian forests

DESCRIPTION:
- *Our forests contain large numbers of trees and are one of our major natural resources.*
- *Many trees are cut down each day to make paper, furniture, and building materials.*
- *To preserve our forests, new seedlings are planted in areas where trees have been harvested.*

Seedlings being planted in reforested area

Get Started

1. What does 10 000 look like? Here are three ways to show 10 000 trees. There are other ways to show 10 000. Work with a partner to show 10 000 in other ways.

10 000 Trees:

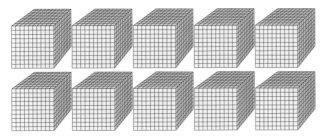

2. Think of a real-life situation where you saw about 10 000 of something. Share your response with the class.

10 000 Trees:

10 000 trees

10 000 Trees:

Lesson 1: Place Value to 10 000   **107**

Build Your Understanding

Numbers to 10 000

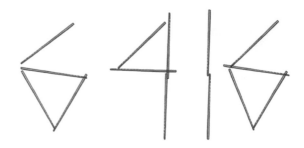

You Will Need
• place-value chart

Fort Nelson is a town of 4500 people located in a heavily forested area in the northern part of British Columbia. It is also home to the world's largest chopstick factory.

While visiting Fort Nelson, you visit the factory daily to record how many chopsticks were produced. Here are the numbers you record for one week. Record these numbers on a place-value chart.

Day 1 six thousand four hundred sixteen	**Day 5** five thousand one hundred twenty
Day 2 nine thousand nine hundred ninety	**Day 6** three thousand eight hundred ninety-one
Day 3 nine thousand thirty-four	
	Day 7 seven thousand six hundred two
Day 4 four thousand seven hundred ten	

1. On which days were the largest and the smallest number of chopsticks produced? How do you know this?

2. On which two days were the numbers almost the same? Explain how you know.

3. Write the expanded form of the number of chopsticks produced each day. (For example: Day 4 = 6000 + 400 + 10 + 6)

4. For each day, estimate how many more chopsticks had to be produced to make 10 000 chopsticks.

What Did You Learn?

1. To what place value did you estimate in question 4? Give reasons for your answer.

2. Would you need to estimate the number of chopsticks needed to make 10 000 on Day 2? Why or why not?

Practice

Identify the value of the underlined digits. Here is an example to get you started: 3<u>8</u>04: eight hundred.

1. <u>1</u>0 000   **2.** 607<u>2</u>   **3.** 9<u>2</u>40

4. <u>7</u>51   **5.** 40<u>3</u>8   **6.** <u>5</u>391

Compare the following numbers using < or >:

7. 8402 ■ 4835   **8.** 5923 ■ 7192

9. 9998 ■ 9899   **10.** 644 ■ 6044

11. Explain how you got your answer to question 9.

Write the following numbers in expanded form:

1902   3820   9874   6003

12. Explain what happens to the number 9 999 when you add 1. Use pictures, numbers, and words.

13. Write the numbers from question 11 in words. (For example: 1902 = one thousand nine hundred two)

14. You discover that more seedlings must be planted to replace trees that have been cut down. Here are the numbers that you have been given:

Year	Trees Cut Down	Seedlings Planted
1	960	800
2	980	840
3	1000	880
4		
5		

a) Describe the patterns that you notice.

b) What will happen in year 5?

c) If 50 seedlings die each year, what will be the total number of seedlings that survive in year 5? Show your work.

d) What will happen in 10 years?

Math Problems to Solve

15. Sri, Dana, Henna, and Ian were playing a game. Sri had 300 more points than Ian but 1000 less than Henna. Dana won the game by 40 points. If Ian's score is 3725, what was everyone else's score? Show your work.

16. Lesley and Daniel decided to count their sports cards. Lesley counted 2956 hockey cards and 4030 baseball cards. Daniel counted 5466 hockey cards and 1768 baseball cards.

    a) Who has more sports cards? Show your work.

    b) Estimate how many more sports cards they would each need to reach 10 000 cards. Explain how you got your estimates.

Extension

17. How many chopsticks do you think it would take to fill your classroom? Work with a partner to solve this problem. Share your results with the class.

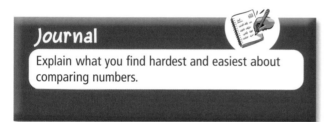

Journal

Explain what you find hardest and easiest about comparing numbers.

Booklink

On Beyond a Million: An Amazing Math Journey by David M. Schwartz and Paul Meisel (Dragonfly Books: New York, USA, 2001). "What is the biggest number in the world?" Travel with Professor X and his dog Y on a journey to find the answer to this question and more!

Lesson 2

Calculating Time Using Hours and Minutes

TRAVEL LOG

PLAN:
You will calculate times in hours and minutes.

DESTINATION:
Whitehorse, Yukon

DESCRIPTION:
- *Whitehorse is the capital of the Yukon.*
- *Winter nights are very long in the Yukon, but summer nights are very short.*

Whitehorse, Yukon

Get Started

If you lived in Whitehorse, you would see as many as 19 hours of sunlight on summer days. In the winter you would see as little as five hours of sunlight each day.

Imagine that you are in Whitehorse on June 21. The sun rises at 7:30 A.M. If there are 19 h of sunlight, what time will the sun set? Show two ways to calculate this. Use A.M. or P.M. and explain in pictures, numbers, and words. Which way was easier? Why?

Vocabulary

sunrise: The time the sun first appears each day
sunset: The time the sun disappears each day

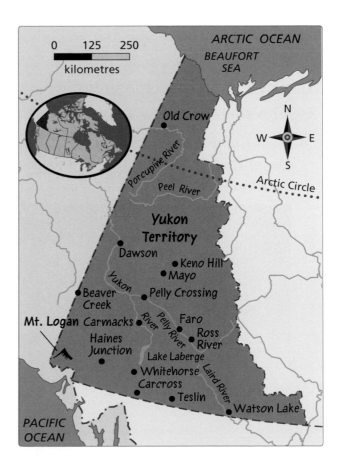

Investigate Time

You Will Need
• clock or a picture of a clock

Use a clock or a picture of a clock to help you answer these questions about time. Give your answers in pictures, numbers, and words.

1. It is the shortest day of the year (there are only 5 h of sunlight). The sun rises 2.5 h before noon and sets 2.5 h after noon.

 a) What time is sunrise?

 b) What time is sunset?

 c) Explain how you calculated the sunrise and sunset.

2. December 21 has the least amount of sunlight in the year. After this date, the sun rises approximately 5 min earlier every 2 days until June 21.

 Imagine that the sun rose at 7:15 A.M. on December 21. What time will the sun rise on January 10? Explain how you calculated the time. (Remember that there are 31 days in December.)

3. Imagine that sunset is at 6:45 P.M. on December 21 in Whitehorse. Sunset occurs approximately 5 min later every 2 days.

 a) What time will sunset be 24 days later?

 b) Is there a quick way to calculate this? Explain.

4. How many minutes earlier does the sun rise 4 days after December 21? 6 days after? 8 days after? 14 days after? 30 days after?

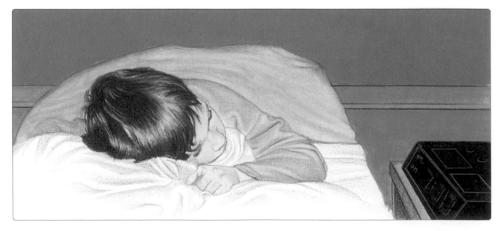

What Did You Learn?

1. Explain how you answered questions 3 and 4 in Build Your Understanding.

2. Is there a pattern to your answers for question 4? Explain.

Practice

1. It is 6:30 A.M. Record the time it will be 13 h 30 min later. Use A.M. or P.M. in your answer.

2. You sleep for 8 h 30 min. You wake up at 6:45 A.M. What time did you fall asleep? Show your work using pictures, numbers and words.

Math Problems to Solve

3. If it is June 25 in Whitehorse, what time is sunset? Explain your calculations in pictures, numbers, and words. (Use details from this lesson to help you solve this word problem.)

4. As a class, find and record your area's sunrise and sunset times for a few weeks. You can use a local newspaper or the Internet. Discuss any patterns you see at the end of the time period.

Extension

5. How many hours of sunlight does your area get on December 21? on June 21? What time is sunrise and sunset on these days?

Lesson 3

Problem Solving

TRAVEL LOG

PLAN:
You will sift through information to solve word problems.

DESTINATION:
Klondike River, Yukon

DESCRIPTION:
- In the late 1890s gold was discovered in the Klondike region of the Yukon and people rushed there to make their fortunes! Dawson City was at the centre of the gold rush.
- Prospectors (people looking for gold) would sift through sand from the rivers to find gold nuggets.

Prospecting in the Yukon

 ## Get Started

Work with a small group. Read the following word problem. Identify facts that are important and facts that are not important. Use a chart like the one on this page to help you.

In 1896, a prospector went to the store at 2:00 P.M. to buy groceries for the next two weeks. In that particular store, imagine that

- dozen eggs cost $2.00
- four oranges cost $1.00
- loaf of bread cost $1.50
- kilogram of meat cost $3.50
- cheese cost $1.00/100 g
- lettuce cost $1.00 each
- 2 kg bag of apples cost $3.00

At 3:00 P.M., the prospector came out of the store with these items:

- 2 kg bag of apples
- loaf of bread
- dozen eggs
- 200 g of cheese

How much change did he receive from a $10.00 bill?

Not Important	Important

Build Your Understanding

Problem Solving

You Will Need
• Important/Not Important chart

Solve the following word problems with a partner using pictures, numbers, and words. Read each question carefully and look for key words. For each problem, record facts on a chart like the one on page 114. Read through each problem, then choose one of these strategies to help you solve it:

• look for a pattern
• draw a picture
• make a table
• use what you have learned from solving a similar problem

1. Patrick wants to build a hexagonal wooden fence for his four horses. Each side of the fence will be 14 m in length. The wood will be 6 cm in thickness. How many metres of fence will Patrick need to buy? Design another fence with the same perimeter.

2. In the first hour after a convenience store opened, 2 customers entered. They spent $50.00. In the second hour, 4 customers came in and spent $65.00. In the third hour, 8 customers came in and spent $80.00. If this pattern continued every hour, how many customers came into the convenience store in the sixth hour after it opened? How much did they spend? Explain the pattern.

What Did You Learn?

1. Describe how you decided if information was important or not.

2. Explain how the problem helped you to decide which strategy to use.

3. Explain how you knew which operation to use.

Math Problems to Solve

Work on your own for this activity. For each problem, list the strategy you used to solve it. Show your work.

1. In one week, Department Store A sent out 4765 flyers advertising a half-price sale. Department Store B sent out 3309 flyers for a 25% off sale. How many more flyers did Department Store A send out than Department Store B? Show two different ways to solve this problem. Use pictures, numbers and words.

2. Create a problem like one that you have solved in this lesson. Give it to a classmate to solve.

3. Create a problem that requires the use of two or more of these numbers: 2614, 985, 4765, 5375. Show a solution to your problem. Switch problems with a classmate.

Show What You Know

Review: Lessons 1 to 3, Place Value and Time

1. Kelly, Hammond, Rachel, and Liam were trading stickers. Kelly had 650 more stickers than Hammond but 2500 less than Liam. Rachel had 4500 more stickers than Hammond. Liam had 6642 stickers.

    a) How many stickers did they each have? Show your work.

    b) Estimate how many stickers they would each need to reach 10 000 stickers. Explain how you got your estimates.

    c) List the strategy or strategies you used to solve this problem.

2. You go to bed at 9:30 P.M. You sleep for 10 hours. What time did you wake up? Show your work using pictures, numbers, and words.

3. It is 11:00 A.M. Record what time it will be 9 h 30 min later. Use A.M. or P.M. and explain how you got your answer.

Lesson 4

Multiplying by 8

TRAVEL LOG

PLAN:
You will multiply by 8 to count how many ravens one birdwatcher counts during the day.

DESTINATION:
Great Slave Lake, Northwest Territories

DESCRIPTION:
• Around Yellowknife, on Great Slave Lake, there are many different types of birds.
• Scientists believe that the raven is one of the smartest birds on the planet.

Raven

Get Started

You Will Need
• hundreds chart
• counters

1. Count by 8s to 100 using the hundreds chart.

2. What pattern(s) do you see?

3. How can you use the 10 times table to help you multiply by 8?

4. Explain why you could or could not use the 4 times table to help you multiply by 8.

5. Create an 8 times table using the hundreds chart.

1	2	3	4	5	6	7	8	9	10
11	12	13	14	15	16	17	18	19	20
21	22	23	24	25	26	27	28	29	30
31	32	33	34	35	36	37	38	39	40
41	42	43	44	45	46	47	48	49	50
51	52	53	54	55	56	57	58	59	60
61	62	63	64	65	66	67	68	69	70
71	72	73	74	75	76	77	78	79	80
81	82	83	84	85	86	87	88	89	90
91	92	93	94	95	96	97	98	99	100

Technology
You can use a computer spreadsheet program to show the multiples of 8.

Look at this array. Create two different arrays for another product from the 8 times tables (for example, 24 or 48). You can use counters to help you. Show two different multiplication sentences for each array.

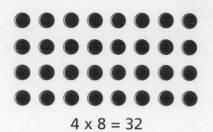

4 x 8 = 32

Build Your Understanding

Multiply by 8

A birdwatcher is on a boat on Great Slave Lake. She has binoculars, a lunch, and a pad of paper to record what she sees. Since there are many ravens in the area, she groups the birds by 8.

Use pictures, numbers, and words to calculate the number of ravens the birdwatcher saw.

1. by 10:00 A.M.
2. by 11:00 A.M.
3. between 10:00 A.M. and 11:00 A.M.
4. by 12:00 P.M.
5. between 10:00 A.M. and 1:00 P.M.
6. by 1:00 P.M.
7. between 9:00 A.M. and 12:00 P.M.
8. between 10:00 A.M. and 2:00 P.M.
9. between 9:00 A.M. and 2:00 P.M.

Time Intervals	Groups of Ravens
9:00 A.M. – 10:00 A.M.	4
10:00 A.M. – 11:00 A.M.	7
11:00 A.M. – 12:00 P.M.	6
12:00 P.M. – 1:00 P.M.	3
1:00 P.M. – 2:00 P.M.	9

What Did You Learn?

1. Describe a strategy to help you remember products in the 8 times table.

2. Which question in the 8 times table is hardest for you to answer? Why?

Practice

Mentally complete these equations:

1. 3 x 8 = ◼ **2.** 7 x 8 = ◼ **3.** 4 x 8 = ◼

4. 9 x 8 = ◼ **5.** 1 x 8 = ◼ **6.** 8 x 8 = ◼

7. 2 x 8 = ◼ **8.** 6 x 8 = ◼ **9.** ◼ x 8 = 80

10. 8 x ◼ = 32 **11.** 19 **12.** 25
                        x 8   x 8

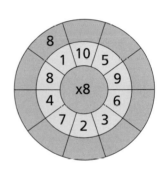

13. With a partner, practise the 8 times table with the numbers 1 to 10 for two minutes. You can use a diagram like the one to the right. Take turns.

14. Show 5 x 8 in an addition equation.

Math Problems to Solve

15. Your class has just finished an art project. To complete the project, the class used 7 boxes of markers. Each box contains 8 markers. 46 markers have been replaced in the boxes. How many markers still need to be returned? Show all your work, and explain the steps you followed.

16. Mark decided to count and record all the stop signs he saw in 3 days. Here are the numbers he recorded:

Day 1   Day 2   Day 3
  8   10   12

How many stop sign sides did Mark see in total? Remember that a stop sign has 8 sides. Show your work in pictures, numbers, and words.

Booklink

Bats on Parade by Kathi Appelt and Melissa Sweet (Morrow: New York, USA, 1999). Bats march in a parade to help you with your multiplication skills!

Dividing by 8

TRAVEL LOG

PLAN:
You will divide by 8 to find out how many dogsleds are competing in a race.

DESTINATION:
Yellowknife, Northwest Territories

DESCRIPTION:
• Yellowknife is the capital of the Northwest Territories.
• Each March, the city hosts the Caribou Carnival where one of the most popular contests is the Canadian Championship Dog Derby.

Get Started

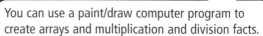

Create a division fact for each of these multiplication facts.

> Here is an example to get you started:
>
> 1 x 8 = 8   8 ÷ 8 = 1   8 ÷ 1 = 8

1. 2 x 8 = 16   **2.** 3 x 8 = 24

3. 4 x 8 = 32   **4.** 5 x 8 = 40

5. 6 x 8 = 48   **6.** 7 x 8 = 56

7. 8 x 8 = 64   **8.** 9 x 8 = 72

9. 10 x 8 = 8

Create a drawing of one of the division facts.

Technology

You can use a paint/draw computer program to create arrays and multiplication and division facts.

Build Your Understanding

Divide by 8

You Will Need
• counters

Imagine that you are at the Canadian Championship Dog Derby. 72 dogs are ready to race in teams of 8. Use counters to represent the dogs. Arrange the counters in groups of 8. Place the groups in rows to represent the dogs lining up for a race. When you have finished, draw how you organized your counters.

1. How many dogsleds are entered in the race?
2. After organizing 32 dogs, how many dogsleds would be in the race?
3. How many dogsleds would there be with 64 dogs? 40 dogs? 48 dogs? 16 dogs? 24 dogs? 56 dogs?
4. After organizing 45 dogs, how many dogsleds would be in the race?

What Did You Learn?

1. Describe how using counters helped you in this activity.
2. Explain which division fact by 8 is easiest for you to remember. Explain which is most difficult. Why?
3. Identify what operations you used to answer questions 1 to 4 in the Build Your Understanding.
4. How does knowing the 8 times table help when you divide by 8?

Practice

Mentally complete these equations:

1. $40 \div 8 = \blacksquare$
2. $8 \overline{)72}$
3. $16 \div 8 = \blacksquare$
4. $64 \div 8 = \blacksquare$
5. $48 \div 8 = \blacksquare$
6. $8 \div 8 = \blacksquare$
7. $8 \overline{)24}$
8. $80 \div 8 = \blacksquare$
9. $8 \overline{)32}$
10. $56 \div 8 = \blacksquare$
11. $8 \times 5 = \blacksquare$
12. $8 \times 7 = \blacksquare$
13. $9 \times 8 = \blacksquare$
14. $2 \times 8 = \blacksquare$
15. $16 \times 8 = \blacksquare$
16. $20 \times 8 = \blacksquare$

Divide these equations by 8 with a remainder:

17. $82 \div 8 = \blacksquare$
18. $44 \div 8 = \blacksquare$
19. $39 \div 8 = \blacksquare$
20. $8 \overline{)19}$
21. $57 \div 8 = \blacksquare$
22. $28 \div 8 = \blacksquare$
23. $8 \overline{)62} = \blacksquare$
24. $19 \div 8 = \blacksquare$

Lesson 6

Multiplying by 9

TRAVEL LOG

PLAN:
You will look at patterns in numbers when you multiply by 9.

DESTINATION:
Northern Canada

DESCRIPTION:
- In parts of Northern Canada, the ground is covered by snow most of the year.
- Snowflakes follow a pattern. Patterns can be natural, like snowflakes and leaves. Patterns can also be created, like patterns in some tiles and fabrics.

Get Started

1. Count by 9s. Begin by using the hundreds chart and then count without using the hundreds chart. What is the pattern of multiples of 9 in the hundreds chart?

2. How can you use the 10 times table to help you multiply by 9?

1	2	3	4	5	6	7	8	9	10
11	12	13	14	15	16	17	18	19	20
21	22	23	24	25	26	27	28	29	30
31	32	33	34	35	36	37	38	39	40
41	42	43	44	45	46	47	48	49	50
51	52	53	54	55	56	57	58	59	60
61	62	63	64	65	66	67	68	69	70
71	72	73	74	75	76	77	78	79	80
81	82	83	84	85	86	87	88	89	90
91	92	93	94	95	96	97	98	99	100

Build Your Understanding

Multiply by 9

Write a list of all multiplication facts on the 9 times table
(1 x 9 to 12 x 9). Look for a pattern in both factors and products.

Share your ideas in small groups of three or four students.
Think of ways you can show a pattern of 9. Decide on one
way and make your pattern. You can use pictures, counters,
or other items in the class (with your teacher's permission).

What Did You Learn?

1. Explain the pattern(s) you found in the 9 times table.

2. Outline how the pattern you discovered might help you to remember the 9 times table.

3. Compare your group's work to the work of other groups. Did the groups show the pattern the same way? Decide which group created the most inventive work. Give reasons to support your decision.

Practice

Mentally complete these equations:

1. 2 x 9 = ▦   **2.** 5 x 9 = ▦   **3.** 1 x 9 = ▦

4. 8 x 9 = ▦   **5.** 10 x 9 = ▦   **6.** 4 x 9 = ▦

7. 9 x 9 = ▦   **8.** 6 x 9 = ▦   **9.** 3 x 9 = ▦

10. 7 x 9 = ▦   **11.** 9 x ▦ = 81   **12.** 9 x ▦ = 45

13. 9 x ▦ = 72   **14.** ▦ x 9 = 36   **15.** 9 x ▦ = 36

16. 27 = 9 x ▦   **17.** 81 = 9 x ▦   **18.** 36 = 9 x ▦

19. 9 x 11 = ▦   **20.** 9 x 12 = ▦

Math Problems to Solve

21. Shakeela is almost finished high school. On Saturdays, she earns $9.00/h pumping gas. She works 6 h each Saturday. How much does Shakeela earn in one week? in two weeks? Show your work in pictures, numbers and words.

22. Shakeela is saving for a stereo that costs $300.00. How long does she have to work to save enough money? Explain using pictures, numbers and words.

A Math Game to Play

Play NADS (Nines Add, Doubles Subtract)

You Will Need
- 2 to 4 players
- 2 number cubes

Object: The first person to get 500 points wins the game.

How to Play

1. Take turns rolling the number cubes.

2. Add the two numbers.

3. Multiply the sum of the two numbers by 9. For example, if you roll a 4 and a 3, the sum is 7. 7 x 9 = 63.

4. Add the total to your score.

Player 1
63

5. If you roll a double, follow steps 2 and 3, but subtract the total from your score. For example, if you roll a 2 and a 2, the sum is 4. 4 x 9 = 36.

Player 1
63
− 36
27

6. Record your score.

7. The first person to reach 500 calls out "NADS!" and wins the game.

Lesson 7

Dividing by 9

TRAVEL LOG

PLAN:
You will count caribou. Your job is to divide the caribou into groups of 9.

DESTINATION:
Nunavut

DESCRIPTION:
- *Nunavut became Canada's newest territory on April 1, 1999. This vast area is very flat with few towns or villages.*
- *Many caribou roam the land.*

Get Started

1. How can knowing about the pattern of multiples of 9 help you divide by 9?

   Think about this as you look at the numbers below. Identify numbers you think can be divided by 9 without remainders.

   | 45 | 53 | 86 | 72 | 36 | 98 | 54 |

   Prove that your choice of numbers was correct.

2. Record the first 10 multiples of 9. Find the sum of the digits for each multiple. For example: 18 is a multiple of 9. 1 + 8 = 9

   What do you notice about the sum of all the multiples of 9? What numbers are they all divisible by?

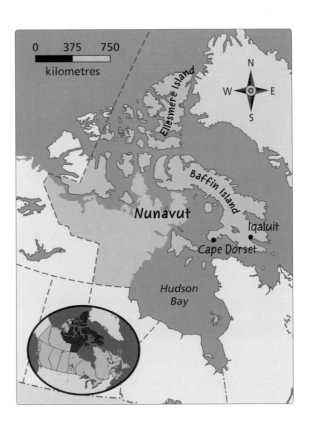

Divide by 9

You will need
• counters or blocks

You see a magnificent herd of caribou, and decide to count them. Counting by 9s, you reach 81 but then you lose track. You start over again, this time reaching 72 before you lose track. Each time you start again, you reach 9 less.

1. How many caribou did you count the third time? You may use counters or blocks to help you.

2. If the herd had 36 caribou, how many groups of 9 would you count?

3. If the herd had 54 caribou, how many groups of 9 would you count?

4. If the herd had 48 caribou, how many groups of 9 would you count? How many would you have left over?

What Did You Learn?

1. When dividing the number of caribou by 9, how did you know there would be no remainders?

2. What is an easy way to remember the quotients of division facts by 9? Explain.

Mentally complete these equations:

1. 36 ÷ 9 = ■   **2.** ■ ÷ 9 = 2   **3.** 54 ÷ 9 = ■

4. 81 ÷ 9 = ■   **5.** 27 ÷ ■ = 3   **6.** 72 ÷ 9 = ■

7. 9 ÷ 9 = ■   **8.** 45 ÷ 9 = ■   **9.** 63 ÷ 9 = ■

10. 90 ÷ 9 = ■   **11.** ■ ÷ 9 = 11   **12.** ■ ÷ 9 = 6

Divide the following and find the remainder. Check each quotient by using multiplication and addition. The first one has been done for you:

73 ÷ 9 = ■

```
      8
9 ) 73          9 x 8 = 72
    72          72 + 1 = 73
    ──
     1          remainder
```

13. 40 ÷ 9 = ■   **14.** 29 ÷ 9 = ■   **15.** 62 ÷ 9 = ■

16. 79 ÷ 9 = ■   **17.** 16 ÷ 9 = ■   **18.** 88 ÷ 9 = ■

A Math Problem to Solve

19. There are 75 linking cubes in a box. Each student needs 9 linking cubes to create a platform of 3 by 3 linking cubes.

a) How many students can create a platform?

b) How many linking cubes will be left over?

Show your work in pictures, numbers, and words.

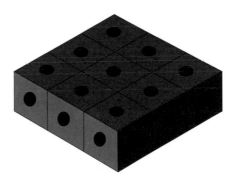

Show What You Know

Review: Lessons 4 to 7, Multiplying and Dividing to 9

1. 8 x 7 = ■   **2.** 9 x 4 = ■   **7.** 72 ÷ 8 = ■   **8.** 54 ÷ 9 = ■

3. 9 x 9 = ■   **4.** 6 x 8 = ■   **9.** 9) 29   **10.** 8) 50

5.   59   **6.**   83   **11.** 8) 49   **12.** 9) 86
       x 8   x 9

Rounding to the Nearest 10 and 100

TRAVEL LOG

PLAN:
You will help Bart figure out how much money he needs to buy winter coats. You will round the prices of more than one coat to the nearest multiple of 10 or 100.

DESTINATION:
Northern Canada

DESCRIPTION:
• When you are in Canada's North during the winter, you must have warm clothes.

Get Started

1. Round these numbers to the nearest 10:

   a) 17   **b)** 14   **c)** 3

   d) 32   **e)** 64   **f)** 96

2. Round these numbers to the nearest 100:

   a) 110   **b)** 235   **c)** 764

   d) 801   **e)** 888   **f)** 949

3. Explain the steps you followed to answer question 1(e).

4. Explain the steps you followed to answer 2(b).

Round up the number when the ones digit is 5 or greater. Round down the number when the ones digit is less than 5.

Round up the number when the tens digit is 5 or greater. Round down the number when the tens digit is less than 5.

Rounding Prices

Bart has saved enough money to buy winter coats for his parents, his brother, and himself. Before buying them, however, he wants to estimate how much money he will need. Here are the prices of the four coats he found:

$189.00, $220.00, $195.00, $275.00.

1. Round each number to the nearest 10, and then to the nearest 100.

2. Record your numbers in a chart like the one shown. The first price is done for you.

	Price	Tens	Hundreds
	$189.00	190.00	200.00
	$220.00		
	$195.00		
	$275.00		
Total			

 3. Total each set of rounded numbers (one total for the numbers rounded to the nearest 10 and one total for the numbers rounded to the nearest 100, as shown in the chart).

 4. Use a calculator to check each rounded total.

5. Use the calculator to figure out the exact cost of the coats.

1. Outline what was simplest for you to do when rounding and what was hardest. Explain your choices.

2. How close was your total rounded price to the exact price? Explain how rounding numbers can be helpful when someone is shopping.

3. List the multiples of 100 from 100 to 1000.

Round each number to the nearest 10:

1. 56   **2.** 72   **3.** 451   **4.** 904

5. 726   **6.** 208   **7.** 186   **8.** 622

Round each number to the nearest 100:

9. 942   **10.** 590   **11.** 357   **12.** 203

Round each dollar amount to the nearest 10, and then to the nearest 100.

13. $187.00   **14.** $253.00   **15.** $564.00   **16.** $921.00

17. $306.00   **18.** $711.00

19. Write down five numbers and give them to a partner. He or she must round each number to the nearest 10, and then to the nearest 100. Check to make sure your partner's answers are correct.

20. Where do you think rounding numbers would be useful outside of school? Make a list of ideas and share them with a classmate.

21. Create a word problem using estimation to purchase a number of the same type of items.

22. Find store catalogues or advertisements that show prices of items. With a partner, practice rounding the prices to the nearest 10, and then to the nearest 100.

Journal

Write your own set of rounding problems and give them to a classmate to solve. Then check to see if the answers are correct.

Booklink

One Hundred Hungry Ants by Elinor Pinczes and Bonnie Mackain (Houghton Mifflin: Boston, USA, 1993). One hundred hungry ants head towards a picnic, stopping along the way to show different divisions of one hundred.

Lesson 9

Multiplying Three-Digit Numbers by One-Digit Numbers

TRAVEL LOG

PLAN:
You will multiply three-digit numbers by one-digit numbers to find the total distance travelled by these animals.

DESTINATION:
Northern Canada

DESCRIPTION:
- The Canadian North is home to many forms of wildlife.
- Grizzlies, muskoxen, and caribou are some of the animals that live here.

Bear

Caribou

Muskoxen

Get Started

Scientists tracked a group of caribou for almost one month. They found that the caribou travelled approximately 9 km each day for 27 days. Use counters or the array below to help you find the total distance they travelled.

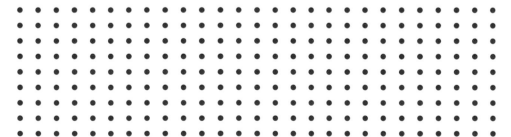

To help you calculate the distance the caribou travelled, divide the array into parts and multiply each part separately: 9 x 7, 9 x 10, and 9 x 10.

Write a multiplication sentence to find the total kilometres the caribou travelled.

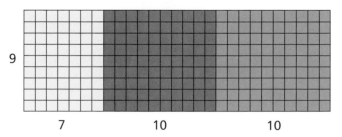

Let's begin multiplying three-digit numbers with one-digit numbers. These are two ways to multiply a three-digit number with a one-digit number:

	2	7	4
		x	8
		3	2
	5	6	0
1	6	0	0
2	1	9	2

	2	7	4
		x	8
1	6	0	0
	5	6	0
		3	2
2	1	9	2

Here is a third way to multiply a three-digit number with a one-digit number:

$$274 \times 8 = ?$$

$$200 \times 8 = 1600$$
$$70 \times 8 = + 560$$
$$4 \times 8 = + 32$$
$$2192$$

$$274 \times 8 = 2192$$

Build Your Understanding

Multiply Three-Digit Numbers by One-Digit Numbers

You Will Need
• 2 number cubes

x
=

1. Copy the boxes above into your notebook. Roll the number cubes. Find the sum of the two numbers. Each time the sum is a single digit, write the number in any one box. Continue until all boxes are full. (Ignore sums that are two-digit numbers.)

2. Find the answer to your question.

3. Rearrange the digits in the boxes to find the largest answer.

4. Rearrange the digits in the boxes to find the smallest answer.

5. Share your results with a classmate.

What Did You Learn?

1. Explain how you multiply a three-digit number by a one-digit number.

2. Write a journal entry that proves that the product of 137 x 6 is 822.

Practice

Estimate the following by rounding, and then check your results. Show your work.

1. 38 x 3	**2.** 57 x 7	**3.** 168 x 8	**4.** 490 x 9	**5.** 705 x 6
6. 92 x 6	**7.** 108 x 4	**8.** 352 x 7	**9.** 601 x 8	**10.** 954 x 3
11. 27 x 6	**12.** 248 x 9	**13.** 509 x 7	**14.** 789 x 2	**15.** 888 x 8

A Math Problem to Solve

16. In one section of a garden store, there are 48 roses. If the roses are organized into rows, how many roses would be in each row? Show your response in pictures, numbers, and words.

Show What You Know

Review: Lessons 8 and 9, Rounding and Multiplying

1. In your notebook, make a chart like the one on the right. Complete the chart by rounding each number to the nearest 10, and then to the nearest 100.

Number	Tens	Hundreds
364		
587		
112		
755		
924		
609		

2. Estimate the following by rounding, and then check your results. Show your work.

   a) 79
   x 8

   b) 461
   x 7

   c) 811
   x 3

   d) 275
   x 9

3. Find the total mass of groups of grizzlies, muskoxen, and caribou.

   Grizzlies are among the biggest bears on the continent. A full-grown male grizzly has a mass of approximately 215 kg. There are 6 full-grown grizzlies in the illustration. Each animal has a mass of 215 kg.

   A full-grown male muskox can have a mass of approximately 350 kg. Each of these muskoxen has a mass of 350 kg.

   Caribou are the lightest of the three animals. A full-grown male will have a mass of between 100 kg and 150 kg each. Four of these animals have a mass of 125 kg each. The remaining four have a mass of 150 kg each.

   Find the total mass of each group of animals by multiplying two ways. Show all of your work.

Lesson 10

Analyzing and Graphing Data

TRAVEL LOG

PLAN:

You will work with a small group to graph distances between places you have visited.

DESCRIPTION:
- You have travelled from coast to coast to coast in Canada and through Canada's North.
- You have travelled short distances and long distances, and visited towns, cities, and places in between.

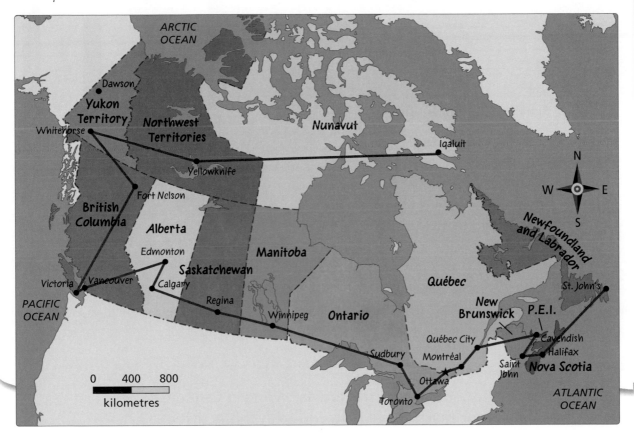

Vocabulary

pictograph: A graph that uses pictures to show the relationship between quantities

Tip

bar graph: A graph that uses parallel bars to show the relationship between quantities

Here are some types of graphs:

Pictograph

Tanya asked her friends to tell her what type of movie they most liked. She showed the information in a pictograph:

Type of Movie	Number of People
Action	🎥🎥🎥🎥🎥 🎥🎥🎥🎥🎥
Comedy	🎥🎥🎥🎥🎥 🎥🎥🎥🎥 🎥
Science Fiction	🎥🎥🎥
Musical	🎥🎥

Note: Each camera represents one person from Tanya's class.

1. Describe three things the information tells you.

2. How could this data be used?

Bar Graph

Barry graphed how long he practised piano each day for a week.

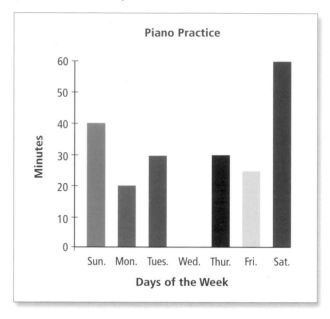

3. Explain three things that the graph tells you.

4. What would does the graph tell you about the time Barry spends practising?

Graph Data

Work with a partner. Choose Eastern Canada, Western Canada, or Northern Canada. Your teacher will help you with this activity.

1. List each city and town you visited in your chosen region. Use the map on page 135 to help you.

2. Find the distances between each city in the order that you visited them. Round your measurements to the nearest cm. For example, the distance between St. John's, Newfoundland and Halifax, Nova Scotia is 2.5 cm. 2.5 cm rounds to 3 cm. Each cm represents 400 km. Therefore the distance from St. John's to Halifax is 1200 km.

3. Calculate each distance until you have found all the distances travelled.

4. Review the graphs in Get Started. Decide what kind of graph you will use to show your information. Graph your information.

5. Present your graph to another pair. Explain why you presented your data this way.

6. Ask the other pair questions based on your graph. For example, ask them to find the two places that are the farthest apart.

What Did You Learn?

1. What type of graph did you choose, and why?

2. With your partner, identify ways you could improve your graph.

3. Why do you think it is important to properly label a graph?

4. What did you find the most challenging when graphing your data? Explain.

Practice

Look at the five graphs on page 138. They show how much precipitation a city received.

1. For each city, name the month that had the most precipitation.

2. For each city, name the month that had the least precipitation.

3. Which city had the most precipitation in a year? Explain how you got your answer.

4. Which city had the least precipitation in a year?

5. Name ways this information could be used.

6. What does this information about precipitation tell you about these cities?

7. Based on the information in the graphs, which city would you like to visit? Explain your answer.

Vocabulary

precipitation: Any form of water falling from the sky or on the ground, such as rain, snow, or dew

Precipitation Graphs Across Canada

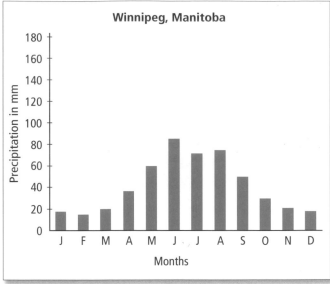

Victoria, British Columbia

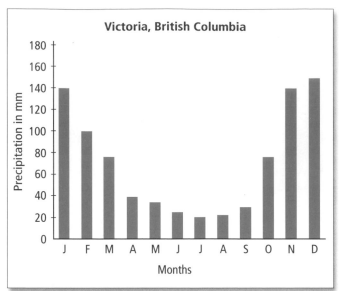

Winnipeg, Manitoba

Québec City, Québec

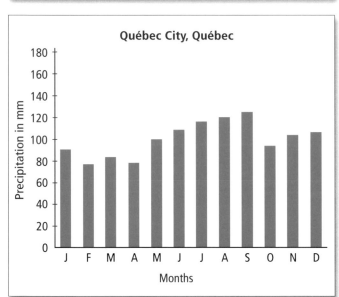

Iqaluit, Nunavut

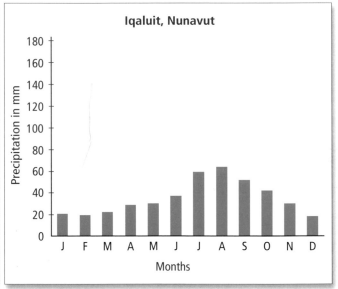

Halifax, Nova Scotia

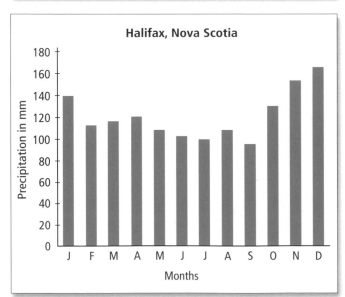

Technology

You can use a computer graphing program to create a precipitation chart for your area. (Use the Internet to research the information.) Compare your results to these locations across Canada.

Lesson 11

Conducting a Survey and Graphing Its Data

TRAVEL LOG

PLAN:
In Chapter 2, you created and conducted a survey. In this lesson, you will conduct a survey and graph the data that you gather.

Get Started

1. In groups of three or four students, discuss what you know about creating and conducting a survey. List the steps you need to follow. Now review what you know about graphing information.

2. As a large group, share your information with the class. Together, develop a plan for creating and conducting a survey.

Lesson 11: Conducting a Survey and Graphing Its Data   139

Build Your Understanding

Create a Survey and Graph Data

Here is the topic for your survey:

Which area of Canada would you like to promote to visitors to Canada: Eastern Canada, Western Canada, or Northern Canada? With a partner from your group, complete the following steps:

1. Review your list of steps to conduct a survey.

2. Plan how you will create and conduct your survey.

3. Predict the possible results of your survey.

4. Conduct your survey!

5. Tally your results.

Tip

A fast way to record responses is to make a tally mark. For example, you can make a chart with these headings: Eastern Canada, Western Canada, Northern Canada. Draw a line to separate the headings. For each vote, draw one tally mark. When you get to five, draw a line through the first four tally marks.

Eastern Canada	Western Canada	Northern Canada
⊥⊦⊦⊦⊦	|||	⊦⊦⊦⊦

Graph Your Results

6. Count the total for each region.

7. Discuss ways you can show your information. Review the graphs you made in the last lesson.

8. Choose one way to display your information.

9. Create your graph.

10. Post your graph where others can view it.

What Did You Learn?

1. Each pair had the same survey topic. Compare your graph to others'. Did you report the same results? If not, give a reason that may explain why the results were different.

2. How alike or different were the graphs? Name the type of graph most groups used.

3. Explain your choice of graph.

4. With your partner, write three questions about your graph.

5. Give your questions to another pair to answer.

6. What conclusions can you make from looking at your graph?

Practice

Create Another Survey

Create a survey to find out something about your family members.
Here are some sample topics you might want to use:

• number of times each person does the laundry in a week or month

• number of phone calls each person receives during one week

• number of times eah person walks the dog during one week

1. Predict the results.

2. Decide how you will collect your data and tally it.

3. How might you record the results for a person who did not want to choose any of your choices?

4. Collect your data.

5. Decide how you will graph it.

6. Give your graph to a partner. Ask your partner to tell you three things she or he learned from your graph.

Chapter Review

1. Sri, Dana, and Bart all have a collection of pennies. Sri has 2405 pennies, Dana has 2045 pennies, and Bart has 5204 pennies. Who has the most pennies? the least? How do you know?

2. Between which two multiples of 100 are each of the following numbers found?

    a) 478   **b)** 792   **c)** 106   **d)** 2840

3. Between which two multiples of 1000 are each of the following numbers found?

    a) 2958 **b)** 9021 **c)** 5603 **d)** 4007

    e) Explain how you know which two multiples of 1000 a number in the thousands is between.

4. Write the following numbers in words:

    a) 3894 **b)** 9065 **c)** 1207

5. Name the value of the underlined digit:

    a) <u>8</u>203 **b)** 24<u>7</u>1 **c)** 503<u>9</u> **d)** 1<u>6</u>93

6. Show 1693 with drawings of base-ten blocks.

7. Name each of the following numbers:

    a) one hundred less than 8483

    b) ten more than 735

    c) one thousand more than 6291

    d) one less than 2560

8. It is 8:00 A.M. Record the time it will be 15 h 30 min later. Use A.M. or P.M. in your answer.

9. You sleep for 10 hours. You wake up at 6:30 A.M. What time did you fall asleep? Show your work.

10. For the following problems, record in your notebook the information that is not important and the information that is important. Then solve the problem.

    a) Mary, who is nine years old, travelled 471 km with her family by car from Halifax to Fredericton. After staying in Fredericton for two days, Mary's family drove to Charlottetown. The total distance was 840 km from Halifax to Charlottetown. What is the distance Mary's family travelled from Fredericton to Charlottetown?

Tip

Remember that a large cube equals 1000, a flat equals 100, a rod equals 10, and a small cube equals 1.

b) Luke is one year old. His brother, Marc, is seven years older. Their combined heights add up to their father's height. If Luke is 0.7 m tall and Marc is 1.1 m tall, how tall is their father?

11. Multiply the following:

a) 7 x 8 = ■ **b)** 9 x 3 = ■

c) 4 x 8 = ■ **d)** 5 x 9 = ■

e) 8 x 6 = ■ **f)** 9 x 9 = ■

g) 10 x 9 = ■ **h)** 30 x 8 = ■

i) 100 x 6 = ■ **j)** 200 x 9 = ■

k) $\begin{array}{r} 25 \\ \times\ 8 \\ \hline \end{array}$ **l)** $\begin{array}{r} 72 \\ \times\ 9 \\ \hline \end{array}$ **m)** $\begin{array}{r} 138 \\ \times\ 8 \\ \hline \end{array}$ **n)** $\begin{array}{r} 407 \\ \times\ 9 \\ \hline \end{array}$

o) Show how you would check the product from question 11 (n).

12. Divide the following:

a) 63 ÷ 9 = ■ **b)** 36 ÷ 9 = ■

c) $8\overline{)48}$ **d)** $8\overline{)16}$

e) $8\overline{)40}$ **f)** $9\overline{)54}$

g) 70 ÷ 8 = ■ **h)** $9\overline{)86}$

i) $9\overline{)17}$ **j)** $8\overline{)25}$

k) Show how you would check the quotient from question 12 (j).

13. Round each number to the nearest 10, and then to the nearest 100.

a) 734 **b)** 155

c) 474 **d)** 811

14. Henna, Christine, Ian, and Evan earned money for chores they did around the house.

Name of Student	Money Earned
Henna	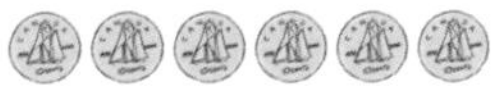
Christine	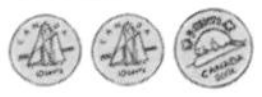
Ian	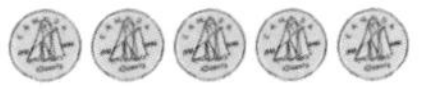
Evan	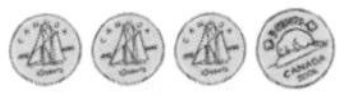

a) How much money did each student earn?

b) Who earned twice as much money as Christine?

15. The students in Carlo's class did the following survey on pets they had at home.

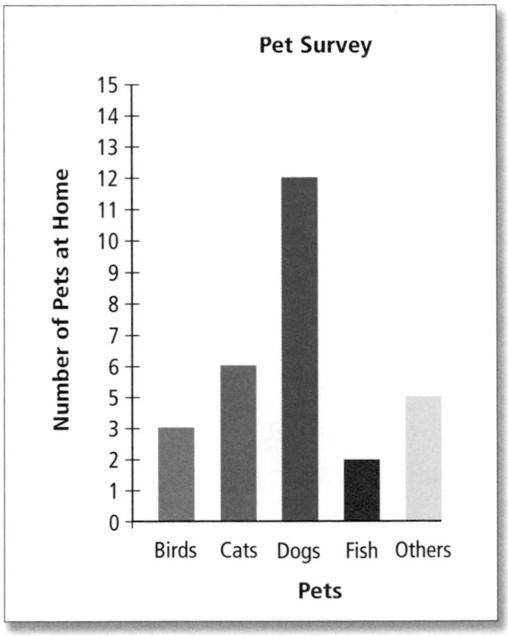

Write three questions that could be answered by this graph.

Chapter 3

Chapter Wrap-Up

You Will Need
• your journal
• materials to make a brochure

You have learned many new math skills while travelling across Canada's North.

Québec City, Québec

Vancouver Island, British Columbia

Iqaluit, Nunavut

Now is your chance to choose an area of the North that you would like to promote in a brochure. You will work with a partner to brainstorm ideas and make a travel brochure. To help you prepare for your brochure, take some time to review Chapter 3 and look at the math ideas you have learned.

You will create your own travel brochure and include

• at least three math skills or topics you have learned or practised

Work on Your Brochure

1. Form small groups.

2. Brainstorm what you will include in your brochure. Here are some things to think about:

- math skills and concepts to include
- illustrations or pictures you will include
- places in the North you will highlight
- tools you can use for research
- what you will say about each place
- what you will need to create your brochure
- how much time you have to work on your brochure
- how you are being evaluated on your brochure

3. On your own, gather the information, the tools, and the materials you will need.

4. Make your own brochure.

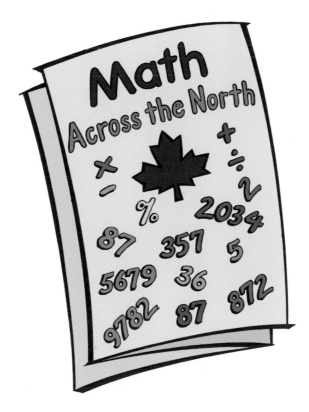

Share Your Brochure

1. Trade brochures with another classmate.

2. Identify the math concepts included in each brochure.

3. If you were a visitor to the North, how would this brochure help you to learn about this part of our country?

4. As a class, identify concepts that were the same in each brochure and concepts that were different.

5. Make a class display in the library or another part of the school, so that other classes can see your work.

Congratulations on completing this journey and good luck for what lies ahead!

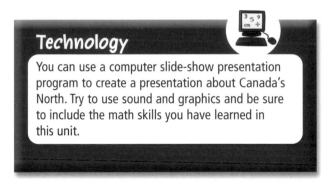

Technology

You can use a computer slide-show presentation program to create a presentation about Canada's North. Try to use sound and graphics and be sure to include the math skills you have learned in this unit.

Problems to Solve

Here are some more fun problems for you to solve. You will be given a helpful problem-solving strategy to use for the first four problems. For the last two problems, you get to choose a strategy from the ones you have learned this year.

Problem 5

Representing and Exploring Fractions

STRATEGY: WORK BACKWARDS

In the "Work Backwards" strategy, you begin working with the information at the end of the problem and work backwards.

OBJECTIVE:

Represent and explore the relationship between fractions

Problem

You Will Need
• counters or unit blocks

The parents at St. Albert School are planning a Donut Day. Seventy-two students ordered one donut each. One-third of the students ordered chocolate donuts, while half of the total students ordered caramel. The remaining one-sixth of the students ordered rainbow sprinkled donuts. How many of each kind of donuts do the parents need to order? Use the "Work Backwards" strategy to help you solve this problem. Show your answer in pictures, numbers, and words.

Reflection

1. What question are you trying to answer?

2. What information do you know?

3. How can you use the counters?

4. What donut order did you figure out first, second, and then last? Why?

5. Was the "Work Backwards" strategy a good strategy to use for this question?

6. Explain your solution to a classmate.

Extension

What would happen to the answer if the number 72 in the problem is changed to 144?

Journal

Write about a time you worked backwards to solve a problem.

Tip

Problem-Solving Steps
1. Understand the problem   2. Pick a strategy
3. Solve the problem   4. Share and reflect

Problem 6

Looking at Probability

STRATEGY: SOLVE A SIMPLE OR SIMILAR PROBLEM

If you find the problem that you are working on to be challenging, you can make it simpler by using this strategy. For instance, you can reduce large numbers to smaller numbers or reduce the amount of items in a problem. You might figure out a pattern or decide on an easier way to figure out the solution.

OBJECTIVE:

Solve a simple probability problem

Problem

Play "Rock, Paper, Scissors" with a classmate to see whose turn it is to be goalie in a floor hockey game. What is the probability of you and your classmate both showing scissors with your hands? Use the "Solve a Simple or Similar Problem" strategy to help you answer this question.

"Rock, Paper, Scissors" is a game for two players. It is usually played to help make a decision. After a count of three, both players show one of the following three hand symbols:

Rock—closed fist

Paper—hand flat

Scissors—index and middle fingers open like scissors

Rock beats scissors, scissors beats paper, and paper beats rock.

Reflection

1. What do you know about the game "Rock, Paper, Scissors"?

2. What are you trying to find out?

3. How can you make the problem similar or easier?

4. How did the problem-solving strategy help solve the question?

Tip

Imagine there are only two choices (rock and paper). Or, create a tree diagram to show all the possible results.

Extension

1. What is the probability of winning "Rock, Paper, Scissors"?

2. Invent a similar game that uses hand symbols.

3. What are your chances of winning the game you invented? How did you figure this out?

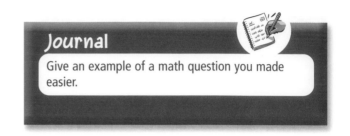

Journal

Give an example of a math question you made easier.

Problem 7

Building Prisms With the Same Volume

STRATEGY: MAKE A MODEL

You can use different materials such as egg cartons, construction paper, or craft sticks to build a model. Using these materials helps you to see a solution to the problem.

OBJECTIVE:

Model three-dimensional figures of specific volumes using blocks

Problem

You Will Need
• cubic centimetre blocks or linking cubes

At the math fair, students were given cubic centimetre blocks and challenged to make rectangular prisms that have a volume of 24 cm³. How many different rectangular prisms could be made? Use the "Make a Model" strategy to solve this problem.

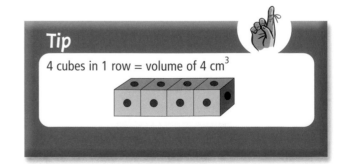

Tip

4 cubes in 1 row = volume of 4 cm^3

Reflection

1. How many cubic centimetre blocks were needed to make one prism?
2. Describe the length, width, and height of each prism.
3. Compare your models. How are they the same or different?
4. Did making models help you solve this problem? Explain.
5. Share your models with a classmate.

Extension

1. Write a math equation for each model.
2. Make a list of the rectangular prism shapes found in your classroom.
3. Find a specific number of cubes from which eight different rectangular prisms could be made. Explain how you got your answer.

Problem 8

Relating Nets to 3-D Objects

STRATEGY: LOOK FOR A PATTERN

"Look for a Pattern" is an important strategy and it can be used for many different kinds of problems. You can identify many different types of patterns, such as patterns in the things you see, or the numbers you are working with. You can then continue the pattern to find the solution.

OBJECTIVE:

Relate nets to three-dimensional objects

Problem

You Will Need
• three-dimensional solids

While visiting an art gallery, you notice an artist making a sculpture of pyramids. The artist would like to know what the net of each pyramid looks like. Use the "Look for a Pattern" strategy while solving this problem.

Reflection

1. What does the word *net* mean in math?

2. What are you trying to solve?

3. Identify the shapes in each net.

4. Name the type of pyramid each net would make.

Journal

How does the "Look for a Pattern" strategy compare to the other strategies you have learned?

5. Explain how pyramids are named.

6. Compare the number of shapes used to make each net.

7. What patterns did you notice? (Hint: How is the base of a pyramid related to the number of faces it has?)

8. How many different nets can be made for each type of pyramid? Draw them.

Extension

1. Pick a three-dimensional solid of your choice. Draw nets for the solid you choose.

2. Make a list of all the three-dimensional solids you know. Draw nets for each solid that you name. Compare your list with a classmate.

3. Are there any three-dimensional solids that a net cannot be made for? Explain.

Problem 9

MEASUREMENT
NUMBER SENSE AND NUMERATION

Estimating and Calculating Sums and Differences

STRATEGY: YOUR CHOICE

OBJECTIVE:
Estimate sums and differences of whole numbers and decimals

Problem

Imagine that you earned the following amounts shovelling snow:

Storm 1 – $11.30   Storm 2 – $23.50
Storm 3 – $ 9.60   Storm 4 – $16.40
Storm 5 – $15.00

1. Estimate how much money you earned. Choose any strategy.

2. Now figure out the actual total.

Tips

1. Round each number to the nearest 10 and then add the rounded numbers together. What estimate did you arrive at using this method?

2. Are there certain numbers that can be clustered together to help you come up with an estimate? Which ones? Why do they go together?

Reflection

1. Explain how you came up with your estimate.

2. Is the actual amount earned higher or lower than your estimate? Explain why.

3. How close was your estimate to the actual total?

4. Which problem-solving strategy did you use? Why?

5. What other problem-solving strategies could you have used?

6. Try the front-end addition method to come up with an estimate. Start by adding the tens numbers together, and then add up the ones numbers in your head. Finally add these two numbers together. What estimate did you arrive at using this method?

Extension

1. Arrange the amounts in order from least to greatest.

2. Make up a similar problem. Give it to a classmate to solve.

Problem 10

Analyzing Patterns

STRATEGY: YOUR CHOICE

OBJECTIVE:
Solve a problem by applying a patterning strategy

Problem

Mario and Heather have a school week (five days) to finish their science project. They both plan to work on the project for 2 hours the first day. Mario will spend 30 minutes more each day working on the project. In the following days, Heather will alternate, first working 1 hour less than the previous day, then 2 hours more. How many hours did they each work on the project by the end of the week? Use pictures, numbers, and words to show your work.

Reflection

1. What strategy or strategies did you use to solve the problem?
2. What other problem-solving strategies could you have used?
3. Did making a picture help you solve this problem? Explain.
4. Discuss this problem with a classmate. What did you find the easiest to do? What did you find the hardest to do? Explain your solution to your classmate.

Extension

1. Create a problem that uses two or more number patterns. Give it to a classmate to solve.
2. Use a hundreds chart. With a partner, find as many different number patterns as you can. List and describe all the number patterns you found. Share your patterns with the class.

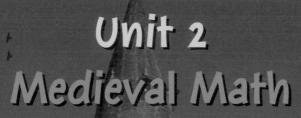

Unit 2
Medieval Math

Mathematics has been used throughout history. Imagine that on a warm, sunny day you stumble upon a time machine that transports you and your class back in time to a world of castles and knights.

In Chapter 4, you will journey through medieval buildings, learn about geometry, and apply what you have learned to make your own two-dimensional plan and three-dimensional castles.

In Chapter 5, you will learn about the mathematics of a medieval feast and will study concepts such as symmetry, shapes, and area. At the end of the chapter you will design a medieval placemat for a royal person to use at a feast.

In Chapter 6, you will use concepts such as time, money, and measurement to plan a medieval festival.

Enjoy your journey!

Math in Medieval Castles

Medieval architects needed math skills to build castles. In this chapter, you will learn some of the math skills they used, so that you too can design and create your own model of a medieval building.

In this chapter you will

- construct and describe two-dimensional shapes (squares, rectangles, parallelograms, trapezoids, rhombuses)
- construct and describe three-dimensional figures (cylinders, cones, pyramids, prisms, cubes)
- measure length
- examine and measure lines

1. Before you travel back to medieval times, look around your classroom for different-shaped and sized objects. Create a chart comparing the objects — their sizes, shapes, and uses.

2. Choose a room in your home to measure. Before you measure the room, estimate the measurements. With a tape measure or ruler measure the dimensions of the room. How accurate were your estimates? Draw a sketch of the room. Try to be as accurate as you can with the measurements.

Now you are ready to explore math in medieval times. Good luck!

This type of castle is called a motte-and-bailey castle.

Lesson 1

Two-Dimensional Shapes

JOURNEY NOTE

PLAN:
You will identify, compare, and construct two-dimensional shapes. At the end of this lesson, you will be able to name the following polygons: squares, rectangles, parallelograms, and trapezoids.

DESCRIPTION:
You begin your journey down a medieval pathway with your teacher and your classmates and notice the countryside around you.

Get Started

This is the layout of a farm in medieval times. What shapes do you see?

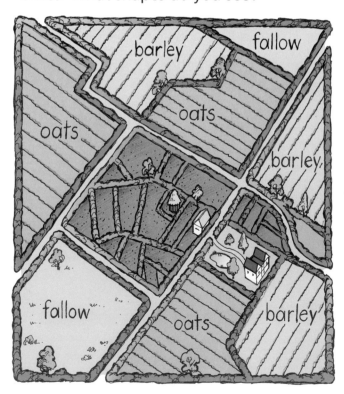

1. In your notebook, make and complete a table like the one below. Remember that 1 cm = 10 mm.

2. Estimate the number of each shape in the farm layout. Check your estimate by counting.

3. Compare your answers with a classmate.

Name of Shape	Number of Sides	Number of Vertices	Length of Sides (mm)

Tip

Refer to the glossary (pp 406–413) for definitions of many two-dimensional shapes.

Build Your Understanding

Construct Two-Dimensional Shapes

You Will Need
- toothpicks

Vocabulary

two-dimensional: Having two dimensions, for example, length and width
vertex/vertices: The point where two lines of an angle or two edges meet in a plane figure, or where three or more sides meet in a solid figure

Construct as many two-dimensional shapes as you can using only four toothpicks each time. Here are some examples to help you. In your notebook, draw each shape that you made. Label your shapes. Compare your shapes with your classmates' shapes. How are your pictures the same? How are they different?

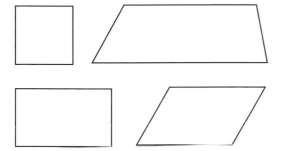

What Did You Learn?

1. What did you learn about the two-dimensional shapes you constructed?

2. How were the shapes similar or different?

Journal

Write a description of a square, a rectangle, a parallelogram, and a trapezoid. Draw a picture to go with each description.

Technology

You can use a paint/draw computer program to create a variety of quadrilaterals and arrange them into groups.

1. Working in groups of four, make a riddle card for each of the two-dimensional shapes in this lesson. On one side of the card, write riddles about the shape. (For example: I have four sides that are the same length.) On the back, draw a picture of the shape. Play the riddle game with your friends.

2. With a classmate, sit on the floor or on chairs with your backs to one another. Partner A makes a two-dimensional shape using four toothpicks, and then describes the shape that he or she made (without naming it). Partner B then tries to draw the shape and name it. Share your results, then switch roles.

3. Explain how a square and a rectangle are the same and different. Use pictures and words.

4. Explain how a parallelogram and a trapezoid are the same and different. Use pictures and words.

Extension

5. Look through magazines and newspapers. Cut out any quadrilaterals that you find. (Make sure you get permission.) Arrange them into groups and display them. Share your final piece with the class.

Lesson 2

Problem Solving With 2-D Shapes

JOURNEY NOTE

PLAN:

You will work on your estimation and problem-solving skills as you continue to investigate two-dimensional shapes.

DESCRIPTION:

As you walk down the medieval pathway, you begin to wonder what year, month, and day it is. You find a calendar to help you.

Get Started

Look at the calendar page. What shapes do you see? Estimate the number of squares on the calendar page. Record your estimation in your notebook. Now, count to see if you were correct.

Tip

Smaller squares may exist within larger squares, for example, four small squares may create one large square.

After you have finished, discuss with a classmate the method you used to be sure that you did not count a square twice. Compare your estimates.

How can multiplication help you find the number of squares on the calendar page? Share your answer with your classmate.

Build Your Understanding

Create Squares

You Will Need
• toothpicks

Continuing on your journey, you see some builders off in the distance. They are positioning wooden beams in just the right places to make a medieval building. Imagine that your toothpicks are wooden beams. Position your imaginary beams on your table or desk to solve the following challenges:

1. What is the minimum number of toothpicks necessary to make 14 squares? Remember that smaller squares may exist within larger squares.

2. What is the minimum number of toothpicks needed to make four parallelograms that are not rhombuses?

Tip

For the definitions of a rhombus and a parallelogram, refer to the glossary.

The marks on the lines mean that the opposite sides are equal.

What Did You Learn?

1. Sketch your toothpick arrangements in your notebook. Label and number the shapes on your sketch. Use a different colour of pencil to highlight each shape.

2. Is a square a rhombus? Explain your answer.

3. What shapes are parallelograms? Explain.

Practice

You Will Need
- graph paper with one-centimetre squares
- letter-sized paper
- marker

1. Use a marker to make a large square on a sheet of graph paper. Now estimate the number of squares inside the square you have created. Count to see if you were correct. Have a classmate check your answer. Repeat this activity with a rectangle. How many squares can you find inside it? What strategy did you use to count the squares inside your shapes? Explain.

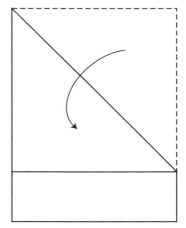

2. **a)** Take a piece of letter-sized paper. Fold one top corner over so that it touches a point on the other side. Cut off the bottom rectangle and recycle it. You should now have a square.

   b) Fold your square in half from top to bottom, and then in half again from side to side.

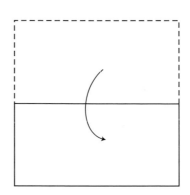

   c) Unfold the paper and cut along the folded lines. You will have four equal squares.

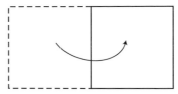

   d) Arrange your four squares in as many ways as possible so that full sides touch full sides. What two-dimensional shapes can you make? Sketch and label your shapes in your notebook.

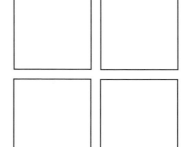

Lesson 3

Constructing Two-Dimensional Shapes

JOURNEY NOTE

PLAN:
You will use a geoboard to explore and construct two-dimensional shapes.

DESCRIPTION:
After your long walk, you finally reach the first castle.

Get Started

You and your classmates look through a front window, and see an artist sitting on a chair. You notice the painting being created.

1. Using the names of shapes, describe the painting in your journal. Share your description with a classmate.

2. What do you think the unfinished shape (letter G) will eventually become when the painter has finished the picture? Why do you think it will become that shape?

Build Your Understanding

Construct Shapes With a Geoboard

You Will Need
- geoboards
- elastic bands

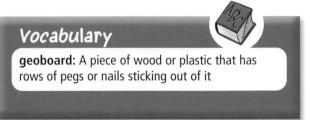

In another room in the castle, you see a person weaving a blanket by threading wool around the pegs on a pegboard. A pegboard is a lot like a geoboard. Many geoboards have 11 rows of pegs with 11 pegs in each row. How many pegs are there in all? How did you calculate your answer?

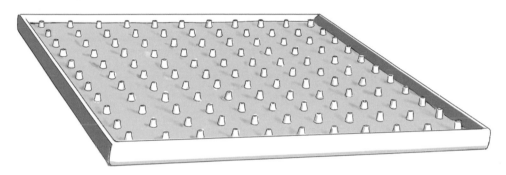

You can stretch elastic bands over the pegs to make shapes. Make a square on your geoboard. Compare the square you made with a classmate's. How are they the same? How are they different? Now make a rectangle. Compare again.

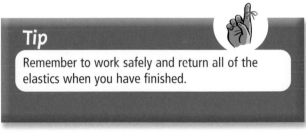

Tip

Remember to work safely and return all of the elastics when you have finished.

Try creating these shapes on your geoboard:

1. Make a square where the elastic touches 8 pegs.

2. Make a square where the elastic touches 12 pegs.

3. Make a trapezoid where the elastic touches 6 pegs.

4. How many shapes can you make where the elastic touches 4 pegs? Share your shapes with a classmate.

5. Show how to make a rectangle larger. How many pegs did you start and end with?

6. Make a large square, and then use elastics to show the smaller squares within it.

7. Create some of your own challenges for a classmate.

What Did You Learn?

1. Which shape did you find easiest to make, and which shape did you find most challenging to make? Why?

2. What was your favourite shape that you made? Describe it in your journal using pictures, numbers, and words.

Practice

1. Pretend you are a geoboard elastic. What shapes can you make with your body? Team up with a partner. What shapes can you and your partner make? Try making shapes in a group of three. In your notebook, record and label the shapes you made.

2. Make a large square on a geoboard using an elastic band. Now make a design in your square using different shapes. Ask a partner to name all the shapes in your design.

Extension

3. Use graph paper to sketch your design from Practice question 2. Colour your design and share it with the class.

Lesson 4

Finding Perimeter

JOURNEY NOTE

PLAN:
You will examine and measure perimeter.

DESCRIPTION:
You and your classmates walk around the outside of the castle.

Get Started

If an object has many bends and turns, the perimeter may be very large. For instance, castles that appear to be the same size can have very different perimeters because some might have different bends and twists.

How can you measure the perimeter of an object that has bends and turns? Share your ideas with the class.

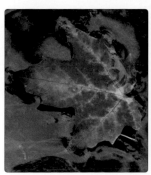 

Vocabulary

perimeter: The distance around an object

1. Think of some everyday objects that look about the same size but have very different perimeters. For example, the tree leaves on the left are about the same size, but they have very different perimeters. Share your examples with the class.

2. With a partner, measure the perimeter of two objects that look about the same size. What did you find out?

Calculate Perimeters

1. First, estimate the perimeter of each of the castles below.

2. Record your estimates. You may want to create a chart to record your estimates and later, your actual measurements.

3. Measure the perimeter of each of the castles. Use a centimetre ruler to measure each side. Then add the lengths of all sides together. If the castle's perimeter is round, use string to help you measure.

4. Look at the scale and figure out the perimeter of each castle in metres. (For these castles, one centimetre equals ten metres.)

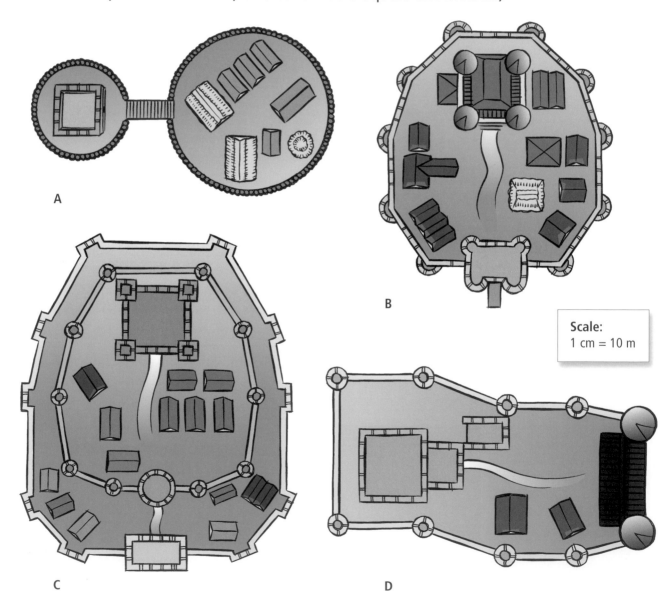

A

B

Scale:
1 cm = 10 m

C

D

What Did You Learn?

1. What steps were needed to figure out the perimeters of the castles in metres? Record the steps in your notebook.

2. Explain how you measured a round perimeter.

3. List the castle perimeters from the smallest to the largest.

Practice

You Will Need
• grid paper

Use grid paper to complete the following challenges. Label the dimensions of each shape you create.

1. Draw a rectangle with a perimeter of 12 squares.

2. Draw a triangle with a perimeter of 15 squares.

3. Draw two different rectangles with a perimeter of 18 squares each.

4. Make a five-sided shape with a perimeter of 30 squares. What is the name of the shape you made?

5. Make a trapezoid with a perimeter of 27 squares.

6. Calculate the perimeter of the following shapes:.

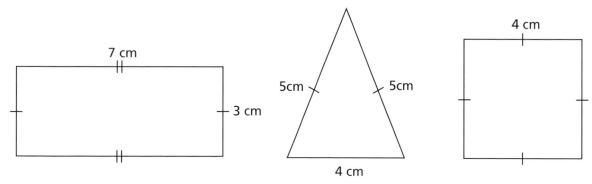

Extension

7. Pick one of the castles shown in Build Your Understanding, and draw a different castle with the same perimeter.

Pretend your school is a castle:

8. Estimate the perimeter using a unit of measurement.

9. Plan how you could calculate it. What unit of measurement will you use? How will you go about this huge task? Is there a way of using a bicycle to figure out this problem? If yes, how?

10. Use your plan to calculate your school's perimeter.

11. The following are more perimeter challenges:

a) What is the perimeter of your playground?

b) What is the perimeter of your classroom?

c) What is the perimeter of a desk, a table, or a bulletin board?

Show What You Know

Review: Lessons 1 to 4, 2-D Shapes and Perimeter

1. Use pattern blocks to build a two-dimensional castle. Create a chart to show the shapes you used.

2. Choose two different pattern blocks. Use a chart to compare how the two shapes are the same and how they are different.

3. A student in grade 5 tells you that a square is a rectangle. Do you agree or disagree? Explain.

4. Imagine that there are two castles in front of you. Castle 1 is much bigger than Castle 2. Does this mean that Castle 1 must have a larger perimeter than Castle 2? Explain your answer using pictures, numbers, and words.

5. In your notebook, draw as many different rectangles as you can with a perimeter of 24 cm. How can multiplication help you find all of the rectangles?

6. Draw or create your own two-dimensional shapes. Calculate their perimeters.

Lesson 5

Investigating Lines

JOURNEY NOTE

PLAN:
You will look for, and then create, different kinds of lines.

DESCRIPTION:
At the back of the castle you and your classmates notice that the castle is undergoing some renovations and repairs.

Get Started

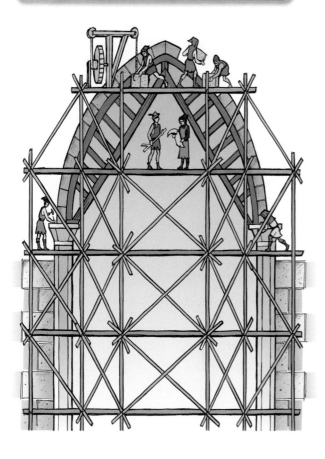

Look at the scaffolding. You will notice several lines going in all sorts of directions. What is a line? What is a line segment? Use the vocabulary box on the next page to help you.

You will need
- coloured pencils
- ruler

Make a copy of the scaffolding, and use coloured pencils to trace the following:
- vertical line segments (red)
- horizontal line segments (blue)
- two sets of parallel line segments (yellow)
- four examples of intersecting line segments (circle their point of intersection in purple)
- two examples of perpendicular line segments (make an orange square around the point where the lines cross)

Build Your Understanding

Explore Your Classroom for Lines

Roll a sheet of paper into a telescope-like tube. Hold the tube up to your eye and examine your classroom for lines. Find examples of lines or line segments in your classroom that are vertical, horizontal, parallel, intersecting, and perpendicular. Make a chart to record your findings. Share your findings with a classmate.

What Did You Learn?

1. What strategies can help you remember what the words vertical, horizontal, parallel, intersecting, and perpendicular mean?

2. When scanning your classroom, which lines were easiest or hardest to see? Why?

Practice

1. Use a geoboard to show examples of vertical, horizontal, perpendicular, parallel, and intersecting line segments. Use your ruler to measure the lines you have created. Record your measurements.

2. Cut several strips of coloured paper. Glue the strips onto white paper to make an interesting design that includes vertical, horizontal, perpendicular, parallel, and intersecting line segments. Record how many of each type of line segment you used.

Lesson 6

Measuring and Comparing Lengths

JOURNEY NOTE

PLAN:
You will measure and compare the lengths of arrow loops.

DESCRIPTION:
You and your classmates notice several slits of different shapes in the castle wall. These slits are called arrow loops and were used by soldiers to shoot arrows through.

Get Started

Look at the arrow loops in the illustration above. Estimate how big you think the slits are if the height of one brick is 15 cm. Share your ideas with a classmate.

Build Your Understanding

Estimate and Measure

1. As a group, use chart paper to design your own arrow loop. Estimate the length and width of your arrow loop, and then use your ruler to measure the length and width of your arrow loop.

2. Measure some arrow loops drawn by other groups. In your notebook, use a chart like the one below to help you record your measurements.

		Length of Arrow Loop		Width of Arrow Loop	
Group Members	Sketch of Arrow Loop	Estimate	Actual	Estimate	Actual

What Did You Learn?

1. Whose arrow loop design was the longest?

2. Whose arrow loop design was the shortest?

3. What unit of measurement did you use? Why?

4. What would you need to add or take away from the length of your arrow loop to make it 50 cm, 3 dm, 1 m, 10 m?

5. How many of your arrow loops would it take to reach the ceiling of your classroom? Explain how you got your answer.

6. How many of your arrow loops would it take to reach 1 m, 100 m, 1 km?

7. Arrange the arrow loop lengths from longest to shortest.

8. Arrange the arrow loop widths from narrowest to widest.

9. Double the lengths of all the arrow loops measured. Now, quadruple the widths.

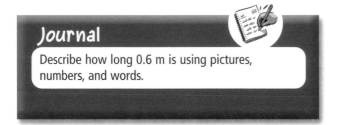

Journal
Describe how long 0.6 m is using pictures, numbers, and words.

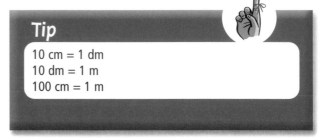

Tip
10 cm = 1 dm
10 dm = 1 m
100 cm = 1 m

Practice

1. Make a list of objects and their measurements that would fit through your arrow loop.

Extension

2. Find the perimeter of your arrow loop. Explain how you calculated your answer.

Rectangular Prisms

JOURNEY NOTE

PLAN:
You will study three-dimensional shapes. In particular, you will learn about rectangular prisms.

DESCRIPTION:
As you and your classmates continue to look at this castle, you notice some workers repairing a stone wall.

Get Started

From a distance, the stones on the wall look as though they have only two dimensions.

1. What three-dimensional shape are most of the stones in the wall?

2. How are the stones different from a two-dimensional rectangle?

3. What are the three dimensions of a stone used to make the castle wall?

4. Estimate the number of rectangular prisms you see in the illustration. Count to see if you are right.

5. As a large group, discuss how three-dimensional shapes are named.

Vocabulary

congruent: Exactly the same size and shape
edge: The line segment where two faces of a figure meet. Edges can be straight or curved.
face: The flat side of a figure. A curved surface can also be considered a face.
prism: A three-dimensional figure with two faces that are congruent and parallel and other faces that are parallelograms

rectangular prism: A three-dimensional shape in which all six faces are rectangles. A square prism is a rectangular prism with two square faces.
three-dimensional: Having three dimensions, for example, length, width, and height
vertex: The point where two lines of an angle or two edges meet in a plane figure, or where three sides meet in a solid figure. If there is more than one vertex, they are called vertices.

Build Your Understanding

Examine a Rectangular Prism

You Will Need
- pipe cleaners
- craft sticks
- toothpicks
- modelling clay

Building Method 1
Create your own rectangular prism. Plan your construction on scrap paper, then cut, tape, or fold a sheet of paper to create a rectangular prism.

Building Method 2
Use a variety of materials to build a rectangular prism (pipe cleaners, modelling clay, craft sticks, toothpicks).

Tip
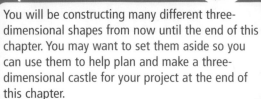
You will be constructing many different three-dimensional shapes from now until the end of this chapter. You may want to set them aside so you can use them to help plan and make a three-dimensional castle for your project at the end of this chapter.

1. How many vertices does a rectangular prism have?
2. How many edges?
3. How many faces?
4. Are the faces the same or different?
5. What two-dimensional shapes are the faces?
6. Why is this three-dimensional shape called a rectangular prism?
7. Display your rectangular prism for the class to see.

What Did You Learn?

1. Write instructions for making a rectangular prism. What did you do first? What did you do next? Discuss your instructions with a classmate. Was making a rectangular prism easy or difficult? Explain. What would you do differently next time?
2. Compare the size of your rectangular prism with one made by a classmate.

Practice

Examine your classroom for rectangular prisms. List all of the objects that look like rectangular prisms. Measure and record the lengths of the edges for each rectangular prism you have found.

Lesson 8

Cubes and Nets

JOURNEY NOTE

PLAN:
You will explore another three-dimensional shape, the cube. You will also learn about nets.

DESCRIPTION:
You and your classmates decide to look for another castle to explore, and it is not long before you find one! As you approach the new castle, you notice a square pattern created by white stones in the wall.

Get Started

Look carefully at the white, square stones in the photograph to the right. What math word is used to describe this three-dimensional shape? What patterns do you see in the photograph?

Look at a sugar cube and imagine that it is a white stone from the castle wall.

1. How many faces does it have?

2. How many edges?

3. How many vertices?

4. What two-dimensional shape are the faces?

Vocabulary

cube: A three-dimensional solid with six congruent square faces

Construct a Cube

This is an illustration of a net for a cube:

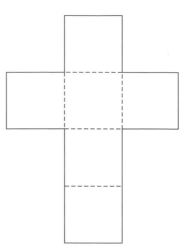

1. Draw and cut out a square.

2. Use your square to make a net for a cube.

3. Cut around the outside edges of your net.

4. Fold on the lines to make a cube. Tape it together. When you have finished, create as many different nets as you can for a cube.

Tip

There are more than ten different nets.

Vocabulary

net: A two-dimensional pattern of a three-dimensional figure

What Did You Learn?

1. Use a piece of chart paper to draw your nets. Post your work in the classroom.

2. Was making nets for a cube easy or difficult? Explain.

3. Is this a picture of a cube net? Explain your reasoning.

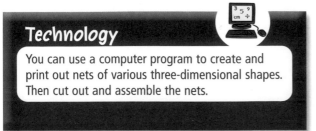

Technology

You can use a computer program to create and print out nets of various three-dimensional shapes. Then cut out and assemble the nets.

Practice

1. Examine the shape of an ice cube. Is this ice cube really a cube? Explain your answer. What factors affect the shape of an ice cube? At home, try to create a real cube of ice. What is your plan?

2. Write a short story about your adventure touring medieval castles and record it on the net for a cube. Number the sides of your cube so your readers can follow the story. Then fold your net into a cube.

3. Investigate the ways in which cubes can be arranged. Arrange three cubes in as many ways as possible. The cubes must touch each other for each arrangement. How many arrangements are possible? Sketch your answers in your notebook.

Show What You Know

Review Lessons 5 to 8, Lines, Measurement, and Shapes

1. In your notebook, draw a picture of a castle that includes vertical, horizontal, perpendicular, parallel, and intersecting line segments. See if a classmate can find examples of each kind of line segment in your drawing.

2. With a partner, make a list of objects and their measurements that would fit on a piece of letter-sized paper.

3. Why are rectangular prisms used for building? Use math language to explain your answer.

4. Examine your classroom and school for cubes. List three objects that look like cubes. Measure and record the lengths of the edges for each of the three cubes listed. If you found real cubes, how many edges would you really need to measure? Explain.

Comparing Three-Dimensional Shapes

JOURNEY NOTE

PLAN:
You will compare and contrast shapes.

DESCRIPTION:
You all go inside the castle and notice the walls in the hallway.

Get Started

You notice both stone cubes and rectangular prisms in the wall.

1. How are cubes similar to other rectangular prisms?

2. How are cubes different from other rectangular prisms?

Build Your Understanding

Construct Three-Dimensional Shapes

You Will Need
- toothpicks
- small marshmallows, soaked dried peas, or straws with pipe cleaners or string inside

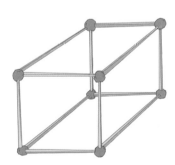

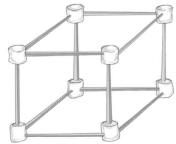

Use toothpicks and small marshmallows or soaked dried peas, or use straws with pipe cleaners or string inside, to make skeletal models of a cube and of a different rectangular prism.

What Did You Learn?

1. How many toothpicks and peas or marshmallows did you use to make the cube?

2. How many did you use to make the other rectangular prism?

3. What building advice would you give to a classmate who was going to try this activity?

4. How are your models the same? How are they different?

5. Put your models on display in your classroom or library.

Practice

1. Using the materials provided in this lesson's activity, make a skeletal tower consisting of cubes.

2. Use a large geoboard to show the net for a rectangular prism or cube.

3. A rectangular prism has 12 edges. Using toothpicks and peas, build a three-dimensional figure that has nine edges. Give your figure a name.

4. How did you name your figure from question 3?

Extension

5. Your task is to build a wall no bigger than a letter-sized piece of paper. Your wall must be made of cubes and rectangular prisms. You may work with a partner or on your own.

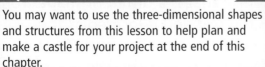

Tip

You may want to use the three-dimensional shapes and structures from this lesson to help plan and make a castle for your project at the end of this chapter.

Pyramids and Nets

JOURNEY NOTE

PLAN:
You will compare and build pyramids.

DESCRIPTION:
You and your classmates enter the courtyard. The courtyard is a central part of the castle that is protected by the surrounding stone walls.

Get Started

As you look up in the courtyard, you are amazed to see a pyramid-shaped roof on the tower of the castle.

Vocabulary

base: The bottom face of a solid figure
pyramid: A solid figure with a polygon base and triangular faces that meet at a common point

This square-pyramid structure on top of the tower is called a spire. The spire or roof would protect the castle guards from stones, arrows, and the weather.

1. What do you know about pyramids?

2. How many faces are on the square pyramid in the illustration?

3. What shapes are the faces? Explain.

4. What do mathematicians call the face that is a different shape from the rest and is located at the bottom of the structure?

5. How are all pyramids alike? How are they different?

6. Why is the pyramid in the illustration called a square pyramid? Explain.

Build Your Understanding

Construct and Compare Pyramids

1. Sketch nets for a triangular-based pyramid and a square-based pyramid. Use the diagrams below to help you.

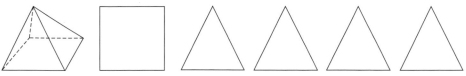

Square-based pyramid

Triangular-based pyramid

2. Cut out your nets, fold on the lines, and tape them together to construct the pyramids.

3. In your notebook, make a chart like the one below. Use your pyramids to complete the first two rows in the chart.

Shape of Base	Name of Pyramid	Number of Faces	Shape of Faces	Number of Vertices	Number of Edges
triangle					
square					
pentagon					
hexagon					
octagon					

4. Complete the chart for the other three types of pyramids.

5. Look at your chart.
   a) What patterns do you see?
   b) What relationships do you see between the name of the shape and the number of vertices or edges? Explain.

What Did You Learn?

1. How are the two pyramid figures that you built the same?

2. How are the two pyramid figures that you built different?

3. Compare your pyramids with a cube or a rectangular prism. How are they the same? How are they different?

Practice

1. Use materials of your choice to build skeletal models of square-based and triangular-based pyramids. You may want to try to roll newspapers into long tubes. Then use masking tape to connect the tubes to make a gigantic skeletal model.

2. Design a skeletal model of a pyramid that has a five- or six-sided base. Name the pyramid that you designed.

3. Design a net for a triangular-based pyramid that is different from the one that you used in Build Your Understanding.

Extension

4. Where might someone see pyramids outside of school? Make a list and share it with your classmates.

5. What modern or ancient structures have you seen, or seen pictures of, that look like pyramids? Try to find illustrations of your answers by looking on the Internet.

Lesson 11

Creating Cones and Cylinders

JOURNEY NOTE

PLAN:
You will continue your investigations of three-dimensional figures focusing on cylinders and cones.

DESCRIPTION:
From the courtyard, you and your classmates climb stairs into one of the high castle towers. You notice a telescope sitting in the corner of the room.

Get Started

When you use the telescope to focus on a castle in the distance, you see the following:

Most towers were built cylinder-shaped so that they would not collapse. Cylindrical towers are stronger than rectangular prism-shaped towers.

1. What shape is the tower in the photograph to the left?

2. What is the shape of the spire on top of the tower?

3. Where else have you seen these three-dimensional figures?

4. As a class, collect some cones and cylinders that can be deconstructed (for example, paper towel tubes or water cooler cups). Take the 3-D shapes apart and discuss your observations.

Create and Analyze Cones and Cylinders

1. To make a cone, first trace a circle. Next, cut a slit from the edge to the middle of the circle. Overlap the sides of the slit and then tape them together. Make another circle to cover the open end of the cone.

2. Draw a net for a cylinder. Cut it out and assemble it.

Look at the figures you have created. Copy and complete this chart:

Figure	Faces	Vertices	Edges

Vocabulary

cone: A solid or hollow, pointed figure that has a flat, round base

cylinder: A solid or hollow figure that is shaped like a can. It has a circular top and bottom.

Tip

Remember that a face is the flat side of a figure. However, a curved surface (like that on a cone and a cylinder) can also be considered a face. Don't forget, edges can be straight or curved.

What Did You Learn?

1. How are cylinders and cones alike?

2. How is a cone different from a triangular pyramid?

3. Which three-dimensional figures can roll? Which ones cannot roll? Make a chart like the one below to record your predictions. Make a ramp to test your guesses.

Will It Roll?		
Figure	Prediction	Test

Practice

1. Make riddles like the example to the right using math language to describe three-dimensional figures of your choice. Prepare an answer, including a drawing of the shape you have chosen. Share your riddles with your class.

2. Explain how to make a net of a cone or cylinder.

I have six sides, and all of them are square?

What figure am I?

_____

Answer: A cube

Show What You Know

Review: Lessons 9 to 11, 3-D Shapes

1. Could you construct a given cube if you only knew its height? Explain your answer in pictures, numbers, and words.

2. How are prisms and pyramids the same? How are they different? Use a chart to show your answer.

3. A new student has moved to your class. How would you explain to the new student the difference between two-dimensional and three-dimensional shapes?

4. You are going to build a castle tower. Use peas and toothpicks to construct at least four three-dimensional shapes. Join the shapes to form your tower. Explain why you chose the shapes you did.

Chapter Review

Chapter 4

You Will Need
- toothpicks or straws
- peas, modelling clay, or marshmallows

1. a) Arrange toothpicks or straws on your desk to make these two-dimensional shapes: square, rectangle, parallelogram, and trapezoid.

   b) In your notebook, compare your shapes by naming and describing them.

2. Use materials to make the following three-dimensional structures: cube, rectangular prism, three-sided pyramid, four-sided pyramid.

3. Copy and complete this chart:

Drawing of Figure	Name of Figure	Number of Faces	Number of Edges	Number of Vertices
	cube			
		5	9	6
(drawing of rectangular prism)				
(drawing of pyramid)				
	square-based pyramid			

4. What are the differences between vertical, horizontal, perpendicular, parallel, and intersecting lines? Use pictures and words.

5. Measure and record five items in your classroom.

6. Sort the following quadrilaterals into the groups below by writing the letter of the shape, and then beside it, writing the group in which it belongs. A shape may fit into more than one group.

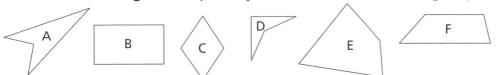

Group 1 Shapes With Parallel Lines	Group 2 Shapes With Four Right Angles	Group 3 Shapes With No Rght Angles

7. Match each net with the three-dimensional figure it creates. Write the letter name of the net in your notebook, and then beside it, write the matching letter name of the shape.

a) 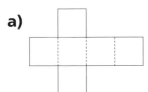   **b)** 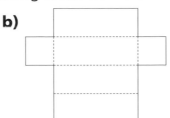   **c)**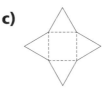

d)   **e)**    **f)**

8. Draw as many rectangles as you can with a perimeter of 36 cm.

9. Estimate, then calculate the perimeter of your classroom clock or garbage bin. Explain how you got your answer.

10. Calculate the perimeter of the following shapes:

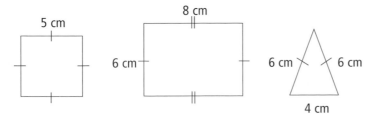

5 cm

8 cm

6 cm

6 cm   6 cm

4 cm

Chapter Wrap-Up

You Will Need
- your journal
- materials to build
  a model of a castle

You have returned from your journey. In this chapter you have learned about medieval times, castles, and the following math concepts: the geometry of two-dimensional shapes and three-dimensional figures, and the measurement of length, and perimeter.

You will apply the math you have learned to make a two-dimensional plan of a castle. When you are finished, you will present your plan to the class.

Start by making a list of what you have learned in this chapter. This list is for you to refer to as you plan. Your plan should show that you understand the concepts you studied in this chapter.

Your plan should include:

- a list of materials needed to build your model
- diagrams of the nets you will need to construct
- a diagram of the finished model. (Label the shapes and solids you will use.)
- the steps you will follow to build your model
- other information you think is useful to know about your model

Use your plan and the materials that you have collected to build a three-dimensional model of your castle.

Math for a Medieval Feast

In this chapter, you, your classmates, and your teacher reach the castle in which the medieval feast will be held. You will learn math by studying the medieval people who live and work in the castle preparing food and making the banquet hall ready for this special meal. At the end of the chapter, you will use the math that you learned to design a placemat for a royal person to use at a feast.

In this chapter you will study
- symmetry and congruency
- two-dimensional shapes (equilateral, isosceles, and scalene triangles)
- angles
- area and volume

Before you begin preparing for the medieval feast, draw two congruent circles in your notebook. Cut out one of the circles and fold it in half. Is your circle symmetrical? How do you know?

Lesson 1

Investigating Lines of Symmetry

JOURNEY NOTE

PLAN:
You will decide if shapes are symmetrical.

DESCRIPTION:
You are introduced to the people who own the castle you are visiting. They leave you alone to get some rest. Your stomach begins to rumble, so you decide to wander out of your room in search of the kitchen.

Get Started

When you first step into the kitchen, you discover a baker removing loaves of bread from the oven. He explains that it is his job to divide food into portions for each person. If he divides a loaf of bread into two parts that are exactly the same, they are said to be symmetrical.

Which of these items are not divided symmetrically?

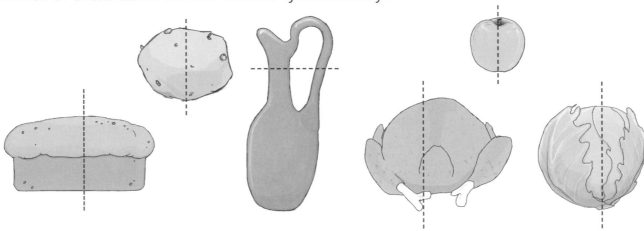

Build Your Understanding

Find Lines of Symmetry

You Will Need
• sheet of clear acetate
• overhead pen or permanent marker
• ruler

1. Find a partner to work with.

2. Use one sheet of acetate for your group.

3. With an overhead pen or permanent marker and a ruler, draw a dotted line vertically down the centre of the sheet. You have just made a symmetry viewer.

4. Use your viewer to determine which of the two-dimensional shapes to the right are symmetrical. Try to position the dotted line so that it divides the object into two symmetrical parts. You may have to turn your viewer to find the line of symmetry. If you cannot divide an object into two exact halves, it is asymmetrical.

5. Draw two large circles of equal size in your notebook. Label the first circle "Symmetrical Shapes" and the second "Asymmetrical Shapes." Record each shape you viewed with your viewer in the circle where it belongs.

1. a) In each of these pictures, which letter represents the line
of symmetry? How do you know?

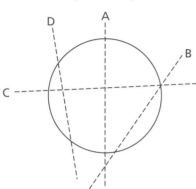 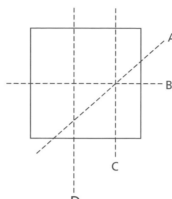 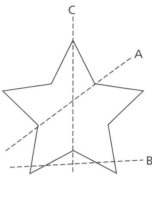

b) Trace the pictures from question 1 a) into your notebook.
Can you find other lines of symmetry for each picture?
If so, draw them and explain how you know they are correct.

Practice

1. Draw a two-dimensional shape that
has at least two lines of symmetry.
Here is an example:

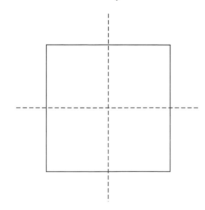

Technology

You can use a paint/draw computer program to
create various shapes and to draw the lines of
symmetry.

2. Explain how you know that the shape you drew for question 1
is symmetrical.

More About Lines of Symmetry

JOURNEY NOTE

PLAN:
You will examine and create symmetrical shapes.

DESCRIPTION:
Across from the baker in the kitchen is a servant preparing seafood for the big medieval feast they are planning.

Get Started

Look at the sea creatures below. Which ones are symmetrical? Explain how you know.

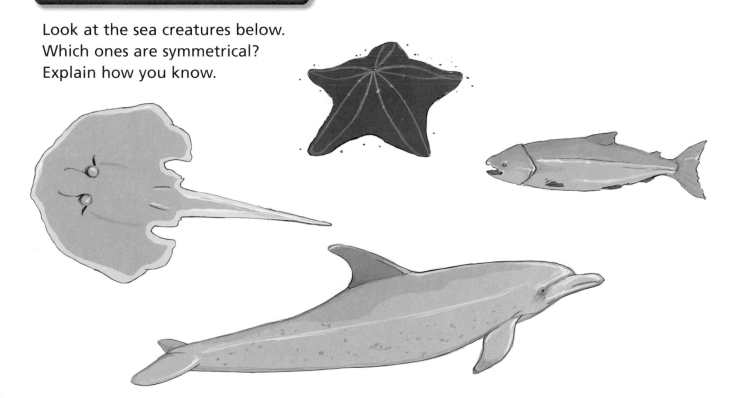

Build Your Understanding

Test for Symmetry

1. **a)** Draw a shape and its line of symmetry on a sheet of paper.

   b) Now fold the sheet of paper on the line of symmetry. Do both halves match up? If they do, your shape is truly symmetrical.

   It is very difficult to draw a shape that is symmetrical. If your halves don't match up, this means that your shape is asymmetrical. Let's try a different way.

2. **a)** Fold a sheet of paper in half vertically.

   b) With the paper folded, cut out a design from the folded edge.

   c) When you have finished cutting, unfold your paper. The fold represents the line of symmetry. If the shapes on the two sides of the line are the same, you have made a symmetrical shape.

3. Repeat question 2, but fold your paper horizontally.

4. Make a chart like the one on the right to record the number of lines of symmetry for each of these two-dimensional shapes. All your shapes must be regular (all sides and angles equal) if possible. The first one has been done for you.
   - square
   - rectangle
   - rhombus
   - parallelogram
   - trapezoid
   - triangle
   - pentagon
   - hexagon
   - octagon

   Analyze your chart for patterns.

Polygon Name	Picture	Line(s) of Symmetry
Square		4

What Did You Learn?

1. Which way of making a symmetrical shape (drawing or cutting) was easiest? Explain why.

2. Write a letter to a friend explaining how to determine if a shape or object is symmetrical.

3. Do all sizes of squares have lines of symmetry in the same place? Explain.

Journal

Using a shape as an example, explain "lines of symmetry."

1. **a)** In groups of four, gather five natural objects and five manufactured objects. Now sort your items into symmetrical and asymmetrical objects.

   b) Are there more or fewer natural objects than manufactured objects in the symmetrical group? Can you explain why?

   c) If you were to do this again, selecting different objects, would your results be the same? Why or why not?

2. Fold and cut paper to design a snowflake that is symmetrical. To do this, try folding the paper in half, then in half again, and even in half again. Cut out pieces from the folded edges.

3. Look for and draw the lines of symmetry for pictures in magazines or newspapers.

4. **a)** Draw two of each of these shapes: squares, rectangles, trapezoids, parallelograms. Use grid paper. Your drawings should be different sizes.

   b) Cut out each shape and fold it on a line of symmetry if you can. Mark the lines of symmetry.

5. Check each printed letter of the alphabet for lines of symmetry. Which letters are symmetrical?

Making Irregular Shapes Symmetrical

JOURNEY NOTE

PLAN:
You will apply what you know about symmetry to irregular shapes.

DESCRIPTION:
Standing in the kitchen of the castle, you notice the variety of fruits and vegetables being prepared for the feast.

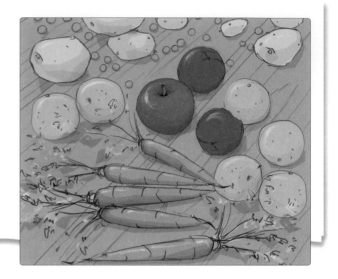

Get Started

Try to find a line of symmetry for each of the foods shown above. Which foods have lines of symmetry?

With a classmate, discuss what an irregular shape is.

Build Your Understanding

Use Miras

1. a) A Mira can help you find a line of symmetry. Place the Mira upright along the side of a picture that has been laid on a blank sheet of paper.

b) Then look through the transparent part of the Mira. Keep your eyes on the same side as the picture. What do you see?

Vocabulary

Mira: A small sheet of reflective but transparent plastic that reflects a drawing back, but makes it look like it's a continuation on the other side

You should see a reflection of the original image that appears to be on the side of the paper behind the Mira.

2. Draw an irregular shape that is open at one side. Now place your Mira upright against the open side of your drawing. Look through the Mira and draw the other half of your irregular shape. Try this procedure again with a different irregular shape.

3. Trade your designs with a partner. Try to find the line of symmetry in your partner's design.

What Did You Learn?

1. What is the difference between a regular and irregular shape? Explain.

2. What do the irregular shapes that you drew remind you of?

3. For which is it easier to find the line of symmetry, a regular shape or an irregular shape? Explain.

Tip

Refer to the glossary for definitions of regular and irregular shapes.

1. Find a picture of a face in a magazine. Cut the face in half along the line of symmetry. Tape one half of the face into your notebook. Place your Mira on the line of symmetry and draw the other half of the face, using your pencil.

2. Compare the half of the face that you drew in question 1 to the real half. What do you notice?

3. Do you think your face is symmetrical or asymmetrical? Justify your answer.

4. What items found in a castle or parts of a castle might be symmetrical?

5. In what careers do you think it would be important to know about symmetry? Make a list and share it with the class.

Extension

6. a) Fold a sheet of paper into four quarters. Mark the vertical line in the centre of the page and the horizontal line across the middle of the page with a coloured pencil.

   b) In one quadrant, draw an irregular shape touching both folds.

   c) Next, use the Mira on each crease to help you complete the three other quadrants of the figure.

Journal

Record the steps to use a Mira to make an irregular shape with symmetry.

Vocabulary

quadrant: One of the four sections of an area that has been divided into four sections

Technology

Use a paint/draw computer program to make an irregular shape that is open at one side. Print your shape and use a Mira to draw the other half.

Lesson 4

Exploring Congruent Shapes

JOURNEY NOTE

PLAN:

You will create and identify congruent shapes.

DESCRIPTION:

Still in the kitchen, out of the corner of your eye you notice someone cutting a pie that will be served with the feast. Each piece of the pie is exactly the same size and shape.

Get Started

Look at the pairs of pictures below. Which pairs of shapes are congruent? Discuss how you know with a partner.

Vocabulary

congruent: Exactly the same size and shape. Orientation does not need to be the same.

A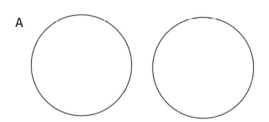

B

C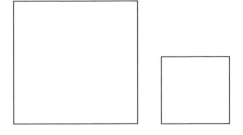

D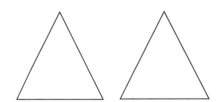

E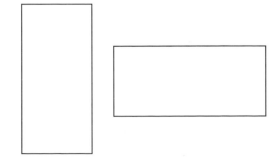

Build Your Understanding

Find Congruent Pairs

1. With a partner, think of a way to cut out two congruent hexagons on white paper (do not colour them). Then cut out your congruent shapes.

2. Next, mix your hexagons with those of your classmates.

3. Once all the hexagons are scrambled together, take turns finding the congruent pairs. Place one shape on top of another to see if they are the same size and shape.

What Did You Learn?

1. Which congruent hexagons were easiest to find? Why?

2. Which congruent pairs were hardest to identify? Why?

3. Identify two objects in the classroom that look congruent. In your journal, explain why you think they are congruent.

4. Draw examples of a pair of figures that is not congruent.

Practice

1. Find the red apple congruent with the green apple. Explain how you know you are correct.

2. Use dot or graph paper to make pairs of congruent irregular shapes. Make a triangle. Make another triangle congruent with the first. Are any tangram shapes congruent? Justify your answer.

3. Use a geoboard to make a shape. Challenge a classmate to make another shape congruent with yours.

A Math Problem to Solve

4. Like people today, those living in medieval times found honey in beehives. A honeycomb grows at a rate of 12 hexagons each day. How many hexagons are there after 3 days, 9 days, 21 days, and 50 days? Show your work in pictures, numbers, and words. Use your calculator to help you.

Extension

5. Add more congruent pairs, or give a person a 30 s time limit to find a congruent match.

Show What You Know

Review: Lessons 1 to 4, Symmetry and Congruency

1. In the picture to the right, identify three symmetrical shapes, two congruent shapes, and one shape that is asymmetrical. Explain how you know your answers are correct.

2. Create your own coat of arms. It must have one line of symmetry.

3. How would you explain symmetry and congruency to someone new to your class?

4. Do all triangles have three lines of symmetry? Explain.

Lesson 5

Comparing Triangles by Side Lengths

JOURNEY NOTE

PLAN:

You will describe and create a design with three types of triangles: equilateral, isosceles, and scalene.

DESCRIPTION:

While you are in the kitchen, the person preparing the seafood for the feast starts to tell you about how the fish were caught in a large fishing net.

She points to the wall, and there you see several lengths of line tied together, forming a fishing net. A closer look reveals that some of the knots in the line have weakened, resulting in three different types of triangles.

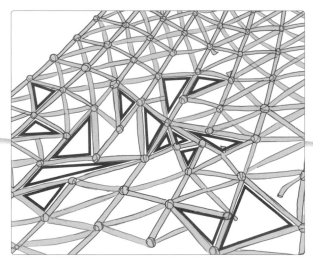

Get Started

Look at the fishing net on this page. Look at the highlighted triangles carefully. In your notebook, name and draw the different types of triangles in a chart like the one below (equilateral, isosceles, and scalene). Now list the characteristics of each type of triangle.

Type of Triangle	Picture	Characteristics

Vocabulary

equilateral triangle: A triangle with all sides equal in length
isosceles triangle: A triangle with two sides equal in length
scalene triangle: A triangle with no equal sides

Build Your Understanding

Continue the Pattern

1. Sketch the following shapes into your notebook. Now continue each pattern, and identify the type of triangle in each pattern.

2. Look at the highlighted shapes from the fishing net picture in Get Started. On a geoboard, create each type of triangle you see in the picture (equilateral, isosceles, and scalene).

Technology

You can use a paint/draw computer program to create a large shape. Then fill it with equilateral triangles.

What Did You Learn?

1. Review and describe the characteristics of each type of triangle (equilateral, isosceles, scalene). Are any parts of these triangles congruent? Explain.

2. Look around your classroom for triangles. Record their locations and types.

Tip

Often, line segments of equal length are shown with small hatch lines across them. This tells you that the lines are congruent.

1. Draw five different triangles. Predict what type of triangle each figure is, then check your predictions by measuring each triangle's sides.

2. Could you draw a given equilateral triangle if you only knew one of its side lengths? Explain using pictures, numbers, and words.

3. How is an isosceles triangle the same as and different from a scalene triangle? Use pictures, numbers, and words.

4. Use graph paper to make a large square. Can you fill the entire square with different types of triangles? Try it and then colour each type of triangle with the same coloured pencil. Share your design with the class.

5. Draw lines of symmetry in different types of triangles.

Extension

6. Use the three types of triangles to make a picture frame for a piece of artwork.

7. Write a poem about triangles and share it with your teacher.

8. Look for triangular shapes in nature books. Keep a record of where they are found.

9. Use playing cards or index cards to make a tower composed of triangles. Count the number of triangles in your tower.

Lesson 6

Comparing Triangles by Angles

JOURNEY NOTE

PLAN:
You will continue to study triangles by analyzing their angles.

DESCRIPTION:
In another corner of the kitchen, you see several workers creating a model of a ship out of sugar. You later learn that a sculpture in medieval times was called a <u>subtlety</u>. This subtlety had a magnificent sail made of coloured triangles and squares.

Get Started

Look at the inside corners of the squares in the picture of the ship. These are angles. How many angles does a square have? What is special about the angles in a square?

Use the square corner of a sheet of paper to find square corners in your classroom. Keep a record of where the square corners are found. A square corner is called a right angle.

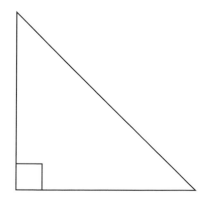

Technology
Think about the different types of angles in everyday surroundings. You can use a paint/draw computer program to draw your pictures.

Build Your Understanding

Make and Analyze Triangles

You Will Need
• geoboards
• straws
• string
• tangram pieces

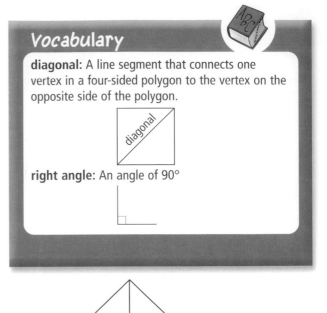
1. Trace your tangram pieces in your notebook. For the triangles, draw a line segment along the line of symmetry to create two new shapes. For the square and parallelogram, draw a diagonal line to create new shapes.

2. **a)** What new shapes did you create?

   b) Describe the angles in these shapes, comparing them with a right angle. Which new angles are larger than the right angle? Which are smaller? Which are the same size?

3. **a)** Use an elastic on a geoboard to make a triangle shape. Make a triangle that has an angle bigger than a right angle.

   b) Now make a triangle that has three congruent angles. What do you notice about each of these angles? Are the angles larger or smaller than a right angle?

4. Look at several different equilateral triangles, isosceles triangles, and scalene triangles. You might make triangles using straws or on a geoboard, or you can look for triangles in your classroom. What do you notice about the size of the angles in each type of triangle? Measure the angles in your triangles, using the corner of a piece of paper to support your observations. Record your observations in a chart and discuss them with the class.

What Did You Learn?

1. Describe three types of angles in your journal.

2. Why do you think triangles are called triangles?

3. Make a list of angles in your classroom. Sort them by right angles, angles larger than right angles, and angles smaller than right angles.

4. Describe the angles in an equilateral triangle.

5. Describe the angles in an isosceles triangle.

6. Describe the angles in a scalene triangle.

Practice

1. Identify the types of triangles in a triangular-based pyramid, a square-based pyramid, and a pentagonal-based pyramid.

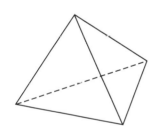 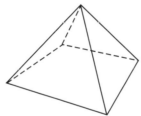 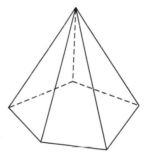

2. Find a pattern between each kind of pyramid and the triangles that make it. Write about this in your journal.

Lesson 7

Comparing and Measuring Angles

JOURNEY NOTE

PLAN:
You will estimate and measure angles using wedges.

DESCRIPTION:
In the kitchen, you see another castle worker cutting a round piece of cheese into portions for the feast.

Get Started

You notice these angles in the wedges of cheese cut from the large round piece:

Is each angle a right angle, greater than a right angle, or less than a right angle? Angles greater than a right angle are called obtuse angles. Angles smaller than right angles are called acute angles.

Look at the angles you worked with in Build Your Understanding in Lesson 6 on page 208. Which angles are right angles, which are acute angles, which are obtuse angles?

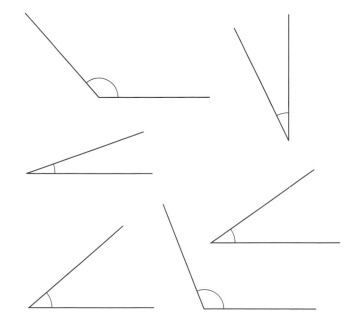

Build Your Understanding

Make and Compare Angles

You Will Need
- modelling clay
- craft stick

1. Pretend you work in a medieval kitchen and have the job of cutting cheese. Use modelling clay and a craft stick to cut pretend pieces of cheese that have obtuse, acute, and right angles.

2. **a)** Trace the right-angle wedge shown on the right on another piece of paper. Then cut it out.

   b) Use your right-angle wedge to determine if your pieces of cheese have obtuse, acute, or right angles.

   c) Copy and complete the following chart to show your measurements.

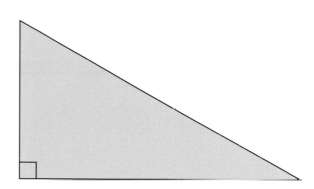

My Clay Piece of Cheese	Measurement Using Right-Angle Wedge	
	Estimate	Actual
Wedge #1	acute	acute
Wedge #2		

What Did You Learn?

1. How accurate were your predictions?

2. **a)** How far do you turn your craft stick to make a right angle?

   b) How far do you turn your craft stick to make a straight line?

3. If you were really hungry, would you prefer a piece of cheese with an acute angle or an obtuse angle? Explain your reasoning.

1. Draw the position of the hands on a clock, and then describe the angles that you see. Do the lengths of the arms affect the angle created?

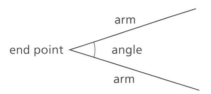

Extension

2. Read "Using a Protractor."

3. Practise using a protractor by measuring the angles in Get Started. Draw more angles. Predict what type of angle they are before measuring them.

Using a Protractor

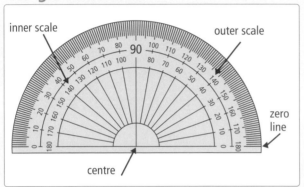

A protractor is used for measuring and drawing angles from 0 to 180 degrees.

1. Draw an angle. Predict how many degrees you think your angle will measure.

2. Place the zero line of the protractor on one arm of your angle, making sure that the other arm is covered by the protractor.

3. Place the centre of the zero line on the endpoint of the angle.

4. Look at the arm that is covered by the zero line of the protractor. Using the scale that starts at the zero on that arm, read the position of the other arm of the angle.

5. What is the size of the angle? How does your prediction compare with the actual measurement?

Show What You Know

Review: Lessons 5 to 7, Triangles and Angles

1. Create a drawing with triangles hidden throughout. Try to hide as many triangles in the drawing as you can. Give your drawing to a partner to find the triangles.

2. Use strips of paper to make triangles that have the following measurements:
- 10 cm, 7 cm, 10 cm
- 8 cm, 12 cm, 10 cm
- 6 cm, 6 cm, 6 cm

Name each type by side lengths and angles.

3. Draw an acute, obtuse, and right angle. Use a protractor to measure your angles. Record your measurements.

Lesson 8

Finding Area

JOURNEY NOTE

PLAN:
You will explore the areas of objects.

DESCRIPTION:
You pick up an apple from the kitchen and start to walk back to your sleeping quarters. Along the way you pass the castle hall. The hall is the largest room in a castle and the place where the feast will take place.

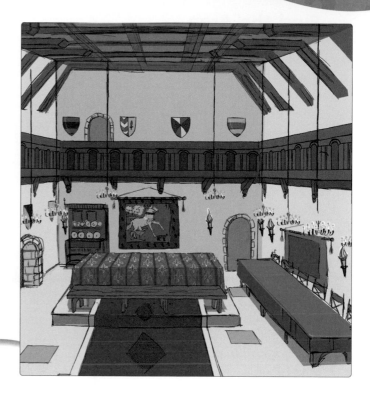

Get Started

In the hall, a worker is repairing the tiles on the floor. She has removed a large area of cracked and broken stone tiles. Help her figure out how many tiles are needed to fix the floor.

Estimate how many tiles are needed to repair the floor in the picture to the right. Use grid paper to draw the section of the floor that needs to be repaired. How many tiles are needed to repair the floor?

What are the dimensions of the area that needs to be repaired? How could you use multiplication to help you find the number of tiles needed to repair the floor? Discuss your answers with the class.

Find the Area

You Will Need
- grid paper

Vocabulary

area: The amount of surface inside a two-dimensional shape. Area is measured in square units: mm², cm², dm², m², km².

1. Find the area of the tiles below. The area for Tile A has been calculated for you.

To calculate the area of a square or rectangle, multiply the length by the width for the given shape. The units also get multiplied, which is why area is measured in square units. For example, in question 1, the area of Tile A was calculated by multiplying 5 cm by 5 cm. When a cm measurement is multiplied by another cm measurement, they are shown mathematically as "cm²". Therefore the area of Tile A is 25 cm².

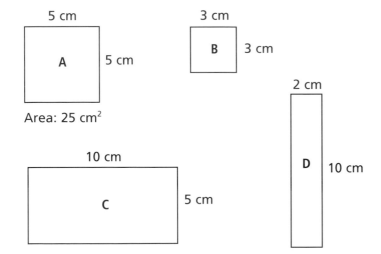

A — 5 cm × 5 cm — Area: 25 cm²

B — 3 cm × 3 cm

C — 10 cm × 5 cm

D — 2 cm × 10 cm

2. If you have a 200 cm² area to fill with tiles, how many A tiles could you fit? Use grid paper or a geoboard to help you. Pretend that one square has an area of 1 cm².

3. How many B tiles, C tiles, and D tiles could you fit? Are there any tiles that don't fit evenly? Explain.

Tip

The area inside a square with sides 1 cm long is 1 cm² (one square centimetre).

What Did You Learn?

1. Explain the method you used to figure out the areas of the tiles.

2. Draw an example of two different shapes with the same area.

3. Shapes with the same area can have different perimeters. Show an example.

Practice

1. What size of square (cm², dm², m²) would you use to measure the following areas? Explain your choices.
   - classroom
   - textbook cover
   - eraser
   - playground
   - computer screen
   - window

2. On grid or dot paper, draw as many different rectangles as you can that have areas of 12 cm².

3. Explain how you would find the area of a rectangle with a length of 6 cm and a width of 8 cm. Use pictures, numbers, and words.

4. Can you draw a rectangle that has a different perimeter than your rectangle in question 3, but has the same area? Use pictures, numbers, and words to explain your answer.

Extension

5. Use a square that has an area of 1 dm² to calculate the approximate area of the top of your desk.

6. Use masking tape on the floor of your classroom to figure out how many squares with areas of 1 dm² fit into a square with an area of 1 m².

Lesson 9

Looking at Perimeter and Area

JOURNEY NOTE

PLAN:
You will continue to examine the perimeters and areas of different shapes as you learn about factors.

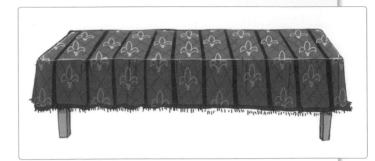

DESCRIPTION:
In the grand hall a maid is putting tablecloths on the tables. You and some of your classmates go over and lend a helping hand with the large tablecloth. The maid tells you about each magnificent tablecloth.

Get Started

1. Copy and complete the table below. Explain the patterns that you see.

Tablecloth	Perimeter	Area
3 m / 2 m	10 m	6 m²
3 m / 3 m		
4 m / 3 m		

Tip

Perimeter is the distance around an object.
Area is the amount of surface within an object.

Booklink

Spaghetti and Meatballs for All by Marilyn Burns (Scholastic: Markham ON, 1997). What happens to the seating arrangement at a family reunion when chairs and tables are moved around to seat more guests? Read this book to find out!

2. Now extend the pattern by drawing the next two tablecloths.

Build Your Understanding

Calculate Perimeter and Area

You Will Need
• tiles

1. Look at the following shapes:

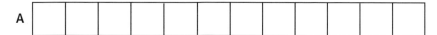

A

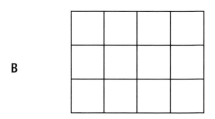

B

2. Calculate the perimeter and area for each shape. Try to make another rectangle with 12 square units.

> The rectangles 3 x 4 and 1 x 12 and 2 x 6 are all the possible combinations that consist of 12 units. The numbers 1, 2, 3, 4, 6, and 12 are all factors of the product 12.

3. Using 16 tiles, create as many different rectangles as you can that use all 16 tiles. The length and width of each of your rectangles are the factors of the number 16. Sketch your rectangles in your notebook. Then try building all the rectangles you can with 20 tiles.

What Did You Learn?

1. Use grid paper to draw an example of two rectangles that have the same area but different perimeters.

2. Is there a relationship between area and perimeter? Explain.

3. Develop a number sentence to help you figure out the area of rectangular figures. Use an example to explain how your number sentence works. Now do the same for perimeter. Share your number sentences with a classmate.

Practice

1. a) Describe all the rectangles you can make with
- 20 square tiles
- 23 square tiles
- 21 square tiles
- 24 square tiles
- 22 square tiles
- 25 square tiles

b) Do you see any patterns? Describe them in your journal.

Some numbers have only one set of factors. These numbers are called prime numbers. Numbers that have more than one set of factors are called composite numbers.

2. Copy and complete this chart of factors:

Number of Square Tiles	Rectangles That Can Be Made (Factors)
10	1 x 10, 2 x 5
11	1 x 11
12	
13	
14	
15	1 x 15, 3 x 5
20	
25	
30	
35	

Vocabulary

composite number: A number that has more than two factors. The numbers 4, 6, 8, 9, 10, 12, 14, and 15 are composite numbers.

prime number: A number that has only two factors: 1 and itself. The numbers 1, 3, 5, 7, 11, 13, 17, and 19 are prime numbers.

3. a) I have the factors 1, 3, 7, and one other number. What number am I?

b) My factors include 2, 3, and 5. What number am I? Can I be more than one number?

c) Make up your own factor riddles like 3a and 3b.

4. Estimate and then calculate the area of the irregular shape shown on the right on graph paper.

5. Explain how you can find the area of an irregular shape. Use pictures, numbers, and words. Share your answer with the class.

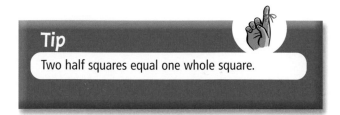

Tip

Two half squares equal one whole square.

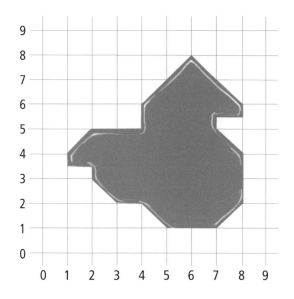

Extension

6. Use a geoboard to calculate the areas of irregular shapes. Make irregular shapes by connecting diagonal pegs. Record your designs and their areas on dot paper.

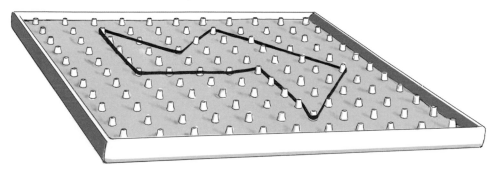

Show What You Know

Review: Lessons 8 and 9, Area and Perimeter

1. You have been asked to create a rectangular wall hanging that has an area of 24 units. How many different dimensions could this wall hanging have? Draw your arrangements on grid paper.

2. Calculate the perimeter for each wall hanging. What do you notice?

3. How would you explain finding area and perimeter to a classmate who was having problems?

Measuring Volume Using Non-Standard Units

JOURNEY NOTE

PLAN:
You will measure the volume of figures using non-standard units.

DESCRIPTION:
In medieval times, eating meat was a common practice. As you wait in the dining hall, you overhear that a main course of wild boar is being prepared for the feast.

Get Started

You Will Need
• containers
• small items such as marbles, macaroni, or dried peas

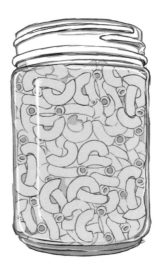
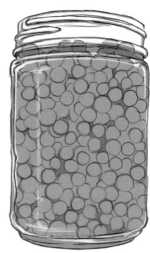

1. Estimate how many pieces of macaroni you think will fit in your container.

2. Pour macaroni into your container until it is full. Then count how many pieces it held. How close was your estimate?

3. Repeat this activity using the same container, but instead of macaroni use dried peas or another small item available in your classroom. You are using non-standard units to measure volume.

4. Record your work in your notebook.

Build Your Understanding

Estimate and Calculate Volume

1. You offer to help bring in some firewood for cooking. The wood is carried in wooden crates. Assuming all of the logs are the same size, how many logs will fit in each wooden crate? Estimate, then calculate.

2. Explain the problem-solving strategy that you used. Why did you use it?

Vocabulary

estimate: To find an answer that is close to the exact answer
volume: The amount of space inside a three-dimensional figure

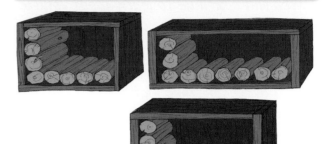

What Did You Learn?

1. What method did you use to count the macaroni?

2. Compare the number of pieces of macaroni and the number of dried peas (or other small objects) that your container held.

3. Explain why there was a difference.

4. Why is knowing about volume important?

Practice

1. Assuming that the items are the same size in each container, estimate and then calculate the volume of the containers below:

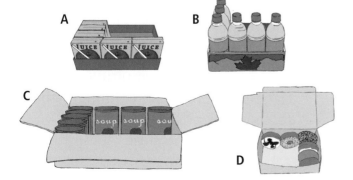

2. Use small blocks or cubes to fill small and medium-size boxes. How many cubes are needed to fill each? Create a chart like the one shown below to help you.

Box	Estimated Number of Cubes	Actual Number of Cubes
A		
B		

Lesson 11

Calculating Volume With Cubes

JOURNEY NOTE

PLAN:
You will continue to learn about volume as you measure the volume of rectangular prisms using centimetre cubes.

DESCRIPTION:
You overhear some maids talking as they begin to set the tables. The feast will begin soon.

During medieval times, salt was a delicacy. Look at a salt crystal with a magnifying glass, and you will notice that it is a cube shape.

Get Started

Centimetre cubes, much larger than salt crystals, are a standard unit of measurement used to measure the capacities of containers. A centimetre cube is a cubic unit.

Tip

Volume is the amount of space an object takes up. It is measured in cubic units.

1. How many centimetre cubes would you need to fill the rectangular prism below?

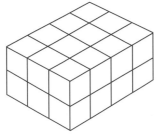

2. What are the dimensions (length, width, and height) of the rectangular prism?

3. How could you use multiplication to help you find the volume of the rectangular prism? Discuss your answers with the class.

Create and Measure Rectangular Prisms

First, use centimetre cubes to make the rectangular prisms described in the chart. Then copy and complete the chart to find the volume of each.

Rectangular Prism	Volume Estimate	Length	Width	Height	Actual Volume
4 5 2					
5 3 2					
3 2 6					

What Did You Learn?

1. Explain how you made an estimate.

2. Explain how you found the volumes of the rectangular prisms.

3. How can you figure out the volume of a rectangular prism if you know its length, width, and height?

4. Write about two ways to calculate volume.

5. Why do you think volume is measured in cubic units? Explain.

1. Use centimetre cubes to design your own rectangular prisms. Record the volume of each structure.

2. Make a different structure using centimetre cubes. It does not have to be rectangular prism. Have a classmate figure out the volume by using the counting method.

3. Does a rectangular prism with a length of 4 cm, a width of 2 cm, and a height of 2 cm have the same volume as a prism with a length of 2 cm, a width of 4 cm, and height of 2 cm? Explain your reasoning. Use pictures, numbers, and words.

4. Calculate the volume of each of these figures. Use the measurements given for each figure.

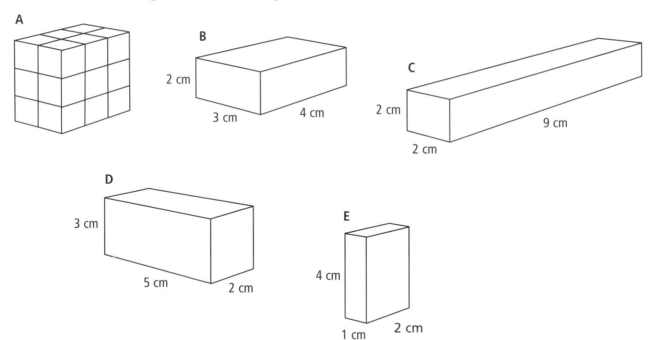

A

B
2 cm
3 cm   4 cm

C
2 cm
9 cm
2 cm

D
3 cm
5 cm   2 cm

E
4 cm
1 cm   2 cm

A Math Problem to Solve

5. Cora needs a box with a volume of 40 cm³. What could the dimensions of her box be? Use pictures, numbers, and words to explain your answer.

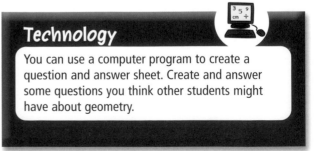

Technology

You can use a computer program to create a question and answer sheet. Create and answer some questions you think other students might have about geometry.

Chapter Review

1. Use a ruler to create a line of symmetry through each object below.

2. Draw three objects in your notebook, and label each line of symmetry.

3. The shapes in Row 1 match up to congruent shapes in Row 2. Match up the number in Row 1 to the correct letter in Row 2. Some of the shapes in Row 2 will be left over.

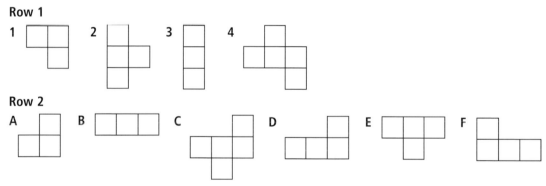

4. In your notebook, draw as many two-dimensional shapes as you can with these triangles. Label your new shapes.

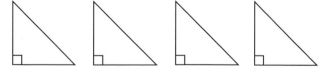

5. In your notebook, write each letter of the angle to the right. Beside it, write if the angle is acute, obtuse, or a right angle.

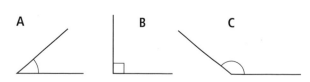

6. In your notebook, make a chart like the one below and complete it by placing the letters for each type of triangle in the chart.

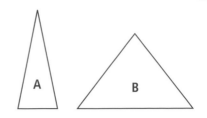
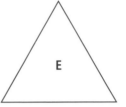

Equilateral	Isosceles	Scalene

7. How did you know how to sort the triangles in your chart for question 6? Explain.

8. Describe the angles in triangles C and E from question 6.

9. a) Find the area of the rectangle on the right:
b) Draw all the rectangles you can with the same area as the rectangle in question 10 (a).

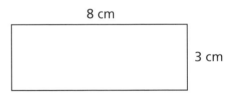

8 cm

3 cm

10. List all the factors of the following numbers: 3, 6, 10, 17, and 30.

11. Use grid paper to create the following:
   a) rectangle that is 8 cm^2 **b)** square that is 9 cm^2
   c) parallelogram that is 16 cm^2
   d) rectangle with a perimeter of 30 cm
   Which shape has the greatest area? Explain how you know.

12. What non-standard unit of measurement could you use to measure the volume of a shoe box? Explain your answer.

13. a) A sugar-cube tower is 4 cubes long, 10 cubes high, and 3 cubes wide. Draw this tower in your notebook and calculate its volume.
   b) What would the volume be if the tower's height is doubled?

Chapter 5

Chapter Wrap-Up

Throughout this chapter, you have learned about symmetry, congruency, triangles, angles, area, and volume while visiting castles.

A medieval feast was a way for the owner of a castle to show off his or her wealth. Your task is to apply some of the math that you learned in this chapter to design a placemat for a royal person to use at a feast. On your placemat, you will create a design using as many math ideas from this chapter as you can. You can create your placemat by drawing, cutting shapes out, and gluing on materials.

1. Sketch two or three possible designs for a placemat. Revise your design sketches to make the math ideas stand out.

2. Gather the materials you will need and create your placemat.

3. On the back of your placemat, list each math idea that you used in your design, and write about how you used it. You will use this information to present your placemat to a "noble" person, such as your teacher, your principal, a classmate, a parent, or a guardian.

Math for a Medieval Festival

As you continue on your adventure, you, your classmates, and your teacher go into town to participate in a medieval festival. What might you see, hear, smell, and taste? Most festivals have food, music, things to buy, and games to enjoy.

In this chapter, you will learn about
- time concepts
- capacity
- money
- measurement
- and collecting data

At the end of this chapter, you will use the math you have been learning to plan and create a medieval festival. You will need to survey your guests to find out what kind of food, drink, and entertainment they would prefer.

Before you learn about math in a medieval festival, answer the following questions:

1. In your notebook, draw what that time looks like on an analog clock and on a digital clock.

2. Now ask three other students in your class what their favourite time of day is, and record their answers in your notebook. Were any of the answers similar to yours?

Lesson 1

Comparing Units of Measurement

JOURNEY NOTE

PLAN:
You will continue to compare lengths using metric units.

DESCRIPTION:
To prepare for the festival, squires (young boys studying to become knights) gather the necessary equipment for the knights. A young squire looks for his knight's sword. Its length measures one metre.

Get Started

1. Identify things in your classroom or school that are approximately one metre in length.

2. Like the clothing of knights, what a jester wore also served a purpose. Bright clothing helped them to be seen in big crowds. A jester's shoes were pointed and twice as long as his feet. How many centimetres long would your medieval jester shoe be? Share your results with a classmate.

Compare Units of Measurement

The metric system is based on the unit 10. For example, if you took one metre and divided it into ten equal parts, you would have ten decimetres. Each decimetre is one tenth (0.1) of a metre. Now, if you took the decimetre and divided it into ten equal parts, you would have ten centimetres. Finally, if you divided a centimetre into ten equal parts, you would have ten millimetres.

Copy and complete the chart. The first line is done for you.

Metres (m)	Decimetres (dm)	Centimetres (cm)	Millimetres (mm)
1	10	100	1000
	1		
		1	
			1

What Did You Learn?

1. How big is a decimetre? centimetre? millimetre? Give an example of each.

2. Find objects, or use parts of your body, to represent one decimetre, one centimetre, and one millimetre. Record your answers.

3. Explain the patterns in the chart you completed in the previous section.

4. In what other words can you hear the prefixes *deci*, *centi*, and *milli* before? Share your words with the class.

5. How can multiplication and division help you convert units of measurement? Use examples to support your answers.

Practice

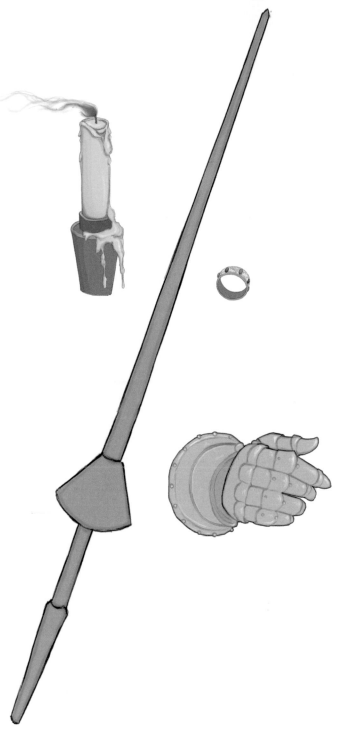

You Will Need
• string

Cut lengths of string to show the following measurements:

1. jousting stick, 2.5 m long

2. candle, 1.3 dm tall

3. ring, 25 mm wide

4. a knight's glove, 8 cm wide

What unit of measurement would you use to measure the following? You can choose from kilometres, metres, decimetres, centimetres, and millimetres. Explain your choices.

5. horse's tail

6. grain of salt

7. shoe

8. oar for a ship

9. mountain trail

Convert each measurement:

10. 150 cm = ■ mm   **11.** 1 m = ■ dm

12. 20 dm = ■ m   **12.** 62 cm = ■ dm

14. 44 mm = ■ cm   **15.** 4 m = ■ cm

A Math Problem to Solve

16. Three friends are measuring the amount of ribbon they each have. Peter has 2500 mm of ribbon. Nicole has 450 cm of ribbon and Abdul has 30 dm of ribbon.

a) Who has the most ribbon? Show your work in pictures, numbers, and words.

b) Each friend needs 5 m of ribbon to wrap presents. How much more ribbon do they each need to reach their goal? Show your work.

Lesson 2

Calculating Distance

JOURNEY NOTE

PLAN:
You will calculate the distances in kilometres that people have travelled.

DESCRIPTION:
The festival is about to begin. A large group of people heads toward the festival grounds.

Get Started

You Will Need
• trundle wheel

The festival grounds are one kilometre away. How far is one kilometre? Estimate how many times you would have to walk around your school to travel one kilometre. Use a trundle wheel to measure your walk. Keep track of the time. How long does it take you to walk one kilometre?

Vocabulary

metre (m) = A unit of length. 1 m = 100 cm
decimetre (dm) = A unit of length. 10 dm = 1 m
centimetre (cm) = A unit of length. 100 cm = 1 m
millimetre (mm) = A unit of length. 1000 mm = 1 m
decametre (dam) = A unit of length. 1 dam = 10 m
kilometre (km) = A unit of length. 1 km = 1000 m
trundle wheel: A small wheel used to measure distances that are too long for a tape measure or that aren't straight.

Build Your Understanding

Calculate Distance on a Map

On the way to the festival, a passerby pulls out a map from his pocket. Use the map to answer the following questions.

1. About how many kilometres is it to Town B from where you are?

2. How far is it to Town A if you travel through Town B?

3. The passerby walked from Town A and passed by the festival on his way to Town C. How far did he walk?

4. A lady left Town B on her way to the festival. Which was the shortest route, through Town C or Town A? Explain.

5. A knight travelled 10 km from Town D to the festival, back to Town D for the night, and then went to Town B in the morning. How far did he travel? Show your work.

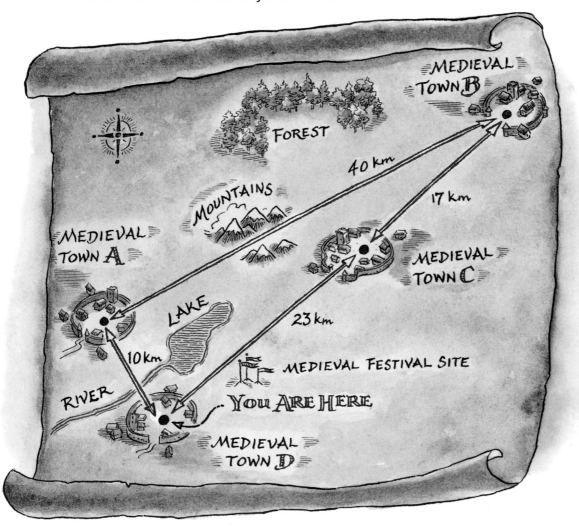

What Did You Learn?

1. How many metres are there in a kilometre?

2. A metre is what fraction of a kilometre?

3. Using kilometres, describe the farthest you have walked, ridden in a car, and flown in a plane.

Technology

With your teacher's permission, you can use the Internet to find some on-line mapping sites to practise calculating distance.

Practice

1. Look at the odometer on your parents' or your teacher's car. Look again at the same time the next day. How far did the car travel in a day?

2. There are various units you can use when measuring something. Here is a saying to help you remember common metric prefixes of length from greatest to smallest. Make up another saying to help you remember them:

"King Henry Drove. Mother Didn't Care Much."

King for kilometre

Henry for hectometre

Drove for decametre

Mother for metre

Didn't for decimetre

Care for centimetre

Much for millimetre

3. How many laps (lengths) of a 25 m swimming pool would you have to swim to travel 1 km? How many laps in an Olympic-sized pool of 50 m? How did you calculate? Use pictures, numbers, and words.

4. Make a scale for the map on page 233. Explain why you chose the scale you did.

5. Examine a road map of your community. Use the scale to make up problems about distance for a friend to solve. For example, how far is it from your house to the nearest shopping mall, fire station, and police station?

Lesson 3

Calculating Capacity

JOURNEY NOTE

PLAN:
You will learn about capacity.

DESCRIPTION:
Someone in the town hall shows you a special clock called a water clock. Water drips from a jar into a cylinder. Inside the cylinder is a float with a rod. Attached to the rod is a pointer that is attached to a ruler marked with different time intervals. As the water level inside the cylinder rises, the pointer indicates a new time on the ruler.

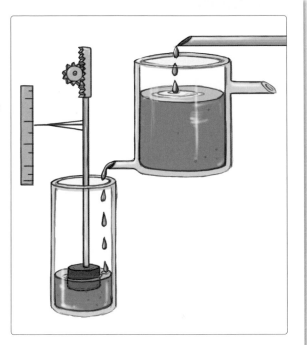

Get Started

Use a container provided by your teacher. Estimate how many centimetre cubes will fit inside. Next, check your estimate by filling the container with centimetre cubes. How close was your estimate?

Build Your Understanding

Measure the Capacities of Containers

You Will Need
- containers that can hold liquids

1. Collect a variety of containers that can hold liquids.

2. Follow these steps to estimate and then measure the capacity of each container.

   Step 1: Estimate the capacity of the container. How many centimetre cubes do you think will fit in the container?

   Step 2: Fill the container with centimetre cubes.

   Step 3: Count the number of cubes in the container. Compare this number with your estimate. How accurate was your estimate?

   Step 4: Imagine the cubes were liquid. Convert their volume to millilitres (mL).

   Step 5: Determine the actual capacity. Fill the container with water, and then pour the water into a graduated cylinder to measure the amount.

3. In your notebook, record your findings in a chart.

Container	Estimated Capacity Using Cubes	Actual Capacity Using Water
juice can	310 mL	350 mL

Vocabulary

capacity: The amount a container can hold when it is filled

litre (L): A unit measure of capacity. It is made up of 1000 mL. 1 L = 1000 mL

millilitre (mL): A unit measure of capacity. It is one thousandth of a litre. 1000 mL = 1 L

Tip

Volume describes how much room something takes up. Capacity describes how much a container can hold. Capacity is measured in litres and millilitres. Volume is measured in litres (L) and millilitres (mL) for liquids, and cubic centimetres (cm³) and cubic metres (m³) for solids.

What Did You Learn?

1. Which step is more accurate for determining a container's capacity? Explain why.

2. Explain the similarities and differences between volume and capacity.

3. How many millilitres (mL) are there in a litre (L)?

4. What comparisons can you use to help you estimate capacity?

5. List items that are sold by the litre (L).

> **Technology**
>
> You can use a paint/draw computer program to explain the activity using pictures, numbers, and words.

Practice

1. Keep track of how much milk or juice you drink in one day.

2. Compare the capacities of different milk containers.

3. How many 250 mL containers full of water could be emptied into a 1-L container?

4. How many 500 mL containers full of water could be emptied into a 1-L container?

5. How many 1000 mL containers full of water could be emptied into a 4-L jug?

6. Check the *Guinness Book of World Records* for the record of the largest container and for other records related to capacity.

7. Experiment with capacity.

   You Will Need
   • plastic pop bottle with a tiny hole at the bottom of the side
   • large, empty container
   • funnel
   • table
   • stopwatch

   a) Place your plastic pop bottle on the edge of a table.

   b) Place an empty container on the floor nearby under the bottle.

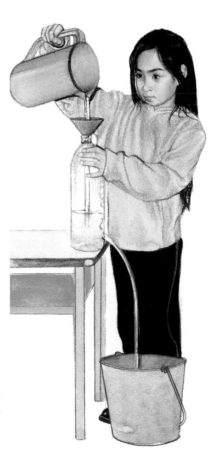

c) Use a funnel to add water into the pop bottle. Make sure you add enough so the water covers the hole on the side of the bottle. Cover the hole with your finger until you are ready to time the experiment.

d) Add a drop of food colouring to help see the liquid. Your water should start flowing through the hole into the container on the floor.

e) Use a stopwatch to time how long it takes the water to flow from the bottle to the pail.

f) Experiment with the amount of water in the bottle. Can you make the flow from the bottle to the container last exactly one minute?

Extension

8. Repeat the Practice section from this lesson but this time change the size of the hole on the plastic pop bottle. Compare your results to the first time you tried this experiment. Graph both sets of results.

9. Estimate then calculate the capacity of an object in your classroom. (Make sure you get your teacher's permission.)

Show What You Know

Review: Lessons 1 to 3, Units of Measurement, Distance, and Capacity

1. What unit of measurement would you use to measure the following? Explain your choices.

a) this book

b) your classroom

c) the distance from your home to your school

d) a pencil

e) your fingernail

f) a bicycle

2. Convert each measurement.

a) 250 mm = ■ cm

b) 650 cm = ■ m

c) 7 ■ = 70 dm

d) 2 m = ■ cm

e) 1 dm = ■ mm

3. How would you explain to a friend how to convert litres to millilitres? Give examples to support your answer.

Lesson 4

Working With Money

JOURNEY NOTE

PLAN:
You will work with different sums of money.

DESCRIPTION:
You walk into the town's marketplace and notice some people using money to buy food.

Get Started

Dollars and cents didn't exist in medieval times. Instead, people used metal coins to buy items like food. Since we use dollars and cents to buy items, the following represents the equivalent in Canadian dollars of the sum of money that was used to buy food for a feast.

How much money was used in total? Explain how you found the answer.

Build Your Understanding

Divide and Count Money

You Will Need
• pretend money (bills and coins)

Food Item	Your Estimate	Actual Amount Counted
A		
B		
C		
D		

1. **a)** Work in teams of two. Pretend your team is buying groceries for a feast. Label four containers A, B, C, and D, representing the items of food you will buy.

   b) Divide the bills and coins that you have into the four containers in any way you like without counting. You must use all of your money.

   c) Work with your partner to estimate how much money you think was spent for each food item. Then count how much money you actually spent on each food item.

   d) Use a chart like the one above to help you keep track of your data.

What Did You Learn?

1. How did you come up with your estimate?

2. Arrange the food items in order from most expensive to the least expensive. What do you think these food items could be, based on their price?

3. How does counting bills compare with counting coins? Which is easier? Why?

Practice

1. You have between $25.00 and $35.00 to spend on a meal for your family. Use grocery store flyers from a newspaper to plan your meal. Show your work in pictures, numbers, and words.

2. Compare your meal with one of your classmate's. How are they similar? How are they different?

Lesson 5

Calculating Change to $50.00

JOURNEY NOTE

PLAN:
You will calculate change up to $50.00.

DESCRIPTION:
In the marketplace, you notice a craftsman who manufactures and sells equipment for knights.

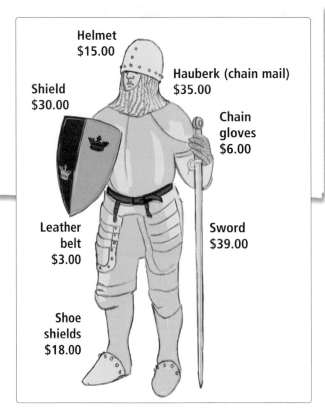

Helmet
$15.00

Shield
$30.00

Hauberk (chain mail)
$35.00

Chain gloves
$6.00

Leather belt
$3.00

Sword
$39.00

Shoe shields
$18.00

Get Started

The items for knights and their prices are shown in the Journey Note. In reality, the cost of these items would be much more. In fact, armour would cost thousands of dollars.

If you had $50.00, what items from the picture above could you buy? Work with a partner and record in your notebook as many shopping combinations as possible. You may buy more than one item.

Build Your Understanding

Work Backwards

Using the information in Get Started, try to calculate what someone purchased who received the following change from his or her $50.00. Use the "Work Backwards" strategy.

1. $14.00

2. $8.00

3. $11.00

4. $5.00

5. $2.00

What Did You Learn?

1. Explain how you used the "Work Backwards" strategy.

2. What other strategy could you have used?

3. Why is knowing how to count money and give change important?

4. Which purchase made the most use of the $50.00? Explain.

Practice

1. a) Figure out the correct amount of change for the amounts listed. Use your pretend money to help you. Put your answers in a chart.

b) Write in your journal about the strategy you used to figure out the correct amount of change.

Money	Cost	Change
$1.00	$0.59	
$3.00	$1.25	
$10.50	$9.49	
$45.02	$29.99	

Math Problems to Solve

2. Your parents give you $5.50 to go shopping. You buy an ice-cream cone for $1.15 and a chocolate bar for $0.99. On the way home you find 2 quarters. How much money do you have now? Use pictures, numbers, and words.

3. At a store, you purchase a cap for $5.95. Show this amount in several different ways using coins and bills.

Extension

4. Why do you think stores sell things with $0.99 endings, as in $9.99?

Lesson 6

Problem Solving With Patterns

JOURNEY NOTE

PLAN:
You will practise your problem-solving skills as you examine a geometric pattern.

DESCRIPTION:
The town is full of excitement. More and more people are crowding into the streets. The medieval festival is just hours away. You notice two people sitting on tree stumps playing a game of chess.

Get Started

Watching these people play chess brings back memories of playing the game with your family. Chess was a popular medieval board game. The chess pieces were often carved from bone or ivory.

What do you know about chess? How many chess pieces are there altogether? Look at the chart on the next page to help you.

Chess Piece	Number of Pieces in a Game of Chess	Type of Move
King	2	One space in any direction (forward, backward, sideways, and diagonal)
Queen	2	Can move many spaces in one direction (forward, backward, sideways, and diagonal in a straight line)
Bishop	4	Can move many spaces on the diagonals only
Knight	4	Two spaces forward, backward, or sideways, then one space to the side (L-shaped moves). The knight is the only piece that can jump over other pieces. All the other pieces can only move if there aren't any pieces in their way.
Castle or Rook	4	Can move many spaces in a straight line forward, backward, and sideways
Pawn	16	One space forward or one space diagonally when capturing another game piece. (A pawn can also move two spaces forward in an opening move.)

Math Problems to Solve

1. Look at the illustration of a chessboard. Estimate how many squares there are. Record your guess in your journal.

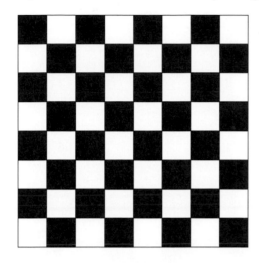

Technology

You can use a paint/draw computer program to create a chessboard with 64 squares and outline all the different squares you see. Use your results to help you answer question 1 in Build Your Understanding.

2. Use a reproducible page of a chessboard.

a) With coloured pencils, outline the 8 x 8 square in red, the 7 x 7 squares in blue, the 6 x 6 squares in green, and so on.

b) How many 8 x 8 squares are there? How many 7 x 7 squares? 6 x 6? 5 x 5? 4 x 4? 3 x 3? 2 x 2? 1 x 1? How many squares are there altogether?

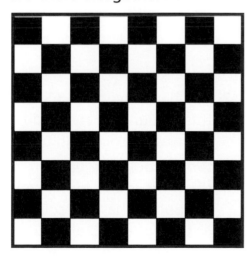

What Did You Learn?

1. How did you come up with your estimates?

2. What is the difference between your estimates and the total number of squares you found?

3. Organize your information into a chart like the one to the right. What patterns do you notice? Discuss your patterns with a classmate.

Type of Square	Number Found
8 x 8	1
7 x 7	
6 x 6	
5 x 5	
4 x 4	
3 x 3	
2 x 2	
1 x 1	64

Practice

1. Play a game of chess.

2. Find a computer game of chess on the Internet.

3. Research another medieval game, backgammon. Explain the rules to a classmate.

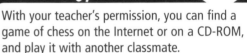

Technology

With your teacher's permission, you can find a game of chess on the Internet or on a CD-ROM, and play it with another classmate.

Show What You Know

Review: Lessons 4 to 6, Money and Patterns

1. Imagine you have $50.00 to spend on a meal for you and a friend. What would you choose to order? How much change would you get back? Use a restaurant menu or create your own. Work with a partner to come up with different meal combinations.

2. You have saved $14.65. Show this amount in several different ways using coins and bills.

3. What would the pattern in the chart above look like if a chessboard has 144 squares instead of 64? Explain using pictures, numbers, and words.

Lesson 7

Calculating Time Intervals

JOURNEY NOTE

PLAN:

You will measure and calculate time intervals using a schedule.

DESCRIPTION:

Many noble people living in and around a medieval town enjoyed hawking—using birds, such as falcons, to catch smaller birds with their talons or claws. Schedules are used to organize many activities like hawking.

Get Started

This is a morning schedule of a hawker:

5:30 A.M. Wake up.
5:35 A.M. Wash and get dressed.
5:45 A.M. Milk the cow.
6:30 A.M. Eat breakfast.
6:50 A.M. Wash dishes.
7:00 A.M. Saddle horse.
7:10 A.M. Gather the falcon.
7:15 A.M. Ride out to the forest.
7:45 A.M. Arrive at the forest.
10:00 A.M. Release the falcon.
11:15 A.M. Attract the falcon.
11:20 A.M. Capture the falcon.
12:00 P.M. Arrive home.

1. How long did it take to milk the cow?

2. How much time passed from the time the hawker woke up until the hawker returned home?

3. Approximately how long did it take to gather the falcon for the hunt?

4. How long did the hawker look for game before releasing the falcon?

5. At what time did the hawker leave the forest to get home at 12:00 P.M. if the hawker travelled the same speed as earlier in the morning?

6. Ask two other questions that could be answered by reading the schedule. What are the answers to your questions?

Technology

You can use a word processing computer program to create your typical weekday morning schedule. Then create questions for a classmate to answer.

Build Your Understanding

Examine Your Schedule

1. Estimate first, then calculate how long you are up before you come to school.

2. Make a schedule of your morning activities until lunch. Start with the time you wake up.

3. About how long does it take you to prepare to go to school?

4. How long does it take you to travel to school?

5. Estimate first, then calculate how long you are in school.

6. How long is your recess break?

What Did You Learn?

1. Using time intervals, how was the hawker's morning like your morning?

2. Using time intervals, how was the hawker's morning different from your morning?

Practice

1. Keep track of what you do every five minutes during math class. Make a chart to record your activity.

2. a) Make a schedule that shows your evening activities (after 6:00 P.M.).

   b) Make up questions that could be answered by reading your schedule. Give them to a classmate to answer.

3. Estimate the amount of time it would take you to
   • walk the length of the gym or athletic field
   • walk, using smaller steps, the length of the gym or athletic field
   • run the length of the gym or athletic field

   Do these activities with a stopwatch or watch to record the actual amount of time it took you.

Math Problems to Solve

4. A hawk took flight at 8:55 A.M. and stayed in the air for 25 min. At what time did it land?

5. a) The neighbour's hawk stayed in the air twice as long as the bird in the previous question. How long was it in flight?

b) If the hawks left at the same time, at what time did the neighbour's hawk return? Show your work in pictures, numbers, and words.

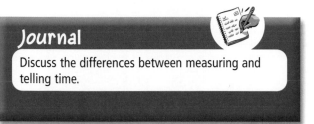

Journal

Discuss the differences between measuring and telling time.

Lesson 8

Reading and Recording Time

JOURNEY NOTE

PLAN:
You will practise reading and writing time.

DESCRIPTION:
In the town you are visiting is a magnificent town hall. The person in charge of ringing the town hall's bell every hour during daylight hours is the official timekeeper.

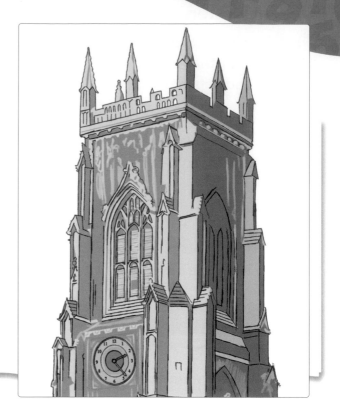

Get Started

You show your wristwatch to the timekeeper. He asks you to read then record the following times in your journal.

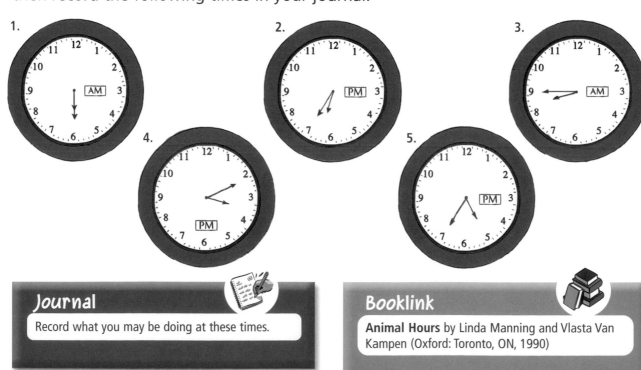

1.
2.
3.
4.
5.

Journal

Record what you may be doing at these times.

Booklink

Animal Hours by Linda Manning and Vlasta Van Kampen (Oxford: Toronto, ON, 1990)

Make a Clock

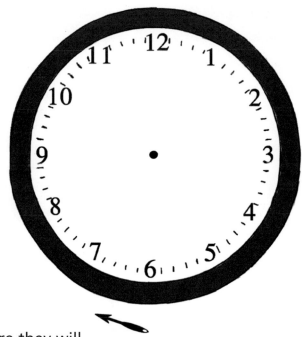

You Will Need
- construction paper
- clock reproducible page
- fasteners

1. Cut out the clock face and hands from the reproducible page.

2. Glue the clock face and hands to construction paper or cardboard and cut them out again. This will make your clock stronger.

3. Punch a hole into each clock hand where they will fasten to the clock.

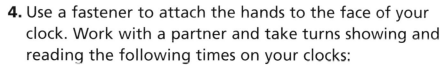

4. Use a fastener to attach the hands to the face of your clock. Work with a partner and take turns showing and reading the following times on your clocks:

   a) 8:35 A.M.   **b)** 12:20 A.M.   **c)** 9:45 A.M.

   d) 5:15 P.M.   **e)** 8:30 P.M.   **f)** 3:55 P.M.

   g) 6:10 A.M.   **h)** 11:40 P.M.   **i)** 2:55 P.M.

5. When you are finished, set your clock to a time of your choice and have your partner read it. Listen carefully. Did your partner tell the time correctly?

What Did You Learn?

1. How many ways can the time 3:15 be said?

2. Record three ways of saying the following time: 4:45.

3. Record two ways of saying the following time: 11:30.

4. What methods or tricks do you use to tell time?

5. What times are easy to read? Why?

6. What times do you find difficult to read? Why?

Practice

Round the following times to the nearest five minutes.
Record your answers.

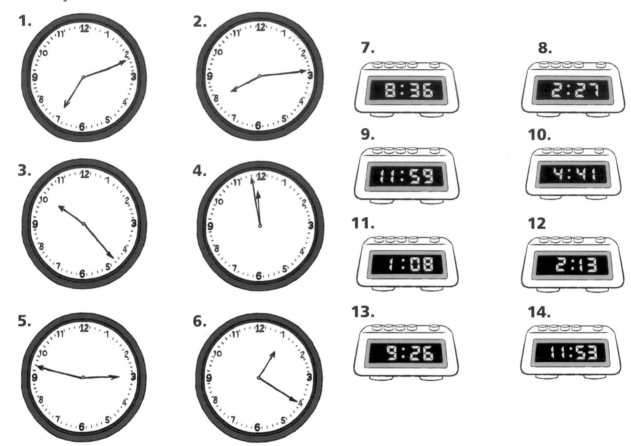

1.

2.

3.

4.

5.

6.

7. 8:36

8. 2:27

9. 11:59

10. 4:41

11. 1:08

12 2:13

13. 9:26

14. 11:53

15. Find a schedule showing arrival and departure times for trains, buses, ferries, or planes in your area. Record some of the times.

16. How do you know when to use A.M. or P.M.? Explain.

Lesson 9

Surveys

JOURNEY NOTE

PLAN:

You will conduct a survey while collecting and organizing data.

DESCRIPTION:

As you continue walking through the town, you come across a group of troubadours. Troubadours were musicians and poets who travelled together, entertaining townsfolk by sharing their stories and news.

Get Started

This group of troubadours is conducting a survey of the townspeople to determine which musical instrument people enjoy listening to most.

It would take too much time to ask everyone in the town, so they are taking a sample of the total population. The results of the survey appear in the chart on page 254.

Make a bar graph of the data in the chart. Remember to label axes and to include a title. Also make sure your scale goes by even intervals.

Townspeople's Favourite Instruments	
Type of Instrument	Number of People
flute	ЖЖ ΙΙ
bagpipes	ЖЖ ЖЖ
harp	ЖЖ ΙΙ
drum	ЖЖ Ι

1. Imagine that you were trying to learn what instrument the people in town liked best. How sure of your results would you be if you asked everyone in the town? Why?

2. How sure of your results would you be if you asked half of the people in the town? Why?

3. How sure would you be if you asked 5 people? Why?

4. If you had enough time to ask 20 people in the town about their favourite instrument, how would you choose which people to ask? Why?

Vocabulary

population: The total number of people in a specific area
sample: A part of a population selected to represent the population as a whole

Technology

You can use a spreadsheet computer program to organize the data and show the results.

Build Your Understanding

Conduct a Survey

Conduct a survey in your class or school to learn students' favourite food, type of book, or sport.

1. Write a title for your survey.

Chapter 6: Math for a Medieval Festival

2. Write five choices on a piece of paper and use tally marks to record people's responses.

3. Survey enough people so that you think the trends in their answers show what the whole group thinks. Choose who you survey (your sample) carefully.

4. Make a bar graph to display your data.

What Did You Learn?

1. You didn't ask everyone in your school to respond to your survey. What makes you confident that trends in your survey results show what the whole group really thinks?

2. How did you choose people to survey?

3. How did you decide when you had surveyed enough people?

Practice

1. Organize the data you collected in your survey in either a chart, table, or pictograph.

2. a) Imagine that you conducted a survey to find out the favourite sport of teachers. You asked three teachers in your school. Explain how reliable or accurate this data is. Why?

b) How could you make the data more accurate?

Show What You Know
Review: Lessons 7 to 9, Time and Surveys

1. A dog, on a morning walk with its owner, picked up the scent of a rabbit in the local park at 6:45 A.M. At 7:15 A.M., the dog lost the rabbit's scent. At 7:35 A.M., the dog found the scent again and resumed following the scent until 8:00 A.M. How long was the dog on the scent of the rabbit? Show your work using pictures, numbers, and words.

2. Write three ways of saying 4:45 P.M.

3. Draw a clock that shows 7:40.

4. Conduct a survey of your choice and display data using a bar graph. Make up questions and ask a classmate to answer them.

5. When someone conducts a survey, why do they usually take a sample of the total population. Explain.

Chapter Review

Chapter 6

1. Convert each measurement:

   a) 120 cm equals ▦ mm

   b) 1 m equals ▦ cm

   c) 10 dm equals ▦ m

   d) 34 cm equals ▦ dm

   e) 76 mm equals ▦ cm

2. How many laps (lengths) of a 40 m track would you have to run to travel 1 km? Explain how you calculated your answer. Use pictures, numbers, and words.

3. Find a container that can hold liquid. Estimate then measure the capacity of the container using cubic centimetre blocks and then water. Explain which method is more accurate.

4. How many 200 mL containers full of water could be emptied into a 2 L jug? Explain using pictures, numbers, and words.

5. Draw in your notebook the different combinations of coins that equal the following amounts:

   a) 4 coins that equal $0.50

   b) 12 coins that equal $0.64

   c) 7 coins that equal $0.23

6. Your aunt and uncle give you $50.00 to go shopping for a new school outfit. You buy a sweater for $16.50, pants for $19.95, and shoes for $11.75.

   a) How much money do you have left? Use pictures, numbers, and words.

   b) Show different combinations of coins that equal the amount of money you have left from the $ 50.00.

7. You have $10.00 to use at a medieval festival. Your choices of activities, the time needed, and the cost are in the chart to the right.

Activity	Time Needed	Cost
Juggling	30 min	$2.70
Jousting	45 min	$3.25
Archery	60 min	$5.00
Chess	50 min	$3.50
Medieval Painting	40 min	$5.50
Weaving	15 min	$0.75

   a) You must schedule three activities and a break between 9:00 A.M. and 11:30 A.M. Create your schedule in your notebook.

   b) Calculate the cost of your activities. Show how much money you have left from your $10.00.

8. Write the following times in your notebook:

A

B
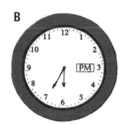
C

D

E

9. Imagine doing a survey about the favourite foods of ten-year-old boys or girls in your school. Answer the following questions about your survey:

   a) What does population refer to when conducting a survey? Estimate the population of ten-year-olds in your school.

   b) What would be a reasonable sample to survey? Justify your answer.

   c) How might the data gathered vary if it was collected before supper rather than after? Explain.

Technology

You can use a computer simulation program to review what you have learned about time, money, volume, capacity, and measurement.

Chapter Wrap-Up

You have reached the end of this chapter. It is time to draw upon what you have learned to plan, as a class, a medieval festival.

Prepare a Schedule

1. Make a list of activities that you might have at the festival.

2. Decide how much time might be needed for each activity.

3. Make a schedule for a festival.

Plan a Meal

4. How much food and drink will you need for your feast? Decide what items of food and drink you will prepare. Use what you know about volume and capacity to decide how much of each you will need. Show your calculations.

5. How much will it cost to buy each item of food? How much money will you need to spend in total?

Arrange the Room

6. Use grid paper to make a floor plan. Draw a room that has an area of 96 square units.

7. You may use up to 25 tables that are each one unit by two units. Each person needs one square unit of table space. How many people can you have at your feast? Show your work.

Make a Map

8. Plan and make a map of your medieval festival. Be sure to include all the activities from your schedule.

9. Decide how far apart all the activities and feasting area(s) will be. Use what you know about measuring distance to help you.

10. Include a scale on your map.

11. Make sure you label your map.

12. Describe on the back all of the math you used to make your map.

Design an Invitation

13. Design and make an invitation for the festival. Use the geometric ideas that you learned in this unit.

14. On the back of the invitation, describe all of the math that you used to make it.

Now you are ready to have your festival. Enjoy!

Technology

You can use a paint/draw computer program to create your invitation for your medieval festival.

Problems to Solve

Here are fun problems for you to solve. You will be given a helpful problem-solving strategy to use for the first four problems. For the last two you get to choose a strategy to use.

Problem 11

Identifying Patterns

STRATEGY: CONSTRUCT A TABLE

You can make a table to organize information, as well as to spot missing information. Constructing a table makes looking for patterns easier, and it also points out important information to help you solve the problem.

OBJECTIVE:

Apply the pattern identified when multiplying by increasing powers of ten

Problem

Monarch butterflies are known for their long migration from east of the Rocky Mountains in North America to Mexico. On her vacation to Mexico, Carla noticed 5 monarch butterflies on the first day of her trip. On day two, she noticed 10 times as many butterflies than on the first day. On the third day she noticed 10 times as many butterflies as the second day. If the same pattern continued, how many butterflies would she notice on the fifth day?

Reflection

1. Make a table of the information presented in the problem.
2. Explain the pattern found in the problem.
3. Explain what happens to a number that is multiplied by 10, then 100, then 1000. Give an example.
4. Explain a short-cut method for figuring out the answer to a multiplication equation when it involves the number 10, 100, or 1000.

Extension

1. Assuming the same pattern continues, how many butterflies would Carla see on the eighth day of her trip? How do you know?

2. Make up a similar problem that involves multiplying by increasing powers of ten (10, 100, and 1000). Give it to a partner to solve.

Comparing Money Amounts

STRATEGY: MAKE AN ORGANIZED LIST

This strategy allows you to organize your thinking and review what you have done. You can identify important steps in a problem, or things you need to figure out to help you solve the problem.

OBJECTIVE:

Compare and order decimals

Problem

You Will Need
• grocery ads from newspapers

You have been asked to help stock the food shelf in the school store. The shelf is 86 cm by 40 cm. The shelf is blue.

What foods will you sell? How much will each food item cost? How will you advertise the prices for customers? Use the "Make an Organized List" strategy to assist you in solving the problem.

Reflection

1. Which problem needs to be answered first, second, and third? Explain why.

2. What additional information could help you solve the problem?

3. What information is not needed to solve the problem?

4. How did you use the "Make an Organized List" strategy?

5. How is your list organized?

6. Share your solution with a classmate.

Extension

1. Organize your price list from least to most expensive food products.

2. The school store is planning a half-price sale. How much will each item cost?

Problem 13

Creating Number Equations

STRATEGY: WRITE AN EQUATION

Sometimes you can come up with a math question to help you solve the problem.

OBJECTIVE:

Demonstrate equivalence in simple numerical equations using concrete materials, drawings, and symbols

Problem

You Will Need
• base-ten blocks

Evan and Henna brought their stamp collections to school. Evan laid out 126 stamps from Asia, 540 stamps from North America, and 246 stamps from South America.

Henna showed 243 stamps from Europe, 389 stamps from Australia, and 280 stamps from Africa.

Sri told the class that he had 467 stamps at home. Who showed more stamps? Use the "Write an Equation" strategy to help you solve this problem.

Reflection

1. What do you know from the information given?

2. What information is not important?

3. What do you need to figure out?

4. Explain your mathematical equation.

5. Show your mathematical equations using base-ten blocks. Draw a picture of your work.

Extension

1. Replace the numbers in the stamp problem with numbers of your choice.

2. Remake the stamp problem so that it involves a different equation or operation. Give your problem to a classmate to solve.

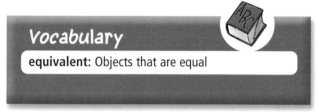

Vocabulary

equivalent: Objects that are equal

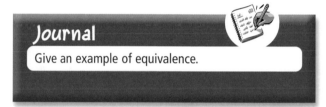

Journal

Give an example of equivalence.

Problem 14

Transformational Geometry

STRATEGY: USE LOGICAL REASONING

You can use a chart to organize your information. Then look at your information and use what you already know to solve the questions you don't know.

OBJECTIVE:

Apply translations, reflections, and rotations using concrete materials and drawings to pose and solve problems

Problem

You Will Need
- felt
- markers
- cardboard
- scissors
- poster paper

Translation

Rotation

Reflection

Ian, Andrea, and Freddie each wanted a poster to hang in their bedrooms. There were three pictures remaining at the video store.

Ian likes designs that look like they have been flipped. Andrea likes designs that look like they have been turned. Freddie likes a poster, but doesn't like what Ian and Andrea like.

Which poster should each person receive? Use the "Logical Reasoning" strategy to solve this problem.

Reflection

1. What is the problem?

2. Complete this like (✔)/dislike (✘) chart to help you with your reasoning:

	Ian	Andrea	Freddie
Translation			
Rotation			
Reflection			

3. Explain who should get each poster.

4. How did the "Logical Reasoning" strategy help you solve this problem?

Extension

1. Use your pencil to demonstrate a translation, rotation, and reflection.

2. Use the materials to design a translation, rotation, and reflection picture. Explain your designs.

3. Using grid paper, draw a polygon or a simple design. Explain what a translation, rotation, and reflection are by using words and your picture.

Problem 15

Problem Solving With Money

STRATEGY: YOUR CHOICE

OBJECTIVE:

Use decimals and money to solve a problem

Problem

While visiting the library to return two library books, you were informed that you had a $1.32 library fine. The penalty for having an overdue book is $0.06 cents per day. How many days were you late returning the books? Choose a problem-solving strategy of your choice.

Reflection

1. List the information you know about the problem.

2. What do you need to figure out?

3. What are some possible problem-solving strategies that could be used to solve this problem?

4. Which strategy did you use? Why?

5. How could you check your answer? Try it.

6. Could drawing a picture help you solve this problem? Explain.

Extension

1. If you paid the fine with a $5.00 bill, how much change would you receive? Show your work in pictures, numbers, and words.

2. Create a similar problem.

Problem 16

Sorting Numbers

STRATEGY: YOUR CHOICE

OBJECTIVE:

Sort numbers into categories, using one or more attributes

Problem

Many people showed up at the same time at Math King's fast food restaurant. Each of the 25 people were given a number.

There are three lines at the restaurant. The first line is for people who have an odd number. The second line is for people who have a number that is a multiple of three. The last line is for people who have an even number. Each line is organized from least to greatest.

Which line is the shortest?

Reflection

1. What do you know about the problem?
2. What numbers would be served first and last in each line?
3. What numbers would be the best to have?
4. Was the line criteria fair?
5. Which problem-solving strategy did you use? Why?

Extension

1. Solve the problem again. This time use a different strategy, such as a diagram.
2. Think of a new criteria for the three lines. Show which numbers would be in each line.
3. What do you think would be served at Math King's restaurant?

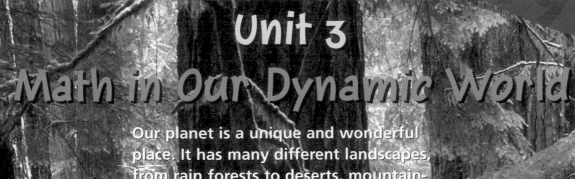

Unit 3
Math in Our Dynamic World

Our planet is a unique and wonderful place. It has many different landscapes, from rain forests to deserts, mountaintops to ocean floors. This diverse planet is our home, but it is also home to millions of other organisms, and we are all interconnected.

In Chapter 7, you will explore large numbers, investigate mass, and analyze the movement of various figures. At the end of the chapter, you will organize data about different organisms living in an area of the forest.

In Chapter 8, you will use fractions and decimals, collect and interpret data on graphs, and study temperature.

In Chapter 9, you will look at maps and study probability. At the end of the chapter, you will create a presentation on extinct and endangered species for your classmates.

Plant and Animal Math

Our earth has many plants and animals living on it. The variety of these organisms is amazing—plant and animal, predator and prey, producer and consumer. The number of plants and animals seems unending, but many of these organisms are in danger of becoming extinct.

In this chapter, we will study plants and animals and explore large numbers and number patterns, investigate mass, make reflections (flips), translations (slides), and rotations (turns), and organize and analyze data.

At the end of the chapter, you will collect data from a particular location, make calculations and comparisons, and then write a description of your findings.

1. How would you describe a pattern?
2. Look around you. Try to find an example of a reflection, translation, and rotation.
3. How can numbers be grouped into patterns? Give an example.

Lesson 1

Representing Numbers up to 10 000

FACT BOOK

PLAN:
You will analyze and compare the populations of different types of animals.

FACTS:
Canada has many different types of animals, including mammals, birds, reptiles, fish, and insects. Canada is home to the largest land carnivores (meat eaters). They are the polar bear and the Kodiak bear.

Polar bear

Get Started

You Will Need
• place-value chart

Look at the following information on the number of different types of animals in Canada.

Type of Animal	Number of Species in Canada
amphibians	45
birds	462
butterflies	284
freshwater fish	230

1. Work with a partner. Use base-ten blocks to make models representing these numbers. Show each model on a place-value chart.

2. Combine your models. In total, how many ones are there, how many tens, how many hundreds, how many thousands? Explain how you got your answer.

Build Your Understanding

Construct Large Numbers

You Will Need
• base-ten blocks

Tip

To make numbers larger than 999, another column is needed on the place-value chart. The number 1274 looks like this:

Thousands	Hundreds	Tens	Ones
1	2	7	4

This number is read as one thousand two hundred seventy-four. It looks like this:

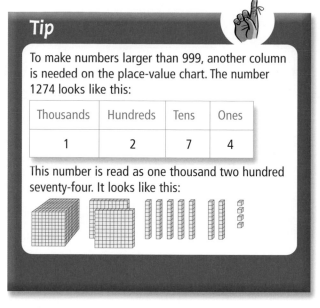

1. Write each numeral. Show the numbers on a place-value chart, and then read the numbers:

a)

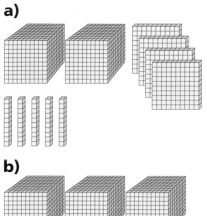

b)

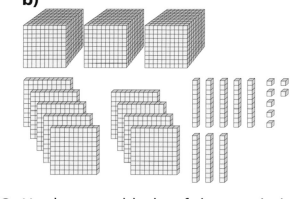

c)

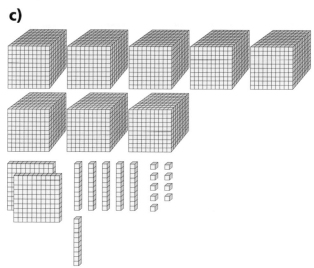

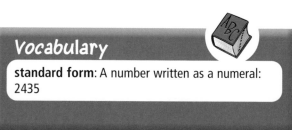

2. Use base-ten blocks of thousands, hundreds, tens, and ones to make the following numbers: 3478, 1023, 8000. Show these numbers on a place-value chart.

3. Show these numbers on the place-value chart:

a) 4 thousands, 3 hundreds, 6 tens, 2 ones

b) 7 thousands, 4 hundreds

c) 5 thousands, 4 tens, 6 ones

d) 2 thousands, 3 hundreds, 8 ones

Write each of these numbers in standard form. Say each number out loud.

4. Order from least to greatest:
1678, 8905, 4567, 3098, 7802

Vocabulary

standard form: A number written as a numeral: 2435

1. How do base-ten blocks help you write numbers in numerical form, say the numbers out loud, and visualize large numbers?

2. What are the advantages of breaking down a number in a place-value chart?

Practice

1. Write each of the following numbers in standard form:

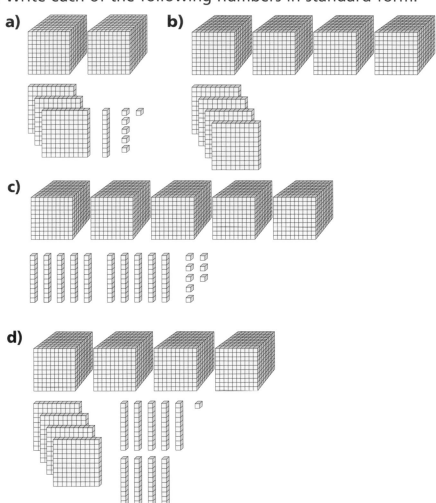

a)

b)

c)

d)

2. Indicate the value of each underlined numeral:

   a) 3<u>2</u>46   **b)** <u>9</u>804   **c)** 67<u>2</u>0   **d)** 541<u>1</u>

Lesson 2

Examining Numbers in Different Forms

FACT BOOK

PLAN:
You will examine numbers to 10000 and analyze the numbers of different species of animals.

FACTS:
There are many more species of animals worldwide than those in Canada. Nearly half of all the different species of mammals worldwide are rodents. The largest animals alive are whales and elephants.

Humpback whale

Get Started

Look at the chart below. The numbers indicate the number of different species found in a specific animal group.

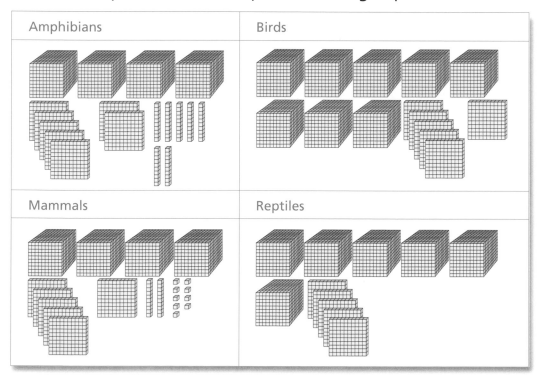

Amphibians	Birds
Mammals	Reptiles

1. Place each of the numbers from the chart in a place-value chart.

2. Write the first number in standard form. Then write the numbers in expanded form. The expanded form of the first number is

   4629 = 4000 + 600 + 20 + 9

Numbers can also be written in words: four thousand six hundred twenty-nine.

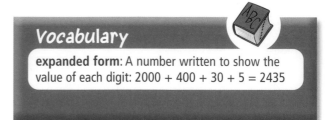

Vocabulary

expanded form: A number written to show the value of each digit: 2000 + 400 + 30 + 5 = 2435

3. Write the other numbers in the chart in standard form, in expanded form, and in words. In your notebook, make and complete a chart like the one below to help you.

4. List the four types of animals in order from the one with the greatest number of species to the one with the fewest species.

Species	Standard Form	Expanded Form	Words
amphibians			
birds			
mammals			
reptiles			

Build Your Understanding

Make More Numbers

You Will Need
• base-ten blocks

Journal

Explain how you would write a number in expanded form.

1. Using the base-ten blocks, create three numbers between 1000 and 10 000.

2. Write each number on a piece of paper.

3. Ask your partner to
   a) put each number on a place-value chart
   b) write the number in expanded form
   c) write each number in words

4. Check to see if your partner was able to identify and describe your numbers correctly.

5. Look at this chart of endangered whales.

Species	Estimate of Number Living in the World
blue whale	
bowhead whale	
northern right whale	
sei whale	
southern right whale	

= 100 whales = 1000 whales = 10 000 whales

   a) What is the most endangered species?
   b) How many right whales are there in total?
   c) How many more blue whales are there than bowhead whales?
   d) Write how many southern right whales there are in standard form and in words.

6. Write another question that can be answered by reading this information. What is the answer to your question?

What Did You Learn?

1. With your partner, explain the difference between the standard form and the expanded form of a number.

2. How many different ways can you show a number? Give an example.

Practice

Write each of the following in expanded form:

1. 2961　　　　**2.** 3049　　　　**3.** 9000

Write each of the following in standard form:

4. 4000 + 20 + 9　**5.** 6000 + 400　**6.** 7000 + 800 + 60

Write the numeral for each of the following:

7. six thousand twelve

8. one thousand three hundred thirty-eight

9. eight thousand one

10. 5 thousands 4 tens

Write each of the following in words:

11. 2600　　　　**12.** 4905　　　　**13.** 6396　　　　**14.** 5217

Write the bigger number in each pair:

15. 4620　4260　**16.** 924　8000　**17.** 3754　3753

What is the value of 3 in the following numbers?

18. 2310　　　　**19.** 9983　　　　**20.** 3075　　　　**21.** 7631

22. Put the following numerals in order from least to greatest. Explain how you decided on your order.

4701　4017　4170　4000　4710

23. Arrange the set of digits below to make the greatest possible number. Explain how you decided on the arrangement.

1709

Lesson 3

Rounding to 10 000

FACT BOOK

PLAN:
You will round numbers as a way to work with and understand large numbers.

FACTS:
There are many different types of insects we know of in the world, and many more we haven't discovered yet! We know there are over 8000 different species of ants and over 7000 species of dung beetles.

Dung beetle

Get Started

Sometimes an exact number is not needed; an approximation will do. There are also times when the exact number is not known. This can be true when we deal with large numbers.

We often use approximations when we talk about numbers of insects because there are so many of them. We can make an approximation by rounding the exact number. For example, we can round 4927 to 5000.

Vocabulary

rounding: A rule used to make an approximation to a number. You should round up when the digit is 5 or higher, and round down when the digit is less than 5.

Use the number line on this page to help you answer the following questions:

1. Read this number: 3999. What thousand is it closest to?

2. Read this number: 2001. What thousand is it closest to?

3. Read this number: 6573. What two thousands is it between? How can you decide which thousand it is closer to?

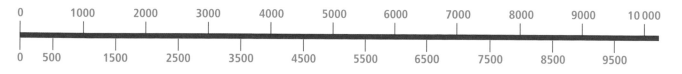

0	1000	2000	3000	4000	5000	6000	7000	8000	9000	10 000

0	500	1500	2500	3500	4500	5500	6500	7500	8500	9500

Build Your Understanding

Explore and Round Numbers

1. Using the number line on page 277, determine which two thousands each number is between, and then select which thousand it is closer to. In your notebook, make and complete a chart like the one below.

Exact Number	Between Which Thousands?	Rounded to Nearest Thousand
2365		
4798		
4590		
6782		
7890		
7403		

2. Put the rounded numbers in order from least to greatest.

3. Put the exact numbers from the table above in order from least to greatest.

4. How would you round 9999 to the nearest thousand? Explain.

5. Work with a partner. Name numbers up to 10 000 for your partner to round to the nearest thousand. Check on a number line to see if she or he is correct.

What Did You Learn?

In your journal, explain how to round numbers to the nearest thousand. Use pictures, numbers, and words, to explain your method. Share your method with the class.

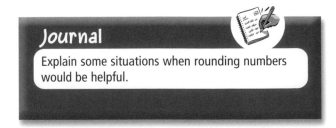

Journal

Explain some situations when rounding numbers would be helpful.

Create your own number line in your notebook. Use the number line from this lesson as a reference. Put each of the following numbers in its approximate location on your number line.

1. 4361 **2.** 5026 **3.** 7902 **4.** 2849 **5.** 1430 **6.** 9567

7. Work with a partner and check that you both agree on where each number goes.

8. Round each of the numbers in questions 1 to 6 to the nearest thousand.

9. For each number and its rounded number, circle the number in the pair that is closest to 1000.

A Math Problem to Solve

10. Your family decides to buy a computer system. The monitor costs $1390.00. The hard drive costs $2564.00 and the printer costs $790.00. Approximately how much money will your family need to buy the whole computer system? Explain how you got your answer.

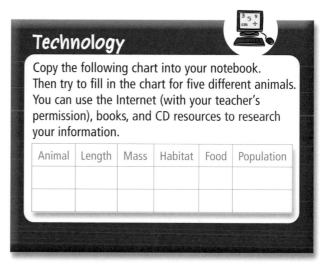

Technology

Copy the following chart into your notebook. Then try to fill in the chart for five different animals. You can use the Internet (with your teacher's permission), books, and CD resources to research your information.

Animal	Length	Mass	Habitat	Food	Population

Extension

11. Suppose there are exactly 4563 ants in an anthill. Round this number to the nearest ten, hundred, and then thousand. Each of the rounded numbers is an approximation. Which approximation is closest to the exact number? Why might you choose to round this number to the nearest thousand?

12. If you were estimating the number of ants in 100 anthills, why might you round the number for one anthill to the nearest 100?

Lesson 4

Place Value With Ten Thousands

FACT BOOK

PLAN:
You will investigate place value as you analyze the large numbers of different types of plants.

FACTS:
There are many different types of plants in the world. Trees are the largest plants. The largest tree is the sequoia. The sequoia may grow to over 90 m tall, and it takes about 15 people holding hands with their arms stretched out to reach around a sequoia.

Sequoia

Get Started

There are many more types of plants in the world than mammals, birds, reptiles, and fish. In fact, the total number of different plant species is so large that it can only be estimated.

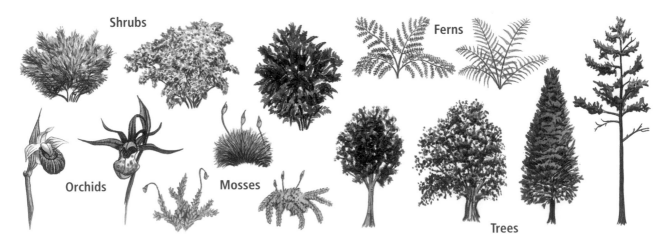

Shrubs

Ferns

Orchids

Mosses

Trees

Look at the following model of the estimated number of types of ferns in the world:

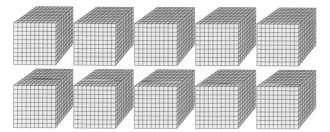

Orchids are considered some of the most beautiful flowers. Here is the estimated number of orchid species found so far:

Here is the estimated number of different types of mosses:

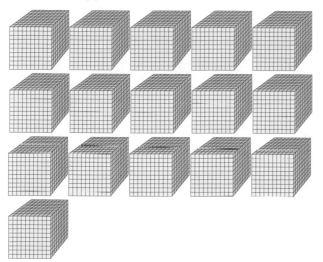

1. a) How many types of ferns, mosses, and orchids are there?
   Use a place-value chart like the one below to help you:

Plant	Ten Thousands	One Thousands	Hundreds	Tens	Ones
ferns					
mosses					
orchids					

b) What strategy did you use to calculate how many types of ferns, mosses, and orchids there are?

2. How many ones are there in this number? How many tens? How many hundreds? How many thousands?

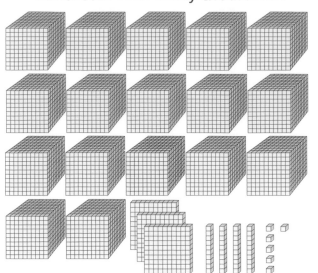

We say "seventeen thousand three hundred forty-six." We write in numerals, 17 346.

3. Look at the following number. Say the number and write it in numerals.

Build Your Understanding

Explore Large Numbers

You Will Need
• base-ten blocks or pictures of base-ten blocks

1. With a partner, make a large number using base-ten blocks.

2. Exchange your model with another team of your classmates. Write each other's numbers in numerals.

3. Make a list of six other numbers made by your classmates. Put these numbers in order from least to greatest.

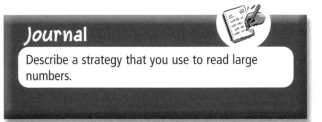

Journal

Describe a strategy that you use to read large numbers.

What Did You Learn?

1. How do base-ten blocks help you understand large numbers?

2. Write the numbers from Build Your Understanding question 3 in words and in expanded form.

Write each of these models in numbers and words:

1.

2.

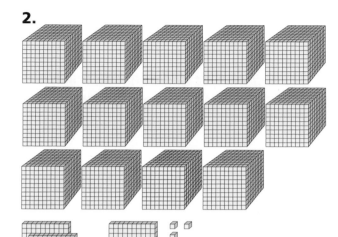

Write the following numbers in standard form:

3. 47 thousand 5 hundred twenty-one

4. thirty-six thousand seven hundred ninety-three

5. 67 thousand 8 hundred

6. eighty-eight thousand three hundred seven

7. 99 thousand sixteen

8. a) Order the following numbers from least to greatest:

   47 321   96 000

   83 492   30 996

   56 201

   b) Explain how you know your order is correct.

Show What You Know

Review: Lessons 1 to 4, Representing and Rounding Numbers

1. Gather data from *The Guinness Book of World Records.* Select data with numbers in the thousands and ten thousands.

2. Show the numbers that you find in various forms.

3. Round the numbers that you find to the nearest thousand and ten thousand.

Graphing Large Numbers

FACT BOOK

PLAN:
You will analyze and graph information about different animals who migrate each year.

FACTS:
People have always wondered what happened to the creatures that seemed to disappear for part of the year. Some people thought that one type of animal changed into another type of animal for a certain part of the year. Other people suggested that many animals hibernated. Some people thought that some birds hibernated under water!

Get Started

One of the great mysteries in the animal kingdom is migration. This chart lists some migratory species and the total distances they travel each year.

1. Why would it be difficult to be exact when calculating the distances an animal migrates?

2. Put all the numbers in the chart in order from least to greatest.

3. Which creatures travel more than 10 000 km?

Animal	Length of Migration
Arctic tern	40 200 km
Atlantic leatherback turtle	15 000 km
Barren-ground caribou	2400 km
Female fur seal	9600 km
Grey whales	19 300 km
Monarch butterfly	4800 km
Pink salmon	8000 km
Ruby-throated hummingbird	5900 km
Short tailed shearwater (a type of puffin)	32 000 km

Analyze the Data

Make a bar graph of the information on the chart. For your scale, draw a bar 1 cm long for every 2000 km that the animal migrates. Remember to title and label your graph.

1. How much farther does the grey whale travel than the Atlantic leatherback turtle?

2. How many times farther does the turtle travel than the monarch butterfly?

3. Which two creatures travel similar distances?

4. The arctic tern travels this distance by making a round trip. It goes from the Arctic to the Antarctic and then back again. How far is the one-way trip?

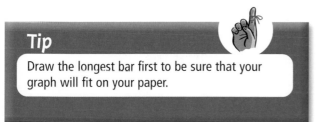

Tip

Draw the longest bar first to be sure that your graph will fit on your paper.

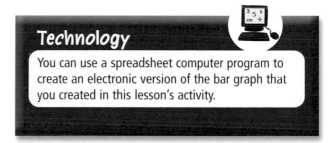

Technology

You can use a spreadsheet computer program to create an electronic version of the bar graph that you created in this lesson's activity.

What Did You Learn?

1. In a small group, discuss when it is necessary to use exact numbers when collecting data to display on a graph.

2. What other questions might be answered from the data on your bar graph? Take turns asking your questions in a small group.

1. What are some of the advantages of rounding numbers?

2. What are some other examples where rounding would come in handy?

3. What are some examples of numbers that we should not try to round? Why?

4. How did your bar graph differ from the chart on page 284? What are some of the advantages of placing data on a bar graph?

5. What are some advantages or disadvantages of using rounded numbers in a chart or graph?

6. Make a list of things you need to remember when making a bar graph.

Extension

7. Research the length of migrations for animals other than the ones listed in the chart on page 284. Create a bar graph of the information. Make up questions that might be answered from the data on your bar graph. Give your questions to a classmate to answer.

Lesson 6

Measuring and Comparing Mass

FACT BOOK

PLAN:
You will measure and compare the mass of different things.

FACTS:
Scientists are interested in all aspects of an organism, including how heavy it is. The mass of a human baby is about 3 to 4 kg at birth. The mass of a baby lion is about 1 to 2 kg at birth. By the time a human is 9 years old, his or her mass is about 40 to 50 kg. The mass of a 9-year-old lion is about 200 kg!

Get Started

We measure mass in grams or kilograms. A gram is about the mass of a raisin or a jellybean. A kilogram is about the mass of a small bag of flour and is equal to 1000 g. Approximately how many jellybeans would there be in a kilogram?

What other items do you think have the mass of about one gram or one kilogram? Share your ideas with the class.

Vocabulary

mass: The amount of matter in an object

Tip

The unit "gram" is abbreviated using "g." The unit "kilogram" is abbreviated using "kg."

Build Your Understanding

Compare Mass

You Will Need
- container
- sand
- small container of sand with a mass of exactly 1 kg
- small plastic bag of sand with a mass of exactly 40 g
- a balance
- several small plastic bags

Gerbil

Raccoon

A raccoon has a mass of about 9 kg, while a gerbil has a mass of about 120 g.

Working with a partner, make your own kilogram mass using the material provided:

1. Fill the container until you estimate its mass to be about a kilogram.

2. Compare it, by holding it in your hand, with the kilogram mass that is provided. How do you think it compares? Do you need to add more mass or remove some mass?

3. When you have what you feel is about a kilogram, measure its mass on a balance. Add or remove material until your container has a mass of one kilogram.

4. Combine your kilogram mass with that of eight other pairs of students. Lift all nine containers. This mass is approximately that of an average raccoon.

5. A gerbil has a mass of about 120 g. Now use the materials provided to make the mass of a gerbil.

What Did You Learn?

1. What else do you think might have a mass equal to a raccoon?

2. How did you make a mass of 120 g using the materials you had to work with?

3. Why do you think the gerbil's mass is given in grams? Why do you think the raccoon's mass is given in kilograms? Explain.

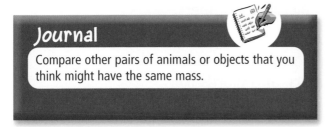

Journal

Compare other pairs of animals or objects that you think might have the same mass.

Practice

Tip

1 kg = 1000 g

Which would be the better unit, grams or kilograms, to measure the mass of each of the following objects? Explain your choices.

1. dime

2. house cat

3. math textbook

4. package of gum

5. person

6. magazine

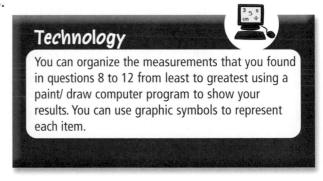

Technology

You can organize the measurements that you found in questions 8 to 12 from least to greatest using a paint/ draw computer program to show your results. You can use graphic symbols to represent each item.

7. Measure three objects around your classroom, and record the mass of each. In a group of four students, put all of your recorded masses in order from least to greatest.

In your notebook, write the most appropriate mass for each of the following:

8. wristwatch: 3 g, 30 g, 300 g

9. hockey player: 9 kg, 90 kg, 900 kg

10. spoon: 44 g, 440 g, 4200 g

11. apple: 15 g, 150 g, 1500 g

12. your textbook: 7 g, 170 g, 700 g

How many grams are there in each of the following?

13. two kilograms = ■ grams

14. three kilograms = ■ grams

15. 9 kg = ■ g

16. 0.5 kg = ■ g

17. 1.5 kg = ■ g

18. An orange has a mass of about 250 g. How many of these oranges would it take to make 1 kg? Use pictures, numbers, and words to explain your answer.

19. How many 100 g boxes of tacks would have the same mass as a 2 kg box of nails? Use pictures, numbers, and words to explain your answer.

A Math Problem to Solve

20. In one month, Allison consumed about 850 g of cereal. In the same month, Zoe ate about 0.9 kg of cereal. Who consumed more cereal? Show your work in pictures, numbers, and words.

Extension

21. Research the mass of each animal from the chart on page 284. Put the animals in order from least mass to greatest mass. Does the mass of each animal relate to the distance it travelled? Be prepared to justify your answer.

22. About how many grade 4 students would it take to balance an elephant with the mass of 6000 kg? Explain your answer.

Lesson 7

Graphing Mass

FACT BOOK

PLAN:
You will analyze and graph data on the
mass of different animals.

FACTS:
Different types of animals can have a
range of different masses. While a polar
bear has a mass of approximately 300 kg,
a golden eagle has a mass of only 5 kg.

Polar bear and golden eagle

Get Started

A group of students researched the
masses of different kinds of animals.
This table shows what they found.

1. What do you find to be the most
   surprising piece of information in
   this table? Why?

2. Do you think that every walrus
   has a mass of 900 kg? Explain.

Build Your Understanding

Graph the Mass

1. Create a pictograph or a bar graph
   of the information in the table.
   Why does it help to graph the
   greatest mass first?

2. What animal was the most difficult
   to fit on your graph? Why?

Mass of Animals	
Animal	Mass
African elephant	6000 kg
Cheetah	58 kg
Chimpanzee	75 kg
Golden eagle	5 kg
Gorilla	140 kg
Komodo dragon	100 kg
Moose	364 kg
Octopus	25 kg
Polar bear	300 kg
Porpoise	47 kg
Raccoon	9 kg
Tiger shark	800 kg
Walrus	900 kg

Lesson 7: Graphing Mass

What Did You Learn?

1. What was the most difficult part of making your graph? Explain.

2. What are the advantages of using a pictograph or a bar graph?

3. Why does a pictograph need a scale?

4. What do you think is the most challenging part of making a pictograph? Explain.

Technology

You can complete the activity in this lesson electronically by using a spreadsheet or graphing computer program. Which way is better to make the graph: by hand or electronically? Why?

Practice

Here is information about the masses of some smaller animals.

1. a) Create a pictograph of this information.

Mass of Small Animals	
Animal	Mass
Rat	450 g
Gerbil	124 g
Pygmy shrew	5 g
Helena's hummingbird	2 g
Vampire bat	28 g
Eclectus parrot	450 g

b) Now create a bar graph of the information in the table.

c) Which graph was more difficult to make? Explain.

2. Make up questions that might be answered by looking at the data on your pictograph.

3. Give your questions to a classmate to answer.

Lesson 8

Analyzing Data

FACT BOOK

PLAN:
You will investigate, explain, and analyze data about birds.

FACTS:
The female chickadee scares off intruders by making a sudden snakelike hissing sound. The bird species that prey on chickadees are usually found in Papua New Guinea.

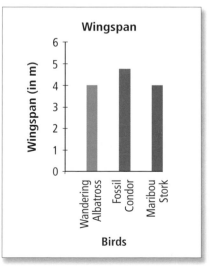

Chickadee

Get Started

Welcome to the world of birds. With a partner, study the graphs on this page. Be prepared to tell the rest of the class about a piece of information you find most interesting, or to share some questions you might have.

Bird	Mass
Elephant Bird * of Madagascar	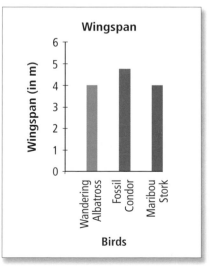
Emu	
Ostrich	

* extinct since at least the sixteenth century

= 50 kg

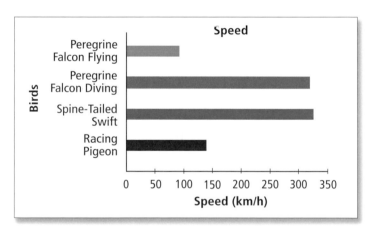

Calculate the Data

Work with a partner to answer the following questions.
Use pictures, numbers, and words to explain your thinking.

1. a) What is the mass of five emus?

   b) How does the mass of five emus compare with the mass of one ostrich?

2. a) How far could a racing pigeon travel in four hours?

   b) How far could a spine-tailed swift travel in four hours?

   c) If the pigeon and the swift started at the same spot, how much farther would the swift be than the pigeon at the end of four hours?

   d) A car is travelling at 80 km/h. A swift started flying at the same time and is travelling in the same direction. After four hours of travel, how far behind the swift will the car be?

   e) If a peregrine falcon were to dive for 15 min, how far could it dive?

3. What is the total mass of three ostriches, four emus, and one elephant bird?

4. a) What is the total wingspan of eight fossil condors?

   b) How does the wingspan of a marabou stork compare with the wingspan of a wandering albatross?

What Did You Learn?

1. Which graph on page 293 did you find the most challenging to read? Explain.

2. With your partner, make up three questions of your own for a pair of classmates to answer, based on the data in Get Started. Be sure to have answers to your questions.

1. How many albatrosses with their wings spread out would it take to stretch the length of your classroom? Explain how you got your answer.

2. How might you show on the pictograph the mass of a bird that weighs 25 kg?

Extension

3. Research the mass of three birds different from the ones in the pictograph on page 293. Add the birds to the pictograph. Use the given scale. (You may need to round the mass of the birds you choose.)

Show What You Know

Review: Lessons 5 to 8, Mass and Graphs

1. Measure the mass of different objects in your classroom. Will you use grams or kilograms? Explain.

2. Round the mass numbers to the nearest 10, 100, and 1000.

3. Design and complete a chart to organize your information.

4. Make a graph of the masses you found.

5. Record three questions about your graph for a classmate to answer.

Lesson 9

Number Equations

FACT BOOK

PLAN:

You will solve some equations using the fact book numbers as well as other numbers.

FACTS:

If we look at numbers, insects lead the world. There are more species of insects in the world than of any other group of living things.

Here is some insect information:
- Insects have six legs.
- There are about 5000 different species of dragonflies.
- There are about 14 000 species of ants.
- A cricket will lay 300 eggs each fall.
- A caterpillar uses over 700 m of silk thread to spin its cocoon.
- In one bee's eye, there are 6900 lenses. A human eye has only one lens.

Ladybugs

Get Started

Here are some equations for you to solve based on the information in the Fact Book:

1. 12 ÷ 6 = ■

2. 5000 − ■ = 1000

3. 14 000 = ■ + 900

4. 6900 x 2 = ■

5. ■ − 300 = 300

6. ■ x 5 = 3500

With a partner, describe a situation or write a sentence for each of the equations above. For example, "I can see 12 cricket legs. Each cricket has 6 legs, so there are 2 crickets."

Solve Equations

Solve the following equations:

1. $56 + 112 = \blacksquare$

2. $96 + 12 + \blacksquare = 138$

3. $98 - 29 = \blacksquare$

4. $784 - \blacksquare = 432$

5. $9 \times 7 = \blacksquare$

6. $\blacksquare \times 10 = 120$

7. $280 \div 4 = \blacksquare$

8. $48 \div \blacksquare = 6$

9. $3968 = \blacksquare + 900 + 60 + 3$

10. $9000 + \blacksquare + 3 = 9603$

Now make up five equations of your own. Include at least one addition, one subtraction, one multiplication, one division, and one of your choice. Have a classmate solve your equations.

Make and Solve Equations Game

You Will Need

- number cards from 1 to 10 (Aces can be used as ones if you are using a real deck of cards.)
- 2 players
- pencil and paper for each player to record equations and keep score

Object: The first person to reach 10 points wins the game.

How to Play

1. The first four cards from the top of the pile get flipped over. Each player makes and records an equation for the other player to solve, using all four numbers shown. (You are allowed to include one more number of your own choice.)

2. Players trade equations and solve them. Correct equations get one point. Incorrect equations do not get any points.

3. Record your scores.

4. Continue playing until the first person reaches 10 points and wins the game.

What Did You Learn?

1. Describe in your own words how to solve an equation such as $96 + \blacksquare = 452$.

2. The answer is 544. Use some of these numbers to create an equation: 136, 4, 356, 188, 68.

Practice

Solve the following equations:

1. $8764 = 8000 + 70 + \blacksquare + 4$

2. $106 + \blacksquare = 246$

3. $280 + \blacksquare + 55 = 479$

4. $\blacksquare \times 45 = 90$

5. $300 - 50 - 50 = \blacksquare$

6. $100 \div \blacksquare = 20$

7. $428 - \blacksquare = 169$

8. $7000 - \blacksquare = 6500$

9. Show the different ways any insects could be combined to form groups of 16. Use pictures along with an equation.

10. Knowing that a cricket lays 300 eggs each fall, how many years would it take this cricket to lay 900 eggs? 1800 eggs? Show your work in pictures, numbers, and words.

11. You have 7 magnifying glasses to use. Show the ways you could divide 20 students into small groups to observe insects using one magnifying glass per group. How many students would be in each group?

12. Create more equations or word problems for another classmate to solve.

Extension

13. Make up a game that involves number equations. Play your game with a partner.

Journal

Create a problem that could be solved by using addition. Now create a problem that could be solved by using subtraction. Do the same for multiplication and then for division. Be sure to also record the answers for each problem.

Technology

You can use a word processing computer program to create your own equations for your classmates to answer. Also create an answer key.

Lesson 10

Number Patterns

FACT BOOK

PLAN:
You will look at the patterns found in various groups of numbers.

FACTS:
Spiders are in a different grouping than insects. They are called arachnids. Spiders have eight legs. Most spiders reproduce by laying eggs. Different species lay different numbers of eggs. One species lays only two eggs at a time; others can lay up to several hundred at a time.

Black and yellow argiope spider

Get Started

Use the data in the chart to answer the questions that follow it:

	Imaginary Species A	Imaginary Species B
Number of Spiders	Number of Eggs	Number of Eggs
1	90	120
2	180	240
3	270	360

1. What is the pattern in the number of eggs for Species A?

2. What is the pattern in Species B?

3. How many eggs will there be if there are five spiders of each of these species in a garden? How many eggs will there be if there are ten of each of these species?

4. a) Now imagine a new species of spider. Create a pattern for the number of eggs that spiders of the new species would lay.

   b) Have a partner determine what the pattern is and how many eggs will be in the garden if there are five and then ten spiders in the garden.

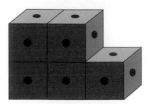

Build Your Understanding

Investigate Patterns

You Will Need
• linking cubes

1. a) Use linking cubes to create the pattern above.

   b) Continue to use linking cubes to extend this pattern twice more. What do you notice? Explain the rule.

   c) How many linking cubes would there be in the tenth pattern? Show your work.

You Will Need
• counters

2. a) Let each counter represent one spider and ten eggs. Explain the relationship between the number of spiders and the number of eggs laid. What is the pattern rule?

   b) How many spiders would it take to lay 210 eggs?

   c) How many eggs would 28 spiders lay?

3. a) Use linking cubes to create and extend the pattern shown in the chart:

Number of Spiders	Number of Eggs Laid
1	2
2	4
3	6
4	

   b) How many spiders that lay 100 eggs at a time would it take to lay 1000 eggs? Present your data in chart form.

4. Look at the following sets of numbers. Copy and complete the patterns. Write the pattern rule for each set of numbers.

12, 23, ■, ■, 56, 67, ■, ■

340, 440, ■, 640, 740, ■, 940, ■

1950, 1975, ■, ■, 2050, 2075, ■, ■

5. Look at these numbers:

269, 279, 289, . . .

What is the rule for this pattern?

What would the next three numbers in the pattern be?

6. Patterns can also be more complicated. What is the rule for the next set of numbers?

120, 260, 160, 300, 200, 340, . . .

What are the next three numbers in this pattern?

7. Work with a partner to create patterns. Start with the same number and create three different patterns. Share your patterns with another pair of classmates. Have them determine the rule for each pattern, and add three more numbers to each pattern.

8. Create three more patterns with your partner. This time begin with the number 3456. Share your patterns with another pair of classmates. Have them determine the rule for each of your patterns and add three more numbers to each pattern.

What Did You Learn?

1. List the numbers in a classmate's pattern that you solved. Explain in words and numbers how you determined what the pattern was.

2. What strategy or strategies do you use to find the pattern rule for a given set of numbers?

3. How can presenting data in chart form help someone find a pattern?

4. What operations are most likely used in number patterns that increase? What about number patterns that decrease? Explain.

Practice

Copy and complete the pattern:

1. ■, 16, 24, ■, 40, ■

2. 1600, 1700, 1800, ■, ■, 2100, ■

Copy and complete the following patterns and state the pattern rule:

3. 692, 694, 696, ■, ■, ■

4. 932, 922, 912, ■, ■, ■

5. 5762, 5862, 5962, ■, ■, ■

6. 9940, 9730, 9520, ■, ■, ■

7. Look at the following pattern:

1250, 1275, 1300, . . .

  a) Will you get to 1450 in this pattern? How do you know? You can use a calculator to help you.

  b) Will you get to 1640? How do you know? You can use a calculator to help you.

8. Look at the following pattern:

2300, 2600, 2900, . . .

  a) Will you get to 4000 in this pattern? How do you know? You can use a calculator to help you.

  b) Will you get to 5000 in this pattern? How do you know? You can use a calculator to help you.

  c) What multiples of 1000 will you get to in this pattern up to 10 000? Explain how you know.

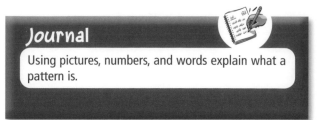

Journal

Using pictures, numbers, and words explain what a pattern is.

A Math Problem to Solve

9. Jenna starts baby-sitting to save money for a new jacket that costs $93.00. She charges $3.00 the first time she baby-sits. Every time after, Jenna charges twice as much money as the time before. How many times will Jenna need to baby-sit before she can buy the new jacket? Present your data in chart form.

Lesson 11

Flips, Slides, and Turns

FACT BOOK

PLAN:

You will investigate and analyze different types of movement that are part of geometry.

FACTS:

Animals have different ways of getting from one spot to another. Some animals, like cheetahs, move very fast. A cheetah can travel up to to 110 km/h. Other animals, like turtles, move much slower. The average turtle only travels anywhere from 4.5 km/h to 6.5 km/h.

Get Started

Some animal movements can be described in mathematical terms. Here is an alligator moving along in a river.

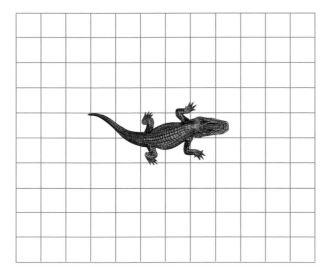

1. How would you describe the following change in motion?

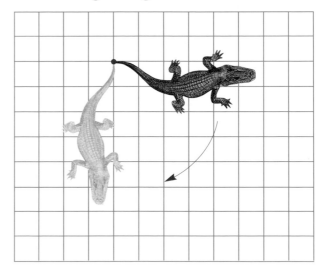

2. How would you describe the
motion now?

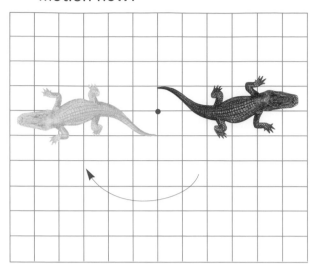

3. What about now?

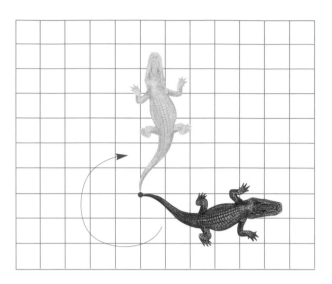

4. If the alligator kept swimming in the same direction, would
you describe its movement as a flip, slide, or turn?

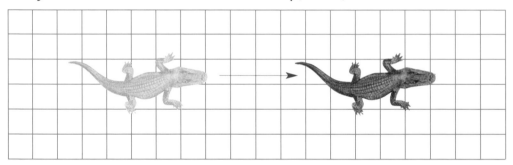

5. Here is a very interesting catfish that lives in the Nile River
in Egypt. This catfish has a habit of swimming on its back.
How would you describe this movement?

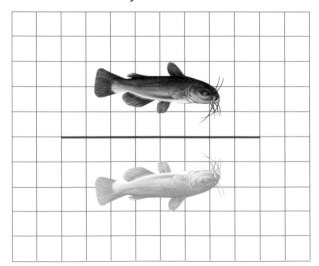

Vocabulary

reflection (flip): The mirror image of a figure
rotation (turn): To turn a figure around a centre
point in one direction
transformation: The movement of a figure by a
slide, flip, or turn
translation (slide): To slide a figure from one
position to another position of fixed distance

In mathematics, we talk about translations (slides), rotations (turns), and reflections (flips).

Translation

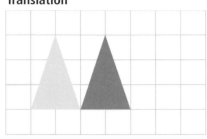

Rotation

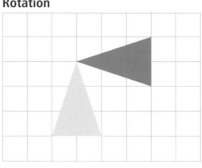

Reflection

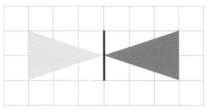

Build Your Understanding

Transform the Arrow

You Will Need
• graph paper

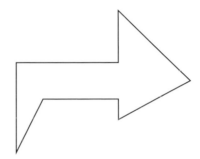

Trace this arrow onto another piece of paper and cut it out.

Now complete the following steps by using your arrow and a piece of graph paper. Place your arrow on a starting point, and make sure your arrow is positioned back on the same starting point for each question:

1. Draw a vertical mirror line. Flip the arrow. The image must be the same distance from the mirror line (or line of symmetry) as the original arrow.

2. Slide the arrow from left to right 10 squares.

3. Use the given point and turn the arrow $\frac{1}{4}$ turn clockwise.

4. Use the given point and turn the arrow $\frac{3}{4}$ turn counterclockwise.

Tip

A clockwise turn goes in the same direction as the rotating hands of a clock. A counterclockwise turn goes in a direction opposite to the rotating hands of a clock.

1. Using pictures and words, describe a translation (slide).

2. Using pictures and words, describe a rotation (turn).

3. Using pictures and words, describe a reflection (flip).

Practice

1. Describe the motion in each drawing.

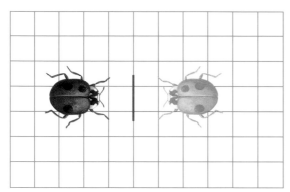

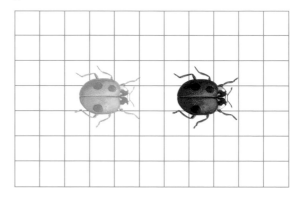

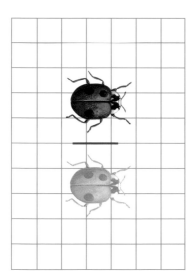

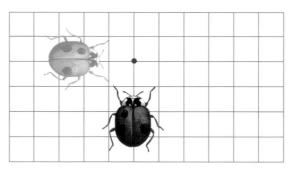

Make each of the following transformations:

2. translation (your choice)

3. $\frac{1}{4}$ rotation counterclockwise

4. a reflection (vertical or horizontal)

5. Describe your translation from question 3.

Tip

When you are rotating a figure, imagine there is a pin or nail at the centre of rotation and the shape turns around it. If there is no centre of rotation on the figure, imagine that the shape is attached to the centre with a stick (like the hands of a clock).

Chapter Review

1. Write the numeral for

a)

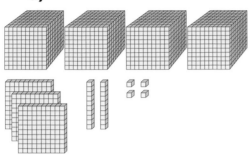

b)

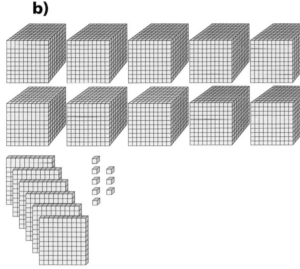

2. Write the numerals for
   a) 7 thousands, 3 hundreds, 6 tens
   b) 14 thousand 10
   c) sixty-three thousand seven hundred twelve
   d) eight thousand two

3. Write each number in words:
   a) 3469 **b)** 8700 **c)** 9604

4. State the value of the underlined digit:
   a) 834<u>3</u> **b)** 5<u>9</u>96 **c)** <u>1</u>243

5. Write the following in expanded form:
   a) 3294 **b)** 4406

6. Write the following in standard form:
   a) 9000 + 800 + 3 =
   b) 10 000 + 10 + 9 =

7. Write the number that is 10 more than each of these numbers:
   a) 9657 **b)** 8403 **c)** 17 594

8. Write the number that is 100 more than each of these numbers:
   a) 36 481 **b)** 7509 **c)** 8970

9. Order the following numbers from least to greatest. Explain how you know your order is correct.
   9604 9460 6499 4600 9600

10. a) Make the greatest possible number with the following digits: 4 6 3 0 7
   b) Make the least possible number with the above digits.
   c) What strategy did you use to answer a) and b)?

11. Round each number to the nearest thousand:

    a) 6472 **b)** 7700 **c)** 9501

12. Circle the number in each pair that is closer to 5000:

    a) 4963 or 5150

    b) 4001 or 5098

13. Continue the following patterns:

    a) 1650, 1660, 1670, ■, ■, ■

    b) 2600, 2700, 2800, ■, ■, ■

    c) 3496, 4496, 5496, ■, ■, ■

14. a) Name three things you would measure the mass of in grams.

    b) Name three things you would measure the mass of in kilograms.

15. Circle the most appropriate mass for each:

    a) A dime might have a mass of
        3 g   30 g   300 g

    b) A light bulb might have a mass
        of   5 g   50 g   500 g

16. Complete:

    a) five kilograms = ■ g

    b) 0.5 kg = ■ g

    c) 3500 g = ■ kg

17. Choose five different books. How many pages does each book have?

    a) Design and complete a chart to organize your information.

    b) Make a graph of the data.

    c) Record three questions about your graph for a classmate to answer.

18. Copy and complete each number sentence:

    a) 12 + ■ + 10 = 30

    b) ■ − 30 = 45

    c) 9 x ■ = 27

19. Copy and complete the pattern and state the rule:

    a) 2788, 2792, 2796, ■, ■, ■

    b) 3, 9, 8, 14, 13, ■, ■, ■

    c) 110, 120, 140, 170, 210, ■, ■, ■

20. With a two-dimensional shape, make each of the following transformations. Draw the shape you start with and the shape you end with.

    a) translation (slide)

    b) rotation
        ($\frac{1}{4}$ turn clockwise around a point)

    c) reflection (flip)

    d) Describe your translation and reflection.

Chapter 7

Chapter Wrap-Up

A group of scientists counted the number of living organisms in an area of a forest. They divided the site into five sections and counted the number of trees, mammals, birds (both migratory and breeding), reptiles and amphibians, and specimens of mosses. This is the data they gathered:

Number of Organisms	Section 1	Section 2	Section 3	Section 4	Section 5
Birds	331	124	143	296	83
Mammals	326	188	290	156	96
Mosses	3670	1960	950	3500	2860
Reptiles and Amphibians	344	250	112	404	466
Trees	1581	763	575	1960	393

Your task is to create a display of the forest that will be shared with your classmates.

Your display will include
- a graph of the data
- questions based on your graph that other classmates will answer
- answers to your questions on a separate piece of paper
- a flag for the forest
- a description of the flag

Organize and Describe the Data

1. Add up the totals of each type of organism and then round the total to the nearest thousand.

2. Create a graph to display the information. Include all of the necessary labels.

3. Develop three questions that could be answered by analyzing your graph.

4. Write the answers to your questions on the back of your display.

Design and Describe a Forest Flag

1. You will need to design a flag for your display. Use some or all of the following shapes to create a flag using slides, flips, and turns.

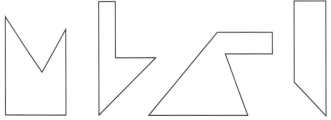

2. Describe your flag in your journal.

Share Your Work

1. Share your work with a partner. Use your partner's graph to answer his or her questions.

2. In your journal, describe the transformations (slides, flips, turns) that your partner has used on his or her flag. Be as specific as you can.

Chapter 8

Habitat Math

All living things are part of an ecosystem. An ecosystem is a natural area that includes living and non-living things that interact with one another.

In this chapter, we will examine some of the places organisms live. We'll look at natural ecosystems and "homes" for the organisms created by people. During our investigations we will use fractions and decimals, collect data, interpret data on line graphs, and study temperature. At the end of the chapter, you will design and conduct a survey to determine what type of wildlife recreation facility people like to visit most.

1. Why do you think conducting a survey is a useful way to find out information?
2. Why do you think organizing data into graphs is important?
3. What temperature do you think is most comfortable. Why?

Lesson 1
Proper, Improper, and Mixed Fractions

FACT BOOK

PLAN:
You will use fractions to divide and analyze gardens.

FACTS:
Gardens are planted by people to grow vegetables, flowers, and plants. Plants can serve many different purposes. Plants give us oxygen (which is the air that we breathe in) and take in carbon dioxide (which is the air that we breathe out).

Get Started

1. Look at figure A. Answer the following questions in a large group.

   a) What fraction is being represented?

   b) How can you show this using numbers?

   c) How did you know what numbers to put on the bottom?

   d) How did you know what number to put on the top?

   e) What are the names given to each part of a fraction?

   This fraction is called a proper fraction.

2. Now look at figure B. How can it be written using numbers? Can you show it another way?

A

B

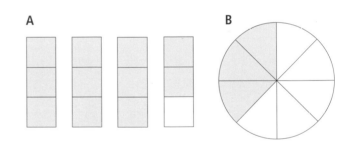

Vocabulary

denominator: The bottom number in a fraction, which tells the number of parts in a whole — $\frac{3}{8}$

improper fraction: A fraction with a numerator that is larger than the denominator — $\frac{11}{3}$

mixed number: A number that is part whole number and part proper fraction — $3\frac{2}{3}$

numerator: The top number in a fraction, which tells the number of parts referred to — $\frac{3}{8}$

proper fraction: A fraction with a numerator that is smaller than the denominator — $\frac{3}{8}$

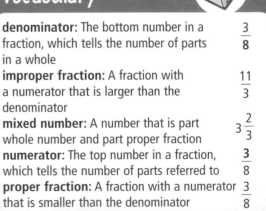

3. Look at these tomato gardens. The gardeners have divided their plots of land into pieces or fractions to separate the different plants they would like to grow.

For each garden, write the fractions that represent tomatoes, orange marigolds, and yellow marigolds. For example, in Garden A, there are 4 sections of tomatoes out of 6 total sections. So the fraction of the tomatoes would be $\frac{4}{6}$.

Garden A

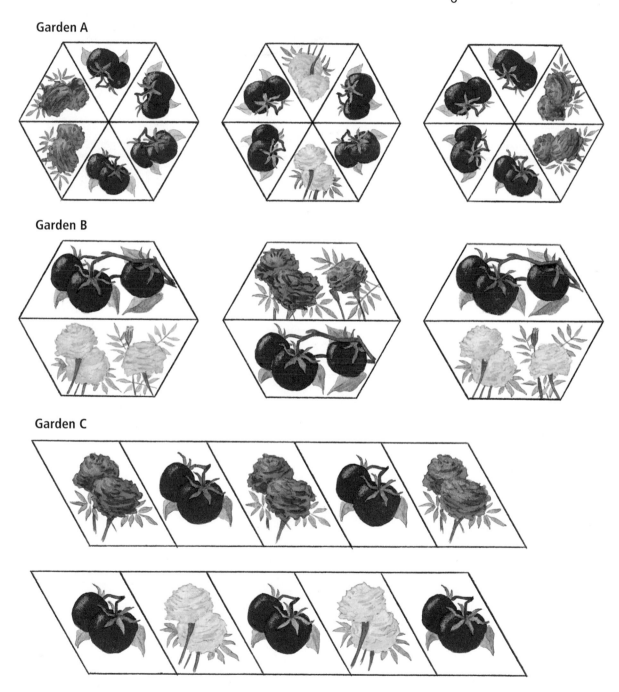

Garden B

Garden C

Calculate Fractions

You will need
• grid paper

To change an improper fraction to a mixed number, use grids to help you. For the improper fraction $\frac{17}{10}$, you would use two ten-square grids (because 10 is your denominator), and you would shade 17 squares in total.

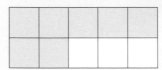

The grid that is completely shaded represents a whole number. Now count the squares that are shaded in on the second grid, and that is your numerator. Your denominator stays the same.

To change a mixed number to an improper fraction, use grids to help you. For example, for the mixed number, $1\frac{3}{5}$, you would use five-square grids to help you, because 5 is your denominator. How many fifths would you shade in total?

Your answer is the numerator of the improper fraction. The denominator stays the same. In your notebook, change the following improper fractions to mixed numbers. Use grids to help you.

1. $\frac{17}{3}$ **2.** $\frac{7}{2}$ **3.** $\frac{15}{4}$ **4.** $\frac{23}{5}$

Change the following mixed numbers into improper fractions. Use grids to help you.

5. $2\frac{2}{3}$ **6.** $3\frac{1}{2}$ **7.** $1\frac{1}{3}$ **8.** $3\frac{3}{4}$

9. a) Take a sheet of paper and fold it into halves, then quarters, and then eighths. Pretend that your sheet of paper is a large piece of land waiting to be planted. You decide to plant your field one eighth at a time. You will grow corn in over half your field and in the rest of your field you will grow soya beans and wheat.

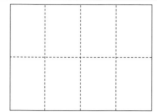

b) Decide which eighths are going to be planted with corn, which with soya beans, and which with wheat.

c) Show your decisions on your paper field. Use fractions to record how much of your field is planted in corn, how much in soya beans, and how much in wheat.

10. Compare your field with that of a classmate. Add up how many eighths in the two fields are planted with corn. Write your answer as a fraction.

11. Cut out all the eighths in the two fields that are planted with corn. Put them together. How many whole fields of corn can you make? What fraction of a field is still left?

12. Write the size of your corn field as a mixed number. Explain how you got your answer.

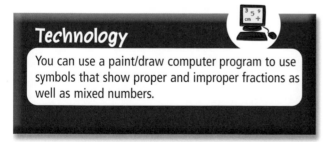

Technology

You can use a paint/draw computer program to use symbols that show proper and improper fractions as well as mixed numbers.

What Did You Learn?

1. In your journal, explain the terms *proper fraction, improper fraction,* and *mixed number* in your own words. Give some examples of each, and use diagrams for each example.

2. Show the relationship between improper fractions and mixed numbers using pictures, numbers, and words.

Practice

Use squares or rectangles to draw the following fractions.

1. $\frac{3}{4}$ **2.** $1\frac{1}{2}$ **3.** $\frac{14}{4}$ **4.** $5\frac{1}{6}$

Write the fraction shown by each diagram. If an improper fraction is shown, write it as a mixed number as well:

5.

6.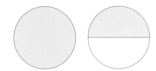

7.

8.

Write each fraction as a mixed number. Use grids to show a picture for each fraction you make.

9. $\frac{3}{2}$ **10.** $\frac{6}{4}$ **11.** $\frac{12}{6}$ **12.** $\frac{13}{5}$

Write each mixed number as an improper fraction. Use grids to show a picture for each fraction you make.

13. $3\frac{1}{2}$ **14.** $2\frac{4}{5}$ **15.** $6\frac{1}{3}$ **16.** $7\frac{1}{8}$

Compare the following fractions using < >, or =:

17. $4\frac{3}{5}$ ▪ $\frac{22}{5}$ **18.** $\frac{6}{4}$ ▪ $\frac{3}{4}$

19. $\frac{18}{8}$ ▪ $2\frac{2}{8}$ **20.** $\frac{9}{6}$ ▪ $1\frac{4}{6}$

21. $\frac{11}{10}$ ▪ $1\frac{1}{10}$ **22.** $2\frac{1}{2}$ ▪ $\frac{7}{2}$

23. This circle graph shows how an allowance is spent. Write the fractions for each section:

Lesson 2

Adding Fractions

FACT BOOK

PLAN:
You will use fractions to analyze and compare leaves and land affected by the gypsy moth. You will also learn how to add fractions.

FACTS:
The larvae of small white moths called gypsy moths like to eat the leaves of at least a hundred different types of trees throughout southern Canada and the northern United States. The larvae are particularly fond of oak, aspen, and elm leaves.

Gypsy moth larva or caterpillar

Get Started

1. Which fraction shows the number of leaves totally eaten and partially eaten? Put your answers in a chart.

Tip

When we add fractions with the same denominators, we total the numerators, but the denominators stay the same.

Fraction of Number of Leaves Totally Eaten	Fraction of Number of Leaves Partially Eaten	Fraction of Leaves Not Eaten At All

Build Your Understanding

Investigate and Calculate Fractions

1. The following are diagrams of three wood lots that have been infected with gypsy moths.

Wood Lot A

Wood Lot B

Wood Lot C

Infected area

a) Which wood lot seems to be most affected by the larvae? How would you use fractions to support your answer?

b) Add the fractions of infected area from each wood lot together. Explain how you calculated your answer.

c) Change your improper fraction to a mixed number.

2. Look at the diagram:

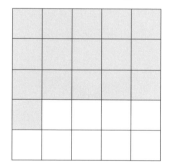

Technology

You can use a paint/draw computer program to draw a tree covered in many caterpillars. Colour some caterpillars blue, some red, some green, and some yellow. Figure out the fraction of each colour of caterpillar according to the total number of caterpillars in your picture.

In a certain area, there are 25 people who own property affected by gypsy moths. A total of 16 of these people want to have pesticides sprayed on the entire area to kill the larvae. The rest do not.

a) What fraction of the people want pesticides?

b) What fraction of the people do not?

What Did You Learn?

Explain in your own words how to add fractions that have the same denominator. Use pictures, numbers, and words.

Add the following fractions. Use grids to help you.
Question 1 (a) has been done for you.

1. $\frac{5}{9} + \frac{3}{9} =$

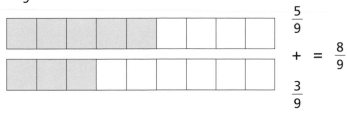

$\frac{5}{9}$

$+$ $=$ $\frac{8}{9}$

$\frac{3}{9}$

2. $\frac{6}{7} + \frac{1}{7} =$ **3.** $\frac{11}{20} + \frac{8}{20} =$

4. $\frac{3}{8} + \frac{4}{8} =$ **5.** $\frac{4}{10} + \frac{2}{10} + \frac{3}{10} =$

Change these improper fractions to mixed numbers.
Make a diagram to help you like the one shown in question 6:

6. $\frac{12}{9}$ $=$ $\frac{9}{9}$ $+$ $\frac{3}{9}$

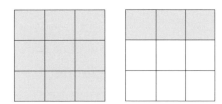

7. $\frac{8}{7} =$ **8.** $\frac{16}{5} =$

Change the following mixed numbers to improper fractions:

9. $1\frac{2}{7} =$ **10.** $2\frac{6}{8} =$ **11.** $5\frac{4}{5} =$

Journal

What do you find easiest about adding fractions,
and what do you find most challenging?

Lesson 3

Decimals to Tenths

FACT BOOK

PLAN:

You will convert fractions of butterfly gardens to decimals.

FACTS:

The butterfly conservatory in Niagara Falls, Ontario has over 2000 butterflies representing 50 different species. There is also a butterfly garden in Victoria, British Columbia.

The Butterfly Conservatory in Niagara Falls

Get Started

Fractions can also be written in another form known as decimals. The fraction $\frac{1}{10}$ can be written as 0.1 (You would read this number as "zero and one tenth," or "zero point one.") Use a calculator to investigate the decimal equivalent of fractions with a denominator of 10. To do this, divide the denominator by the numerator. Begin with $\frac{1}{10}$. Discuss the connections you find.

Butterflies are attracted to some plants, such as the butterfly bush, purple coneflower, and Joe-Pye weed. Here are two plans for garden plots designed to attract butterflies.

Garden Plan A

Garden Plan B

 Coneflower   Butterfly Bush   Joe-Pye Weed

1. In your notebook, make and complete a chart like the one below.

	Garden Plan A	Garden Plan B
Fraction of Garden in Coneflowers		
Fraction of Garden in Butterfly Bushes		
Fraction of Garden in Joe-Pye Weeds		

2. Write each fraction in the completed chart from question 1 as a decimal. For example: the fraction $\frac{6}{10}$ can be written as the decimal 0.6.

3. Decimals can also be written on a place-value chart. Place all your decimals on a place-value chart, like the one below.

Hundreds	Tens	Ones	Tenths

4. Draw a number line like the one below. Place all the decimals in your place-value chart on the number line.

0.0   1.0

Design and Analyze a Garden

1. Design your own butterfly garden by putting the plants mentioned on page 321 in ten sections. (Put one type of plant in each section.)

2. Which flower is in the greatest number of sections? Which flower is in the least number of sections?

3. Write a fraction to represent each type of flower, and then write each fraction as a decimal.

4. Draw a number line like the one you drew in Get Started. Place your decimals and fractions on the number line.

5. Compare your garden with that of a classmate.

What Did You Learn?

Explain in pictures, numbers, and words what 0.3 means.

Practice

For each illustration, write a fraction and a decimal to indicate the shaded part:

1.

2.

3.

4.

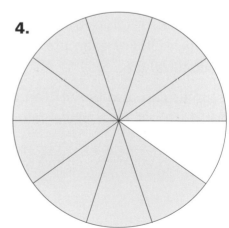

For each decimal, draw a shape and shade part of it:

5. 0.7 **6.** 0.2 **7.** 0.8 **8.** 0.5

Write each of these fractions as a decimal:

9. $\frac{1}{10}$ **10.** $\frac{3}{10}$ **11.** $\frac{7}{10}$ **12.** $\frac{9}{10}$ **13.** $\frac{10}{10}$

Draw a number line like the one below, and place each of these decimals on it:

14. 0.6 **15.** 0.3 **16.** 0.9 **17.** 0.4 **18.** 0.8

Order the following decimals from least to greatest. Explain how you decided on your order.

19. 0.9 **20.** 0.2 **21.** 0.7 **22.** 0.1 **23.** 0.5

24. What do you know about writing a decimal for a fraction that has the same numerator and denominator? Explain using pictures, numbers, and words.

25. Discuss with a classmate how fractions and decimals are similar.

Extension

26. Is your butterfly garden from Build Your Understanding symmetrical? If not, what could you change to make it symmetrical? Explain.

Journal

Explain how you changed the fractions in this lesson into decimals. Use pictures, numbers, and words.

Booklink

Ten For Dinner by Jo Ellen Bogart and Marsha Miceli (Scholastic: Markham, ON, 1989). Margo has a party and invites ten friends. In each situation, a different number of friends chooses different activities such as food and arrival times. This is a great book to help you with your tenths decimal skills.

Working With Fractions and Decimals

FACT BOOK

PLAN:

You will use fractions and decimals to investigate the contents of ten backpacks that are used on nature walks. You will then analyze the information you find.

FACTS:

Often, people like to observe butterflies while on a nature walk. There are many places to go on a nature walk in Canada. In addition to butterflies, people can see many things on a nature walk, such as birds, wildlife, and plants.

Get Started

Look at the following ten backpacks. They are for a group of ten people who want to go on a nature walk to observe butterflies. Some of the packs contain notebooks, some binoculars, some butterfly identification charts, and some first aid kits. All contain bottles of water.

1. in your notebook, make and complete a chart like the one below. The first row is done for you.

Item	Fraction of Backpacks	Decimal of Backpacks
notebook	$\frac{3}{10}$	0.3
binoculars		
identification chart		
first aid kit		
bottle of water		

2. What fraction of the backpacks has a notebook or a chart?

3. What decimal portion of the packs has a notebook or a chart?

4. What fraction has a first aid kit or binoculars?

5. What decimal portion of the packs has a first aid kit or binoculars?

6. How much greater is the fraction of packs with a notebook than the fraction with a first aid kit? Explain how you got your answer.

Build Your Understanding

Calculate the Contents

It turned out that the hike was very popular. Instead of having one group of ten hikers, the naturalists' society had three groups of ten hikers. The groups carried a variety of supplies and equipment. Look at the illustration of the backpacks to determine what each contained.

Group A

Group B

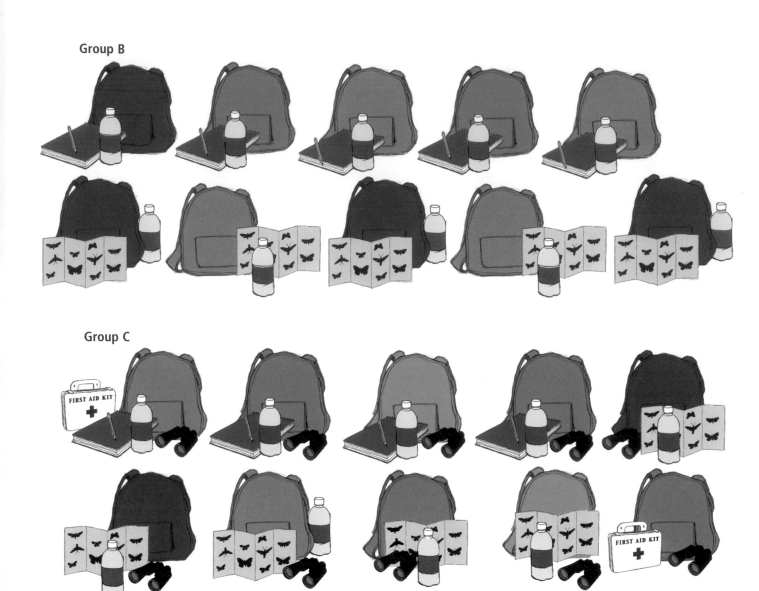

Group C

In a chart, show what portion of the backpacks contained each item.

	Group A		Group B		Group C	
Item	Fraction	Decimal	Fraction	Decimal	Fraction	Decimal
notebook						
binoculars						
identification chart						
first aid kit						
bottle of water						

Work with a partner to answer the following questions.
Write each answer as a fraction and as a decimal. Draw grids to
go with your answers.

1. What is the total number of tenths from each of the three
   groups of backpacks that contain notebooks?

2. What is the total number of tenths from each of the three
   groups of backpacks that contain binoculars?

3. What is the total number of tenths from each of the three
   groups of backpacks that contain first aid kits?

4. What is the total number of tenths from each of the three
   groups of backpacks that contain bottles of water?

5. How much greater is the decimal of packs containing
   binoculars than the decimal containing identification charts?

6. How much greater is the decimal of packs containing bottles
   of water than the decimal containing first aid kits?

What Did You Learn?

1. What is easier for you to understand, fractions or decimals?
   Why?

2. What are the advantages of using decimals and fractions
   to answer the questions?

3. How can drawing grids help you understand fractions and
   decimals?

Practice

Write each as a decimal:

1. 6 tenths   2. one and three tenths

3. 5 and 2 tenths   4. ten and 4 tenths

5. Place all your decimals from question 1 on a place-value
   chart.

6. Use grids to show the decimals from question 1 to 4.

Write each decimal in words:

7. 7.3   8. 0.9   9. 2.5   10. 3.8

Which is the larger number? Write your answer in your notebook.

11. 1.3 0.3 **12.** 0.4 1.2

13. 7.3 3.7 **14.** 2.0 2.1

15. Place each decimal below on your number line.

4.2   5.0   3.9   4.6   3.3

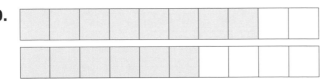

16. Write each decimal on your number line as a fraction.

Write a fraction to describe the shaded part of each diagram. Add the shaded parts of each diagram. Give your answers in both fraction and decimal form.

17.

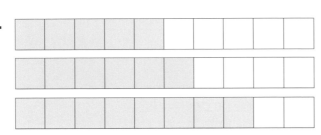

18.

Which decimal describes how much more of the diagram is shaded green than yellow?

19.

20.

A Math Problem to Solve

21. Adjee ate $\frac{6}{10}$ of a chocolate bar. His brother ate 0.8 of a different chocolate bar the same size.

a) Who ate more of their chocolate bar? Use pictures, numbers, and words to show your work.

b) Add the total amount of chocolate eaten by both brothers.

Give your answer in fraction and decimal form. Explain how you got your answer.

Decimals to Hundredths

FACT BOOK

PLAN:
You will convert fractions into decimals and investigate the relationship between fractions and decimals, first using spots on a ladybug, and then using squares.

FACTS:
There are about 500 different species of ladybugs in North America. They are yellow, red, or orange in colour, and most have dots. The number of dots on a lady bug can range from 2 to 13.

Ladybug

Get Started

You are going to design some ladybugs to become part of a set.

1. Design 10 ladybugs. Some should have 2 dots, some should have 7 dots, some should have 9 dots, and some should have 13 dots.

2. How many of your ladybugs have 2 dots? 7 dots? 9 dots? 13 dots?

3. What fraction of the ladybugs have 2 dots? 7 dots? 9 dots? 13 dots? You can use a grid to help you.

4. Convert each of the fractions for the ladybugs into a decimal. Put the decimals in order from least to greatest.

Tip

Remember that $\frac{1}{10} = 0.1$.
Fractions with a denominator of 100 can also be written as a decimal: $\frac{1}{100} = 0.01$. We read this decimal as "zero and one hundredth" or "zero point zero one." Hundredths is the column on the place-value chart to the right of the tenths column.

tens	ones	tenths	hundredths
	0	0	1

5. Use a calculator to investigate the decimal equivalent of fractions with a denominator of 100. First, create fractions with denominators of 100. Then, for each fraction, divide the denominator by the numerator. Discuss the connections you find.

Build Your Understanding

Calculate the Squares

1. Write two fractions to describe each shaded area below.
   Write two decimals to describe each shaded area.
   Remember $\frac{1}{10}$ equals $\frac{10}{100}$.

   a) 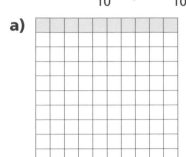   b) 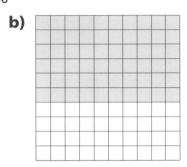   c)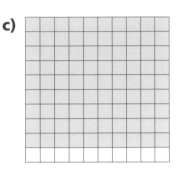

2. Write the following fractions:

   a) 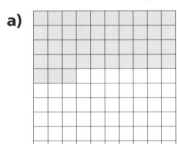   b) 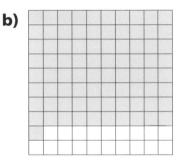   c)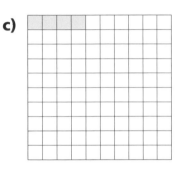

3. Look at the diagrams to answer the following questions:

      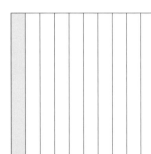   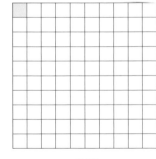

   1.0   0.1   0.01

   a) How many 0.01 sections equal 0.1?

   b) How many 0.1 sections equal 1 whole?

   c) How many 0.01 sections equal 1 whole?

4. Put all the decimals from questions 1 and 3 on a place-value chart.

What Did You Learn?

1. Explain the relationship between 0.01, 0.1, and 1.0 (1 whole) in pictures, numbers, and words.

2. Explain why 0.6 and 0.60 are equivalent. Use pictures, numbers, and words.

Practice

Write a fraction and a decimal that describes each shaded part:

1. 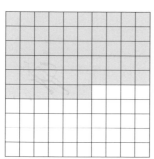   **2.**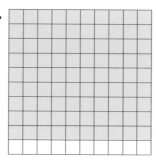

3. 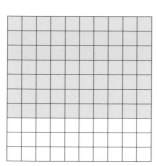   **4.**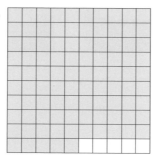

5. 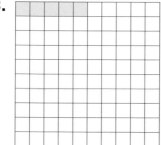   **6.**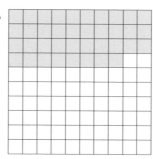

Write each of the following as a decimal:

7. forty-nine hundredths

8. 84 hundredths

9. five hundredths

10. 9 hundredths

Draw 10 x 10 squares on grid paper. Shade in squares to match the decimals below:

11. 0.52   **12.** 0.60   **13.** 0.93   **14.** 0.09   **15.** 0.15   **16.** 0.2

Which is the greater number? Write your answer in your notebook and explain how you know you are right.

17. 0.75 0.80   **18.** 0.07 0.70   **19.** 0.7 0.39

20. Arrange the following numbers in order from least to largest:

0.26, 0.07, 0.83, 0.46, 0.03

Write each of the following decimals in words:

21. 00.36   **22.** 0.12   **23.** 0.80   **24.** 0.99

25. Which is greater: 0.75 or $\frac{7}{10}$? Explain using pictures, numbers, and words.

Extension

26. Ladybugs love to eat aphids. One type of ladybug—the convergent ladybug—can lay 2500 eggs at a time. Each egg can hatch into a very hungry larva. Each larva can eat 25 aphids each day.

Use a calculator to find out how many aphids the 2500 larvae could eat in one day. Show your work using pictures, numbers, and words.

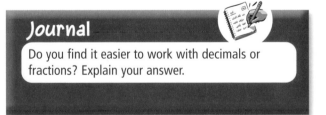

Journal

Do you find it easier to work with decimals or fractions? Explain your answer.

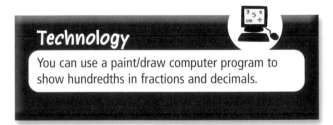

Technology

You can use a paint/draw computer program to show hundredths in fractions and decimals.

Mixed Numbers Using Decimals

Lewis Lake, Yukon Territory

FACT BOOK

PLAN:
You will figure out how big or small a number is by analyzing and using fractions and decimals.

FACTS:
Canada is a large country. Its total land area, is 9 093 507 km². Most of that area is open space. Roughly 90% of the area is not inhabited by people.

Get Started

You can write mixed numbers using decimals. An example of a mixed number as a decimal is 1.29. This mixed number can be read as "1 and 29 hundredths" or "one point two-nine."

1. Look at the following diagrams:

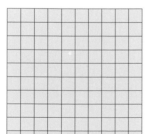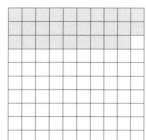

What part of the two grids is shaded in? What part is not shaded in? Use both fractions and decimals to show your answers.

2. What part of the grids is shaded in? What part is not? Use fractions, decimals, and words to show your answer.

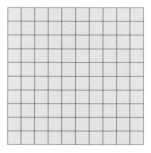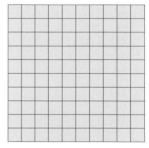

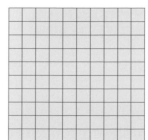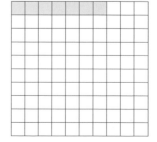

3. a) Read the following numbers out loud:

2.67, 4.67, 17.09, 67.23, 0.89, 1.01

  b) Write down five numbers of your own that include hundredths. Have a classmate read them.

4. a) Using a grid like those shown in questions 1 and 2, show which number is greater, 2.87 or 2.78.

  b) Now use a grid to show which of the following is greater: 1.1 or 1.01.

Build Your Understanding

Order and Compare Decimals

1. Use a grid to show two and four hundredths.

2. Use grids to show which decimal is larger: 2.56 or 1.65.

3. Compare 2.03 and 3.02 using pictures. Which is greater?

4. Compare 1.03 and 2.02 using pictures.

5. Arrange the numbers in each set in order from least to greatest. Explain how you decided on your arrangements.

  a) 0.6, 0.58, 0.61

  b) 0.45, 1.34, 0.56

  c) 1.6, 0.58, 0.66

6. For each pair of numbers, write a number that comes between them:

  a) 1.5, 1.8

  b) 1.05, 1.08

  c) 2.45, 2.78

  d) 3.77, 3.80

  e) 15, 15.04

What Did You Learn?

1. Was it easier to figure out which decimal was greater by using grids? Explain.

2. What strategy do you use to order decimals from least to greatest? Use examples to support your answer.

Chapter 8: Habitat Math

Practice

Write each of the following numerals, using decimal notation:

1. 26 hundredths

2. 2 hundredths

3. 6 and 12 hundredths

4. 93 and 78 hundredths

5. twelve

Write each as a fraction:

6. 0.98

7. 0.08

8. 0.5

9. 0.50

Write each decimal in words:

10. 7.30

11. 2.58

12. 44.01

In each pair, which decimal is greater?

13. 0.78 or 0.87

14. 2.20 or 2.02

15. 3.51 or 2.52

16. 4.5 or 4.05

Write a number that comes between the numbers in each pair:

17. 4.09 and 4.12

18. 5.66 and 5.78

19. 6.7 and 6.75

20. 8.08 and 8.80

21. The organizer of a hike bought 1.5 kg of apples for the participants. In your notebook, shade squares on a grid like the one below to show what 1.5 kg might look like. Explain your answer.

Extension

22. As stated in the fact book at the beginning of this lesson, 90% of Canada's space is not inhabited by people (90% is the same as $\frac{90}{100}$). Draw a picture of Canada as a square or rectangle, and show what part would be lived in by people and what part wouldn't be. Give your answers in both fraction and decimal form.

Now that you have investigated fractions and decimals, use a calculator to change the following fractions into decimals. To do this, divide the denominator by the numerator. The first one is done for you:

23. $\frac{1}{4} = 0.25$ **24.** $\frac{3}{4} = \blacksquare$ **25.** $\frac{1}{5} = \blacksquare$

26. $\frac{3}{5} = \blacksquare$ **27.** $\frac{1}{10} = \blacksquare$ **28.** $\frac{5}{10} = \blacksquare$

29. Arrange the decimals you have written in order from least to greatest.

30. Use pictures to show how $\frac{1}{4} = 0.25$.

Show What You Know

Review: Lessons 1 to 6, Fractions and Decimals

1. In your journal, explain the following using pictures, numbers, and words, and give an example of each:
   • mixed number
   • proper fraction
   • improper fraction

2. Your family is making a quilt. The quilt will have 100 squares.

   a) If your aunt sews 5 squares, your cousin Abdul sews 40 squares, your sister Lisa sews 20 squares, and your grandmother sews 15 squares, what is the fraction of squares that each person sewed?

   b) Convert each fraction to a decimal and arrange the decimals in order from least to greatest.

   c) What is the fraction and decimal of the total number of squares sewed? How many squares are left for you to sew? Show your work.

3. Where might you use fractions and decimals outside of school? Explain.

Lesson 7

Collecting and Analyzing Data

FACT BOOK

PLAN:
You will investigate, compare, and analyze different animals in the grasslands of east Africa.

FACTS:
The Serengeti is a large national park in east Africa that was established in 1929 to protect wildlife. The park is an ecosystem that has more animals than any other place on earth. Roughly 1 000 000 wildebeests, 300 000 zebras, and 300 000 gazelles migrate every year. It is the largest migration of herbivores in the world.

Get Started

The grasslands of east Africa provide a home for a large number of animals. These grasslands undergo a dry season and a wet season. Wildebeests, zebras, and gazelles migrate to follow the rains and find water.

A gazelle is a small animal that looks like a deer. Gazelles have tan skin with black stripes on their sides and have white stomachs and rumps. A wildebeest is a large animal that has a head like an ox, a mane like a horse, and horns like a buffalo.

1. Look at the photograph above. What comparisons can be made between zebras and wildebeests? What are the differences between these animals?

2. Working with a partner, count as many zebras, gazelles, and wildebeests as you can find in the photograph. Record your data on a tally sheet like the example tally sheet below:

Wildebeests   卌 卌 III
Zebras   卌 I
Gazelles   III

Tip

A tally is a mark made to keep count. When using a tally chart, we count in groups of five. To show a group of five, we draw a line through four tallies: ⦀⦀

Technology

You can use a computer spreadsheet program to create an electronic graph to display the animals you counted in Get Started. You can use the text tool to analyze the data.

Build Your Understanding

Analyze the Data

1. Make a chart of the data you have collected.

2. Make a graph showing the total number of animals of each kind in the picture.

3. How many animals are there in total?

4. Which animal has the greatest number?

5. Write the fraction of zebras, wildebeests, and gazelles from the data in your chart. Use a calculator to write each fraction as a decimal. If necessary, round your decimals to the nearest hundredth.

6. What is the fraction of zebras and gazelles? What is the fraction of wildebeests and zebras? Use a calculator to write your answers as decimals. If necessary, round your decimals to the nearest hundredth.

What Did You Learn?

1. What was the most difficult part of counting the animals?

2. a) What are the advantages of using photographs for the collection of data?

   b) What might be the disadvantages of using photographs?

There are many interesting animals that roam the plains of Africa and other parts of the world. Conduct a survey of your classmates to find out which animal they think is the most interesting.

1. Write a question that includes five animal choices and predict what the results might be. Ask ten of your classmates the question.

2. Make a tally of their answers.

3. Graph the data.

4. Use fractions to show the results for each animal. Write each fraction as a decimal.

5. Share your findings with the class. How did your results compare with your predictions?

A Math Problem to Solve

6. Kayla surveyed one hundred students about the kinds of pets they have. Unfortunately, she lost the tally chart she made of her data. However, she was able to find most of her results in fraction form. They are as follows:

Cat: $\frac{2}{10}$

Dog: $\frac{32}{100}$

Bird: $\frac{16}{100}$

Fish: $\frac{1}{10}$

She couldn't find the data she collected on her last choice, which was titled "No pet."

a) Make a new tally chart for Kayla that includes all five of her pet choices. Explain how you made your tally chart.

b) How did you figure out the number of students who did not have pets? Write the number as a fraction.

c) Write each fraction as a decimal.

d) Graph the data

e) Make up three questions about your graph. Write answers.

Lesson 8

Measuring Temperature

FACT BOOK

PLAN:
You will use thermometers to measure and record temperature.

FACTS:
Temperature affects all living things. It greatly affects what can live in a particular place or habitat. The highest temperature recorded in Canada was 45°C in Midale and Yellow Grass, Saskatchewan, on July 5, 1937. The lowest temperature recorded in Canada was –63°C, in Snag, Yukon Territory, and Yellowknife, Northwest Territories, on February 3, 1947.

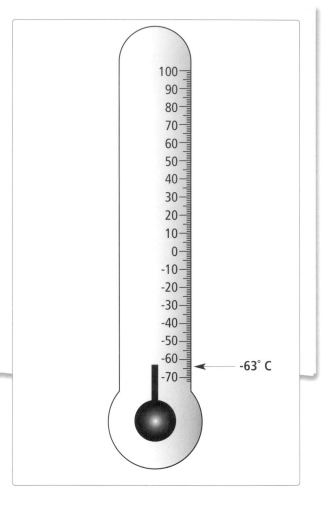

-63° C

Get Started

You Will Need
• thermometer
• reproducible page of thermometers

1. What temperature do you think it is in your classroom? Does it feel hot or cold or just right?

2. We use a thermometer to measure temperature. What units do we use to measure temperature?

3. Predict the temperature in a number of places around the school. Then, use a thermometer to measure the temperature in each place that you picked. Make a class chart of your predictions and the actual temperatures. Discuss the results.

Investigate Temperature

1. Read the following temperatures out loud:

a)

b)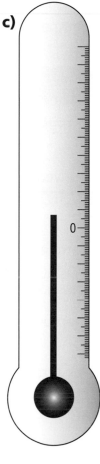

c)

d)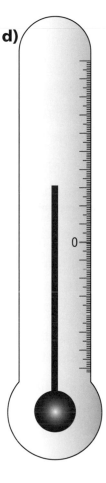

2. Use the reproducible page of thermometers to label the following temperatures on one thermometer:

  a) body temperature (37°C)

  b) room temperature (20°C to 21°C)

  c) the temperature at which water freezes (0°C)

  d) the temperature at which water boils (100°C)

  e) the temperature of a very hot summer day

  f) the temperature of an average winter day

3. Using the remaining four thermometers on your reproducible page, mark the following temperatures on the thermometers. Mark each temperature on a different thermometer.

  a) 20°C   **b)** 25°C   **c)** 9°C   **d)** 2°C

What Did You Learn?

1. What type of clothing would you wear if the temperature were the following?

   a) 30°C   **b)** 2°C   **c)** 22°C   **d)** -15°C

2. Explain how to measure temperature using a thermometer.

Practice

1. In what month is the temperature most likely to reach the freezing mark where you live?

2. Research the months of the year when you can grow plants and food where you live. Why can you only grow plants and food in these months?

3. Research and record the temperature highs and lows for your city for a week. Use a reproducible page of thermometers (given to you by your teacher) to record your findings.

4. Why is there a daily high temperature and a daily low temperature? Explain.

5. Make a list of five different temperatures. See if a partner can label a thermometer with your temperatures. Check to make sure they are correct.

6. What strategy can you use to read a thermometer accurately? Share your strategy with a classmate.

Lesson 9

Graphing Temperature

FACT BOOK

PLAN:

You will analyze line graphs to explain temperature in various cities around the world.

FACTS:

Average monthly temperatures for cities and towns vary throughout Canada. In Victoria, British Columbia, the average temperature for August is 17°C. In Toronto, Ontario it is 21°C. In Charlottetown, Prince Edward Island the average temperature for August is 19°C, and in Iqaluit, Nunavut it is 6°C.

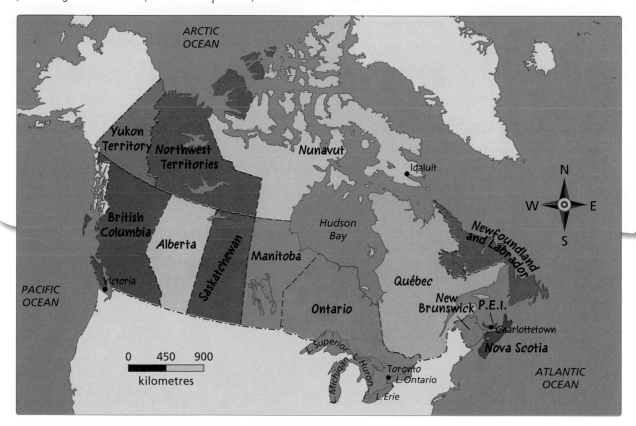

Get Started

The table on page 344 shows the monthly high temperatures for the city of Victoria, British Columbia.

Month	Temperature
January	6°C
February	8°C
March	10°C
April	13°C
May	16°C
June	18°C
July	20°C
August	20°C
September	18°C
October	14°C
November	9°C
December	7°C

This data has been plotted and then turned into a line graph below. The dots for each month's high temperatures have been joined with lines, because the temperature changes gradually from month to month.

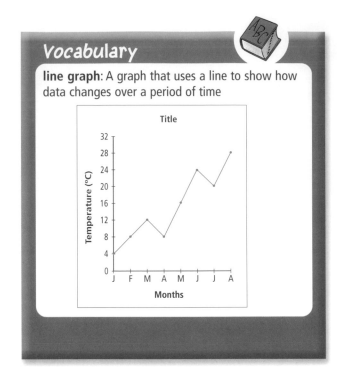
1. Review the graphs. What does the shape of the graph tell you about the temperatures?

2. What is the lowest monthly temperature?

3. What is the highest monthly temperature?

4. What two months have the coolest temperatures?

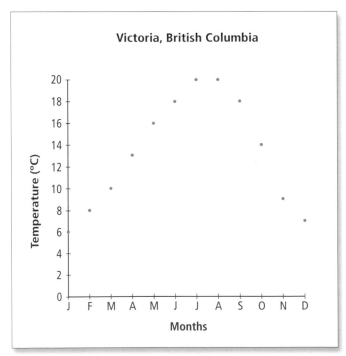

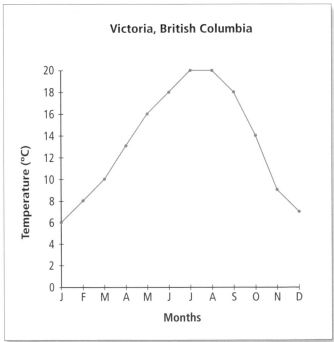

Analyze and Compare

You Will Need
• globe

The following are temperature graphs for the cities of Sydney, Australia, and Nairobi, Kenya:

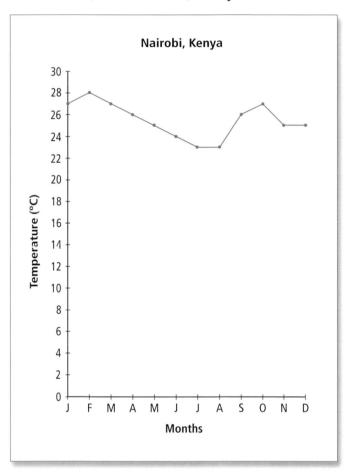

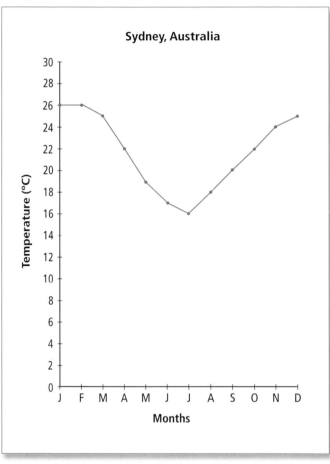

1. Locate Sydney, Nairobi, and Victoria on a globe. Describe where they are in relation to the equator.

2. a) Of the three cities—Victoria, Sydney, and Nairobi—which one seems to have the most constant temperature throughout the year?

   b) How does this city's temperature compare with the highest monthly temperature in the other two cities?

3. a) What is the hottest month in Sydney?

   b) What is the hottest month in Victoria?

   c) Why are these months not the same?

4. a) What is the difference between the temperatures in the hottest and coldest months in Victoria?

b) What is the difference between the temperatures in the hottest and coldest months in Sydney?

c) What is the difference between the temperatures in the hottest and coldest months in Nairobi?

d) Which of these three cities has the greatest range of monthly temperatures? Which has the least? Explain how you got your answers.

5. Look at the temperature graph for Ottawa. What happens to the temperature in January, February, March, November, and December? What does this tell us?

6. Make up three questions that might be answered by looking at the temperature graph for Ottawa. Write the answers to your questions.

7. Look at the graph of the monthly temperatures in another city. Unfortunately, there was no data for February to April. Look at the graph and the direction of the line. Predict what you think the temperatures might have been for February, March, and April. Explain your predictions.

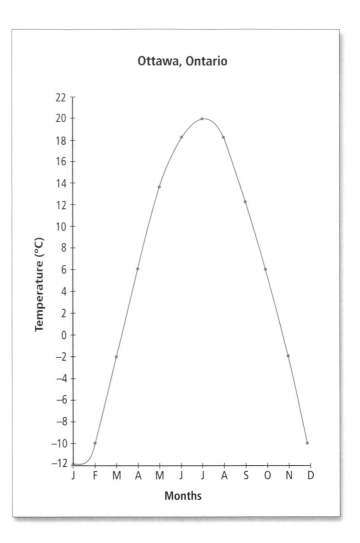

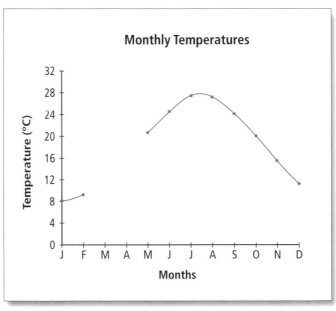

What Did You Learn?

1. Looking at temperature alone, which city looks more appealing to you: Victoria, Sydney, Nairobi, or Ottawa? Why?

2. How is a line graph different from a bar graph?

Practice

1. Why is it helpful to record data in a line graph?

2. When might you use a line graph, other than for temperatures?

3. Look in a local newspaper to find examples of line graphs.

4. Imagine you are helping your classmate plan her vacation. Your classmate tells you that she wants to go somewhere warm, but she can only go in March. What would be the best travel spot for your classmate to visit? Explain your choice.

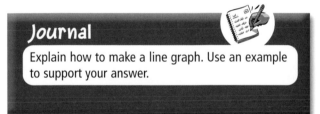

Journal

Explain how to make a line graph. Use an example to support your answer.

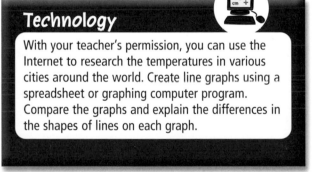

Technology

With your teacher's permission, you can use the Internet to research the temperatures in various cities around the world. Create line graphs using a spreadsheet or graphing computer program. Compare the graphs and explain the differences in the shapes of lines on each graph.

Chapter Review

Chapter 8

1. What part of each diagram is shaded?
   Write your answer as a fraction.

   a)

   b) 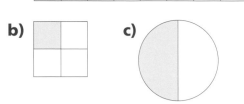   c)

2. Draw your own shapes and shade in the part indicated by the
   following fraction or mixed number:

   a) $\frac{5}{8}$ b) $3\frac{5}{6}$

3. Change these improper fractions to mixed numbers.
   Use grids to help you.

   a) $\frac{17}{4}$ b) $\frac{12}{5}$ c) $\frac{19}{3}$

4. Change the following mixed numbers to improper fractions.
   Use grids to help you.

   a) $1\frac{3}{4}$ b) $2\frac{1}{2}$ c) $3\frac{5}{6}$

5. Add the following:

   a) $\frac{1}{4} + \frac{1}{4} = \blacksquare$ b) $\frac{2}{8} + \frac{4}{8} = \blacksquare$ c) $\frac{2}{6} + \frac{3}{6} = \blacksquare$

6. What portion of each diagram is shaded? Write your answer as
   a decimal.

   a)

   b)

7. Write these fractions as decimals:

   a) $1\frac{5}{10}$ b) $6\frac{7}{100}$ c) $3\frac{6}{10}$ d) $9\frac{34}{100}$

8. Write these decimals as fractions:

    a) 5.6   **b)** 4.1   **c)** 0.73   **d)** 2.98

9. Order these numbers from least to greatest.
Explain how you know your orders are correct.

    a) 10.3, 10.9, 8.4, 7.6, 4.2, 6.5

    b) 7.02, 7.9, 3.42, 3.07, 2.99, 2.19

10. Write these fractions in words:

    a) $\frac{72}{100}$ **b)** $5\frac{8}{10}$

11. Write these decimals in words:

    a) 3.66   **b)** 1.1   **c)** 4.90

12. Write each question as a decimal addition question with its answer. Copy the last diagram of each question into your notebook and shade it to show the answer.

a)

c)

b)

13. Write each question as a fraction addition question with its answer. Copy the last diagram of each question into your notebook and shade it to show the answer.

a)

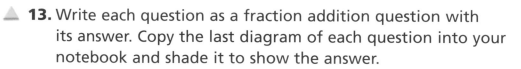

b)

c)

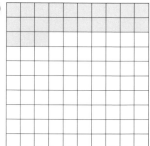

14. Express the shaded part both as a fraction and as a decimal:

a)

b)

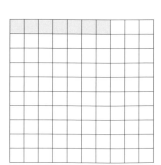

15. Show the following decimals on grids by shading the appropriate number of squares:

a) 1.03   **b)** 2.75

16. Look at the following line graph. It shows how many times Henna's class went for a nature walk each month.

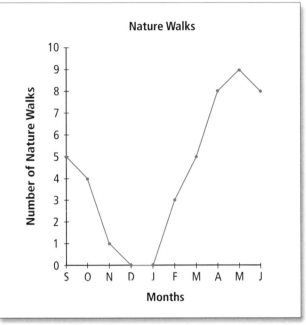

Nature Walks

a) In which month did the class go on the most nature walks? Why?

b) In which month did the class go on the least nature walks? Why?

c) How many nature walks did the class go on in total for the whole year? Show your work.

17. Write the following numerals as fractions and as decimals:

a) thirty-five hundredths

b) four and eleven hundredths

c) ten and two hundredths

18. Write a number that comes between the numbers in each pair:

a) 0.6 ▦ 0.9   **b)** 0.63 ▦ 0.67   **c)** 1.42 ▦ 1.5

19. How would you write the number 13 in tally form?

20. In your notebook, write the temperatures shown on the thermometers on the right:

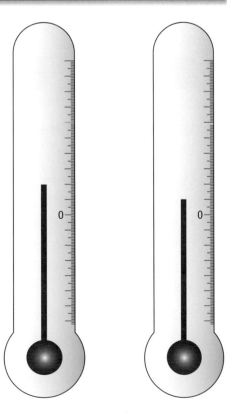

Chapter Wrap-Up ●▲■⬠

What types of places will people visit in to order to see plants and animals? Wildlife facilities protect wildlife and their living spaces.

Wildlife facilities, like the Delta Beach Waterfall Research Centre in Manitoba, are found throughout Canada.

Looking at Wildlife

Imagine that in one school year your class went on ten school trips to the wildlife centre shown above. The following diagram shows the different types of animals that you saw on one visit:

■ Canada geese
□ Caribou
■ Moose
■ Tundra swan

1. Use decimals and fractions to explain how often each type of animal was seen.

2. Work with a partner and make another similar diagram to show $\frac{2}{10}$ of the visits seeing owls, 0.4 of the visits seeing hummingbirds, and some of the rest of the visits seeing chipmunks and raccoons. Use decimals and fractions to explain how you know that your diagram matches what was seen.

3. Use the diagram shown above to figure out the total number of animals that your class would see for all ten visits. Show your answer on a hundreds grid like the one on the next page, and explain your answer in fractions and decimals.

Graph the Information

1. Create a graph of the information given to you in the diagram on page 352.

2. Now create a graph of the information from the diagram that you and your partner created.

3. Write three questions about your graphs for another classmate to answer.

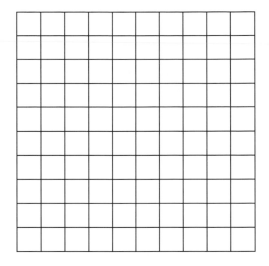

Temperature

Your class noticed that the temperature was different each time you visited the wildlife park. The following chart shows the temperatures that were recorded during each of your visits.

Visit 1	Visit 2	Visit 3	Visit 4	Visit 5	Visit 6	Visit 7	Visit 8	Visit 9	Visit 10
18°C	15°C	8°C	3°C	2°C	6°C	12°C	16°C	21°C	25°C

1. Display the data using a line graph. Remember to label and title your graph.

2. During which visit was the temperature the hottest? What month do you think this visit took place in? Explain.

3. Do you think there were any visits during winter? Explain your answer.

4. One of your classmates says that it was more often cooler than 10°C at the park than it was warmer than 10°C. Do you agree or disagree with your classmate? Explain your answer using decimals and fractions.

5. Create three questions about your line graph and write answers.

Measuring People's Impact

You have learned that the living world has many parts, and that each part is connected with other parts. Any event that affects one part affects many.

In this chapter, you will look at a few of the ways that people affect the world. You will

- see how people sometimes harm and sometimes help the environment
- explore more ways of organizing and analyzing data

- Use maps to locate things
- explore probability

In your journal, explain probability and give an example of something that is most likely to happen, and something that is least likely to happen. Explain your reasoning.

At the end of the chapter, you will create a presentation about extinct or endangered species using the math you have learned.

Lesson 1

Exploring Maps

FACT BOOK

PLAN:

You will explain direction and distance when you analyze maps of ponds and islands.

FACTS:

Many organisms make their homes around ponds. Some of these creatures are frogs, fish, snails, mosquitoes, dragonflies, worms, and ducks. The mallard duck is found mainly in Saskatchewan, Alberta, and Manitoba.

Mallard duck

Get Started

Look at this map of a pond environment. Many organisms make their homes here:

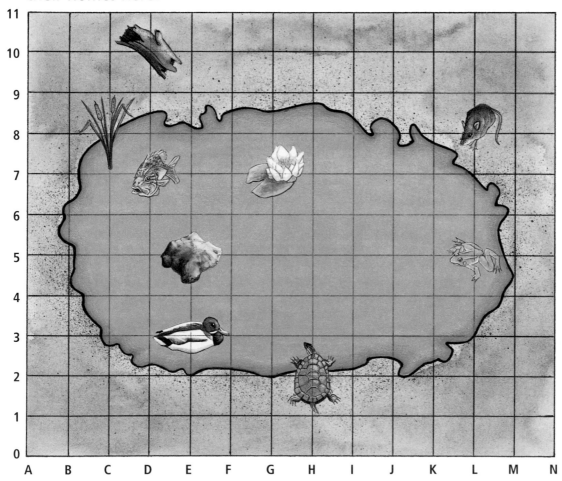

1. Describe the various things you see.

2. How would you label the four directions (north, south, east, west) on the map? Explain.

3. Name something that is directly north of the duck.

4. Name something that is east of the fish.

5. What is at each of the following locations: C8, H2, D10?

6. The frog is at L5. If the frog wishes to go to the rock, how many spaces west will it move?

Build Your Understanding

Master the Map

You Will Need
• grid paper

1. Draw your own map of a pond on grid paper. Label vertical lines to N and horizontal lines to 11. Include a legend.

2. Place a rock at L2. Draw a frog far from a water lily.

3. Plan a short path for the frog to get to the water lily. Your frog can hop or swim only on the grid lines. Draw a coloured line on your grid to show the frog's path.

4. **a)** Draw a mouse far from an old log.
   b) The mouse wants to go to its summer home in the old log. Plan a route so that the mouse won't have to swim.
   c) Draw a coloured line on your grid to show the mouse's path. Use a different colour than you used for the frog's route.

5. Add the routes of the mouse and the frog to your map legend.

What Did You Learn?

In your journal, use words to describe the frog's route and then the mouse's route. Include directions and distances.

Copy this map of an island onto grid paper.

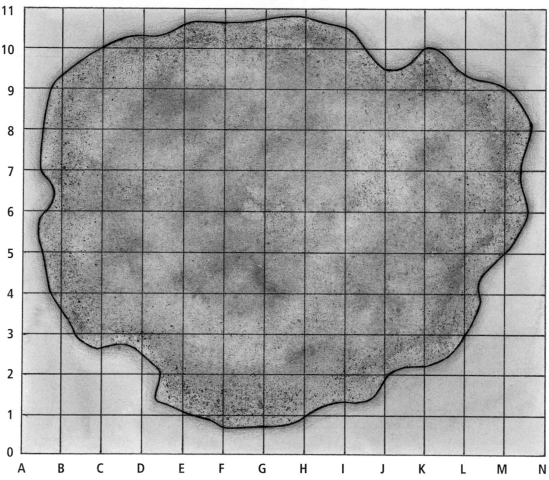

1. Place a tree at F4.

2. Place a rock at C2.

3. Place a water hole at J7.

4. Add three more items to your map. Name and locate each item.

5. Add the four cardinal directions (**N**orth, **S**outh, **E**ast, **W**est).

6. a) Place a monkey on your map.

   b) Plan a route for the monkey to get to the water hole. Remember, it can travel only in straight lines going north, south, east, or west. Draw your monkey's route on the map.

   c) Describe your route in words. Be sure to include direction and distance.

   d) Add a legend to your map.

Technology

You can use a paint/draw computer program to create a grid. Then you can complete Practice electronically, and use symbols to represent each object to be placed on the map.

Lesson 1: Exploring Maps   **357**

Lesson 2

Designing Maps

FACT BOOK

PLAN:
You will create your own map to track the paths of animals.

FACTS:
Scientists are always looking for ways to track the paths of animals to learn more about them. Such information is crucial to protect these creatures.

Satellite transmitters attached to leatherback turtles help scientists learn about their migration routes.

Get Started

You are going to plan and make a map of a different environment. You may choose your backyard, your schoolyard, or a place you might like to visit, such as a field or a beach.

Your map must have three animals, several plants, and at least two objects, such as a rock, sandbox, or garbage can. Draw your map on a piece of grid paper. Be sure to add the directions (north, south, east, west) and a legend.

Build Your Understanding

Design Some Paths

1. Plan and draw a path for one of the animals on the map you created in Get Started.

2. On a separate piece of paper, describe the path for another one of the animals for a classmate to draw on your map.

3. Exchange maps with a partner.

   a) On a separate piece of paper, describe the path of the animal marked on your partner's map.

   b) Using the description written by your partner, draw the path of the second animal.

4. Check the accuracy of your partner's work on your map. Share your observations with your partner.

What Did You Learn?

As a class, discuss the challenges involved in creating your own maps.

Practice

1. Was it easier to make a path on the map by following your own instructions, or was it easier to follow your partner's instructions? Explain.

2. Could you have made your instructions to create a path on the map clearer for your partner? How?

Lesson 3

Exploring Probability

FACT BOOK

PLAN:
You will decide what you think the chance is of something happening based on information you already know.

FACTS:
Is there a solution to the problem of harming natural habitats? You might have thought it was impossible, but nature is often able to heal many of the problems in the environment on its own. For example, cattails are tall plants with brown tops that can quickly absorb materials that can pollute the water, leaving pure, clean water.

Cattails often grow in wetlands.

Get Started

1. List three things that you think are impossible.
2. List three things that you think are possible.
3. List three things that you think are certain to happen.

Look at the illustrations on this page. For each statement below an illustration, choose a word from this list to describe the situation:

- possible
- impossible
- certain

1. The butterfly bush attracted the butterflies.

2. The polar bear is a good dancer.

3. The polar bear enjoys freezing cold water.

4. Recycling is a good idea.

5. The duck enjoys a long bike ride.

6. Putting trash in the trash can keeps the park cleaner.

Likely or Not Likely

1. With a partner, write

   a) two sentences that tell things that are certain

   b) two sentences that tell things that are impossible

   c) two sentences that tell things that are possible

2. With a partner, write

   a) two sentences that tell about things that are equally likely

   b) two sentences that tell about things that are not equally likely. Use the words "more likely" and "less likely."

What Did You Learn?

1. How did you decide whether various things would happen?

2. Use examples to explain the meaning of certain, possible, and impossible.

Vocabulary

certain: When something will happen
impossible: When something cannot happen
probability: The part of mathematics that looks at the chances or likelihood that an event will happen
possible: When something can happen

Journal

Think of other situations where you could use possible, impossible, certain, and uncertain. Record them in your journal.

Practice

1. State whether the following statements are true or false. Justify your choice.

    a) It is less likely that it will snow than rain tomorrow.

    b) It is equally likely that the students in grade 4 and grade 5 will play outside at recess.

    c) It is more likely that the principal will teach your math class than your regular teacher.

2. Choose a word to describe each statement below: possible, impossible, certain.

    a) You will run in the next Olympics.

    b) The sun will come up tomorrow.

    c) It will snow tomorrow if it is 30°C outside.

    d) It will be cloudy tomorrow.

    e) You will see a giraffe one day.

    f) You will have pizza for supper.

3. Make up three statements that tell about things that are equally likely, more likely, and less likely. (Use Practice question 1 to help you.) Give your statements to a classmate to decide if they are true or false. Make sure your classmate justifies his or her choice.

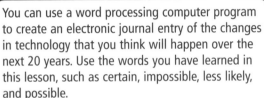

Technology

You can use a word processing computer program to create an electronic journal entry of the changes in technology that you think will happen over the next 20 years. Use the words you have learned in this lesson, such as certain, impossible, less likely, and possible.

Lesson 4

Examining Likelihood

FACT BOOK

PLAN:
You will investigate how likely it is that things will happen.

FACTS:
Butterflies and moths are a group of insects called Lepidoptera. Butterflies are usually found in warmer months, and they can be found all over the world. If you went on a nature walk in January to see butterflies, would you see any? What if you walked in a field of wildflowers in July?

Black swallowtail butterfly

Get Started

In math, something that happens is called an event. For any event, there are two extremes:

1. no chance at all that it will happen

2. absolute certainty that it will happen

The middle position is an even chance that the event will happen or will not happen.

No chance	Even chance	Absolutely certain

Less probable ⟵——•——⟶ More probable

We can describe these possibilities in numbers as well.

$0 \longleftarrow \qquad \frac{1}{2} \qquad \longrightarrow 1$

You are told that a bag contains 4 blue blocks. What is the probability of picking a blue block? What is the probability of picking a red block? Give your answers in numbers and words.

1. In a small group, create and complete a chart like the one below. In each column, enter things that you think have that particular probability.

No chance that these things will happen (impossible)	About even chance that these things will happen (possible)	Certain chance that these things will happen (certain)
0	$\frac{1}{2}$	1

2. Copy the blank spinner face to the right into your notebook three times.

   a) On your first spinner, colour in a space that a player will have almost no chance of landing on.

   b) On your second spinner, colour in spaces that a player will almost certainly land on.

   c) On your third spinner, colour in the space that a player will have an even or $\frac{1}{2}$ chance of landing on.

3. For the first spinner you drew, describe, as a number, the probability of landing on the section you coloured.

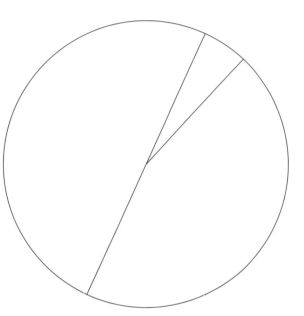

Build Your Understanding

A Chance to Win?

You Will Need
- paper clip
- paper
- pencil

With a partner, follow the steps that you used in Chapter 2, Lesson 4 on page 76 to make a spinner. Divide the spinner into four equal sections. Two should be dark and two should be light coloured. You can see a completed spinner on the top right of page 365.

1. Use your spinner. Take turns with your partner and spin your spinner ten times. What is the chance of landing on a dark section? Use numbers and words.

2. What is the chance of landing on a light section? Use numbers and words.

3. Create another spinner and design a game so that a player has almost no chance of winning. Include the following in your game:

a) number of players

b) object of the game (or how to win)

c) rules of the game

Predict the chances of a player winning. Invite classmates to play your game, and see if your predictions about the chances of winning were correct.

What Did You Learn?

How would you explain probability to someone new in your class? Use examples to help the student understand.

Practice

1. Look at this spinner.

a) Decide whether a player has almost no chance of landing on the yellow portion, has an even chance of landing on the yellow portion, or will almost certainly land on the yellow portion. Explain your decision.

b) Is the chance of landing on the red portion closest to 0, to $\frac{1}{2}$, or to 1? Explain.

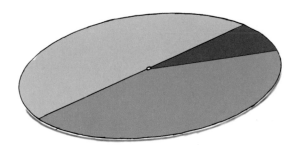

Lesson 5

Investigating Probability

FACT BOOK

PLAN:
You will continue to investigate probability.

FACTS:
When searching for wildlife, the probability or chance of seeing a whooping crane used to be very low. In 1941, most of the whooping crane's natural habitats were destroyed, and only 21 birds existed in the world. With the help of many protection programs, however, there were 383 wild and captive whooping cranes in the winter of 1999 to 2000.

Whooping crane

Get Started

You Will Need
• 3 red blocks
• 3 blue blocks
• 3 yellow blocks
• paper bag

Working with a partner, you are going to explore the likelihood of picking a block of a particular colour out of a bag.

Vocabulary

probability: The part of mathematics that looks at the chances or likelihood that an event will happen

1. Place three red blocks, three blue blocks, and three yellow blocks in the bag.

2. Predict how many blue blocks you will pick if you pick one block at a time and you pick nine times. You will return the picked block to the bag each time. Record your predictions with a tally mark in a chart like the one below.

	You		Your Partner	
Block	Prediction	Actual	Prediction	Actual
blue				
red				
yellow				

3. **a)** Take turns with your partner. Pick a block without looking.

   b) Record the colour that you picked with a tally mark in the "actual" column of your chart.

   c) Return the block to the bag. Pick nine times each in total and record the colour each time.

4. How many times did you choose red? How many times did your partner choose red? How close were the results to your predictions?

5. Write the number of times you chose a red block as a fraction with denominator of 9.

Since there are three red blocks, and nine blocks in all, you could say your chances of picking a red block were

$$\frac{3 \text{ (number of red blocks)}}{9 \text{ (total number of blocks)}}$$

$\frac{3}{9}$ is the probability of picking up a red block.

---

6. How close were your results to $\frac{3}{9}$?

7. What is the probability of picking a blue block? Answer in fraction form.

8. What is the probability of picking a yellow block? Answer in fraction form.

Build Your Understanding

Explore Further

You Will Need
- 6 red blocks
- 3 blue blocks
- 3 yellow blocks
- paper bag

This time you are going to change the blocks so that one colour has a better chance than the others of being picked. Use a total of 12 blocks.

1. Place six red blocks, three blue blocks, and three yellow blocks in the bag. Predict how many of each colour block will be picked if you pick 12 times. Write the probability of each colour being picked as a fraction.

2. With your partner, take turns selecting a block, recording your results, and then replacing the block. Each of you should have 12 turns. Record your results in a tally chart.

3. How closely did your results match your predictions?

What Did You Learn?

1. Explain how you predicted what the chances were for each colour to be picked.

2. Why does increasing the number of one colour give it a better chance of being picked?

Imagine that you could pick one marble out of the bowl on the right without looking. What are all the possible outcomes or results?

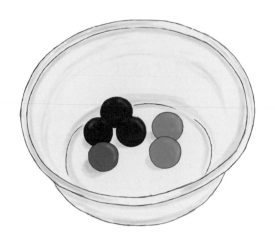

1. What is the probability, in fraction form, of selecting a green marble?

2. What is the probability of selecting a red marble?

3. What is the probability of selecting a blue marble?

4. Which colour are you most likely to pick? Why?

5. What do all the fractions in questions 1, 2, and 3 add up to? Show your work.

6. Draw a bowl of marbles of your own and answer questions 1 to 5, for your own bowl of marbles.

Show What You Know

Review: Lessons 1 to 5, Maps and Probability

1. With your teacher's permission, use the Internet to find a map of the area in which you live. Try to find the street that you live on.

2. Create your own map of the area in which you live, using the map that you found on the Internet for reference. Add some landmarks to your map from your neighbourhood, for example, a park, a store, or a tree. Don't forget to add the cardinal directions (N, S, E, W) and a legend on your map.

3. Create a probability quiz for another classmate to answer.

   a) Create sentences and make sure some are certain, possible, and impossible. Keep a record of the answers on a separate piece of paper.

   b) Give your quiz to a classmate, and have him or her match each statement to a number value: 0 for impossible, $\frac{1}{2}$ for possible, and 1 for certain. Check your classmate's answers by comparing them with your own.

Lesson 6

Reading Double-Line Graphs

FACT BOOK

PLAN:

You will look at double-line graphs to analyze data about ducks and other species.

FACTS:

One reason that species become endangered or extinct is the destruction of their habitat (the areas where they live). Many animals make use of wetlands (an area of land that is covered with water).

Canada is losing many of its wetlands, but we can protect them by restricting human activity (by building a boardwalk, for example) and by decreasing pollution.

A Canadian wetland

Get Started

The double-line graph to the right illustrates the estimated numbers of mallards and wood ducks found in the wetlands in eastern Canada.

1. How many years of data are displayed on the graph?

2. How many mallard ducks were there in 1991? in 1995? What is the difference in these numbers?

3. What is the difference between the population of wood ducks in 1992 and wood ducks in 1993?

4. What other conclusions about mallards and wood ducks can you make?

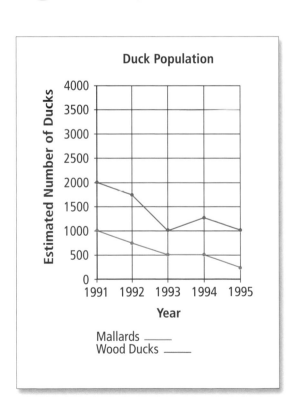

Vocabulary

double-line graph: A line graph that uses two lines to show how two sets of related data change over a period of time. One line must be different from the other.

Build Your Understanding

Analyze the Graphs

The double-line graph to the right provides data on the same estimated duck populations, between 1996 and 2000, after many wetland protection measures were taken.

1. Without counting (that is, by just looking at both graphs), were there more ducks during the first or the second five-year period? How do you know?

2. How many mallards were there at the end of the second five-year period? Describe the change from the end of the first five-year period.

3. What is the difference between the number of wood ducks in 1996 and that in 2000?

4. What other conclusions about the numbers of mallards and wood ducks can you make from this graph?

5. What would you expect the populations to be in 2010? Why?

What Did You Learn?

1. Is using a graph a good way to show information about duck populations? Explain why or why not.

2. What other kinds of information might be displayed using double-line graph? Give some examples.

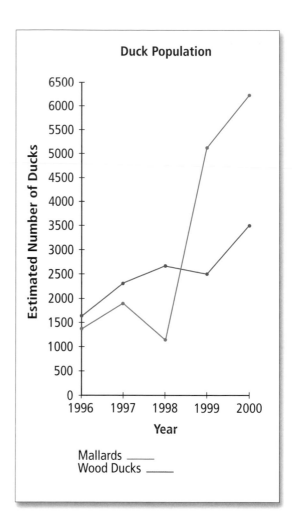

Duck Population

Estimated Number of Ducks

Year

Mallards _____
Wood Ducks _____

Practice

1. What are some advantages of using double-line graphs to analyze the data you learned about in this lesson? Discuss your answers with one of your classmates.

2. The line graph to the right shows the approximate number of butterfly species spotted by park visitors each month for a year throughout parks in southern Ontario. Write three questions about this graph, and then pass your questions to a classmate to answer.

Extension

3. Collect a variety of graphs from your local newspaper or from magazines. Select one to explain the results to a small group or the class.

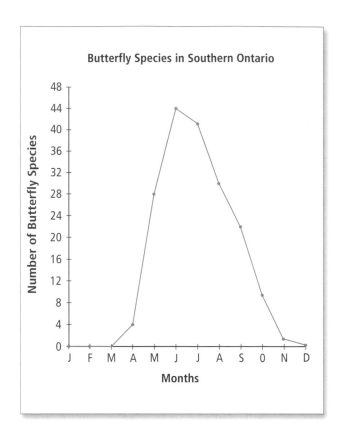

Butterfly Species in Southern Ontario

Booklink

Lifetimes by David L. Rice and Michael Maydak (DAWN: Nevada City, USA, 1997). What is the life-time of a shark? 10 years? 30 years? This book explores the life expectancy of various living things on our planet from ants to plants, with a lot of great information that can be organized into charts and graphs.

Technology

You can use a newspaper template in a desktop publishing computer program to create a newsletter about endangered species. You can research the endangered species on the Internet (with your teacher's permission) or by using books or CD resources. Write a brief article and share it with your classmates.

Lesson 7

Maximum and Minimum

FACT BOOK

PLAN:

You will analyze and graph information about Gros Morne National Park, and explain your results based on the maximum, minimum, range, frequency, and mean.

FACTS:

Canada has many unique national parks. Gros Morne National Park in Newfoundland is so spectacular and has such a unique landscape that the United Nations Educational Scientific and Cultural Organization (UNESCO) declared it a World Heritage Site in 1987. The park is over 1800 km² in size, and is home to many animals.

Gros Morne National Park, Newfoundland

Get Started

Here is a tally of some of the mammals one group of visitors saw at Gros Morne National Park in Newfoundland:

	Moose	Caribou	Snowshoe Hare	Black Bear	Lynx	Beaver
Number of Animals Seen	卌 卌 ///	卌 /	卌 卌 卌 卌 卌 ///	卌 //	//	卌 /

Make a bar graph of this information. Make sure you correctly label your graph, and don't forget to include a title.

Build Your Understanding

Analyze the Results

There are many different ways to examine the information in Get Started.

1. What was the minimum, or least number, of a single type of animal seen?

2. What was the maximum, or greatest number, of a single type of animal seen?

3. What is the range between the maximum and minimum numbers of types of animal seen?

4. What is the mean, or the average number, of animals sighted? Show your work.

What Did You Learn?

Which is the most challenging piece of data to calculate—maximum, minimum, range, or mean? Explain.

Practice

Find the maximum, the minimum, and the range of each set of numbers:

1. 9, 11, 18, 20, 23

2. 10 m, 13 m, 17 m, 26 m, 30 m

Find the mean of each of the following sets of numbers. Show your work. You may use a calculator to help you:

3. 5, 9, 10, 4

4. 63, 75, 47, 27, 18

5. 134, 209, 356

Journal

What are some other situations in which you could use maximum and minimum to organize information?

Technology

You can use the Internet to research the Statistics Canada Web site (www.statcan.ca). Find the heights of various mountains in various provinces and territories. Record the data, and find the maximum, minimum, range, and mean. Organize your results into sentences based on the data.

Lesson 8

Stem-and-Leaf Plots

FACT BOOK

PLAN:
You will use stem-and-leaf plots to
organize data about birdfeeders.

FACTS:
Many people like to feed birds from
a birdfeeder with various types of
birdseed. Some birdseed mixes include
sunflower seeds, peanuts, and safflower
seeds. Some birds have a favourite type
of seed.

Cardinal

Get Started

The numbers 8, 12, and 20 would
be represented on a stem-and-leaf
plot like this:

Stem	Leaf
0	8
1	2
2	0

When there is more than one
number with the same tens digit,
the ones digit is added in that
particular row. For example, if the
numbers 14, 17, 22, 28, 30, and 36
are added to the stem-and-leaf
plot above, it would look like this:

Stem	Leaf
0	8
1	2, 4, 7
2	0, 2, 8
3	0, 6

Vocabulary

stem-and-leaf plot: A chart used to organize a
collection of data. Numbers are grouped according
to their tens digits, from small to large. The stem
represents the tens digits, and the leaves represent
the ones digits.

Josie and her friends counted the number of birds that visited 14 bird feeders in the middle of lawns one morning.

Number of birds seen at each feeder: 12, 6, 9, 14, 20, 10, 17, 8, 3, 4, 6, 8, 15, 14

This information can be organized into a stem-and-leaf plot.

Number of Birds Seen at Each Feeder

Stem (tens digit)	Leaf (ones digit)
0	3, 4, 6, 6, 8, 8, 9
1	0, 2, 4, 4, 5, 7
2	0

What does this particular stem and leaf plot tell us?

Build Your Understanding

Investigate Further

A second set of bird feeders was set up near bushes and trees. These numbers of birds were seen at each feeder: 13, 23, 16, 7, 24, 19, 10, 26, 23, 9, 8, 30, 28, 19

Copy the stem-and-leaf plot below into your notebook, and complete it to display these numbers.

Numbers of Birds at Feeders Near Bushes and Trees

Stem	Leaf
0	
1	7

1. From how many feeders was this data collected?

2. What was the maximum number of birds seen on one day?

3. What was the minimum number of birds seen on one day?

4. What is the range of the data?

5. Which number or numbers had the highest frequency?

6. On how many days were 20 or more birds seen?

7. Which set of feeders had the most birds visit it? Why do you think this happened?

What Did You Learn?

1. Explain how the information in a stem-and-leaf plot is organized.

2. When might a stem-and-leaf plot be better to organize data than another type of graph? Explain.

3. How do you think the stem-and-leaf plot got its name?

Practice

The number of Canada geese wintering in Canada's urban areas has been growing. It seems that, because of interference with their natural habitats, birds that would normally have migrated south no longer do so. There are now generations of birds that have never flown south and don't know how.

These Canada geese were counted in parks in one city in December.

Number of Canada geese counted in each location:

34, 58, 12, 23, 6, 10, 45, 30, 12, 9, 16, 14

1. Make a stem-and-leaf plot to display the data.

2. Use your stem-and-leaf plot to decide about how many Canada geese were in these parks in December. How did you decide?

3. Five years later these numbers of Canada geese were seen in city parks and green spaces in December: 42, 67, 34, 68, 68, 50, 43, 23, 36, 57, 30, 15

   Make a stem-and-leaf plot to display this data.

4. How have the numbers of Canada geese in city parks in December changed over five years? How could you use your stem-and-leaf plots to decide how they have changed?

5. What was the range of the number of Canada geese in the first year? What was the range five years later? Show your work.

Lesson 9

Looking for Trends on Graphs

FACT BOOK

PLAN:
You will compare graphs about animal population and the environment, and look for trends.

FACTS:
The population of our living things, both plants and animals, can change over time. Scientists keep track of animal populations and watch for trends, such as whether the population is increasing in size, staying the same, or decreasing. The muskox is an excellent example of adaptation.

Muskox

Get Started

Here are three examples that show how animals have been tracked by scientists.

Example 1

The muskox is able to survive the harsh winter of the far north, but in the 1930s, scientists estimated that there were only about 500 muskoxen left in the Canadian Arctic.

In 1947, the government enforced laws protecting muskoxen: no hunting of muskoxen was allowed. The population was monitored, and by the 1970s it was estimated that there were perhaps 10 000 muskoxen on the mainland and Arctic islands.

If we were to graph the muskox population from the 1950s to the 1970s, it might look like this:

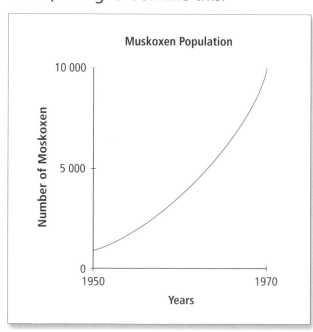

Example 2

The prothonotary warbler is a small yellow, blue, and green bird found in southwestern Ontario and the eastern United States.

There was a slow decline in its population from the 1930s to the 1980s, and a much more rapid decline since then. A graph of these changes would look like this:

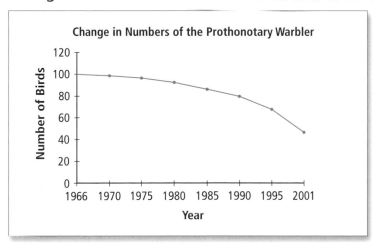

Prothonotary warbler

Example 3

The population of the white-tailed deer has remained steady over a number of years. A graph of the white-tailed deer population would look like this:

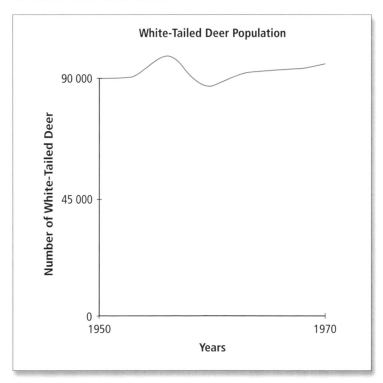

White-tailed deer

Discuss the trends you see in each of the three graphs. Predict how each graph might continue. Share your thoughts with the class.

Build Your Understanding

Investigate Population Changes

1. a) Read these three situations and match each situation with one of the graphs to the right.

Situation A

In one neighbourhood, many people were dumping garbage in a vacant yard. The rat population rose rapidly. Some neighbours got together and cleaned up the area and asked others to find better ways of disposing of garbage. The rat population stopped increasing and started to go down.

Situation B

The frog population in a rural area steadily declined for many years. Better ways were found to dispose of chemical wastes, and the frog population stopped declining and even increased a bit.

Situation C

Scientists are concerned about the rapid destruction of rain forests around the world. Some scientists have said that, if the current rate of destruction continues, rain forests may disappear. People are now protecting forested areas to help keep the size and number of rain forests steady.

b) Explain how you know that you matched each situation to the correct graph.

2. Describe the trends in the two graphs to the right. Copy each graph and complete the missing part. Explain your thinking.

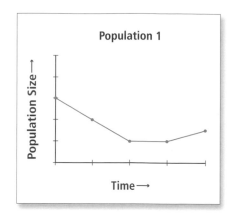

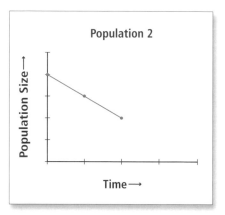

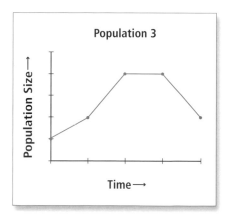

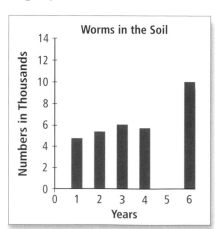

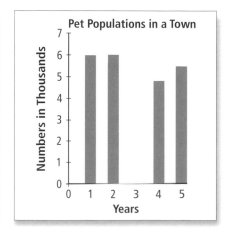

What Did You Learn?

1. How does examining graphs help you to understand some of the problems in the environment?

2. Why is it important to analyze graphs for trends? Give an example.

Practice

In 1944, 29 reindeer were brought to St. Matthew Island. The reindeer did very well. There was enough food to eat, and there were no predators.

By 1957, there were 1350 reindeer on the island. Six years later, there were 6000! But there was very little food left, and some of the reindeer were not very healthy or strong. The winter between 1963 and 1964 was very severe, with a lot of snow, making it difficult for the reindeer to find what little food there was.

In the spring of 1964, when the scientists went to visit again, they made a shocking discovery—many reindeer had died. By 1966, only 42 reindeer remained.

Here is a graph of the reindeer population on St. Matthew Island. Describe what is happening. How is this graph different from other graphs in this lesson?

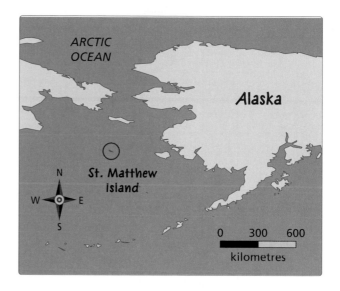

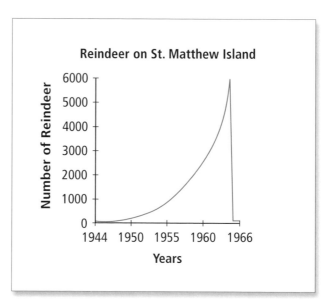

Chapter Review

1. Copy this map of a schoolyard into your notebook:

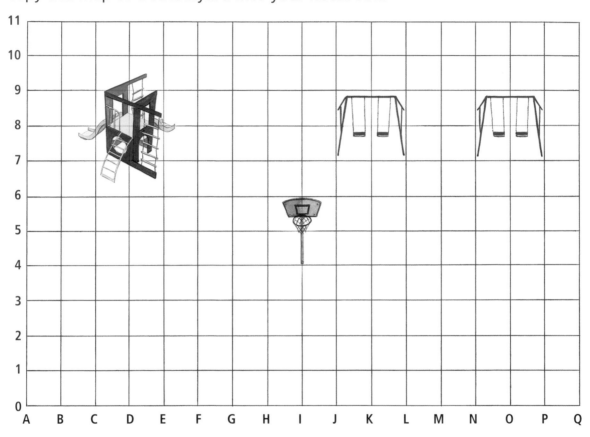

a) Put the cardinal directions (N, S, E, W) on your map.

b) Write the location of the basketball hoop.

c) Put the following on your map, and give their locations:
   (i) another basketball hoop
   (ii) three trees

d) A student enters the yard at A1. Plan a route for this student to reach the swings.
   (i) Draw your route on the map.
   (ii) Describe your route in words, giving both directions and distances.

2. Look at the bowl of marbles on the right.

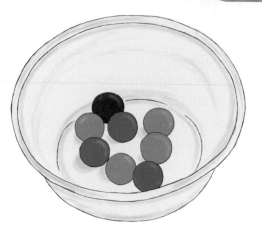

    a) List all the possible outcomes if you wanted to pick one marble without looking.

    b) Describe, as a fraction, your chances of picking a green marble from the bowl.

    c) What is the chance of picking a blue marble? Write your answer as a fraction.

3. For the following situations, use 0, $\frac{1}{2}$, or 1 to indicate the probability that the event will happen:

    a) The next student to join our class will be a girl.

    b) The teacher will start ballroom dancing in the middle of math class.

    c) We will go to sleep on Tuesday night.

4. Look at the following set of student ages:

8, 8, 6, 12, 9, 16, 4

Find the following:

    a) the minimum age

    b) the maximum age

    c) the range of ages

    d) the number with the highest frequency.

    e) the mean

5. The following is a set of data indicating how many birds were seen by each student in a grade 4 class:

16, 12, 37, 26, 30, 22, 23, 9, 12, 36, 39, 18, 43, 29, 17, 27, 30, 9

    a) Make a stem-and-leaf plot to display this data.

    b) What are the maximum and the minimum numbers?

    c) Describe what you can learn from the stem-and-leaf plot.

Chapter Wrap-Up

Create an extinct and endangered species presentation for your classmates. For your presentation, you will need to do the following:

• organize, display, and compare Canada's extinct and endangered species data
• make an extinct or endangered species spinner to analyze and explain probability
• create a map of the endangered species

Organize and Display Data

Status	Mammals	Birds	Reptiles	Amphibians	Fishes	Plants
Extinct	2	3	0	0	5	0
Endangered	18	21	5	5	11	50

1. The chart above shows both the endangered species and the extinct species in Canada as of May, 2002. Make a graph to show the extinct species data and another graph to show the endangered species data. Make sure you correctly label your graphs, and don't forget to include a title.

2. You are going to present your graphs to the class, but first you have to prepare your presentation. Write out the similarities and differences between your two graphs. Now write three questions you could ask your classmates about the graphs, as well as the answers.

Probability

You Will Need
• spinner face like the one shown to the right
• paperclip
• pencil

Follow the instructions on page 76 to make and use a spinner. Divide your spinner into three sections and label your spinner using three of the extinct or endangered species shown in the chart.

1. On your spinner, colour in yellow the space that you would have almost no chance of landing on.

2. Colour in red the space that you would almost certainly land on.

3. Colour in green the space that you would have an even chance of landing on.

4. According to your spinner, use the words "less likely", "more likely", and "equally likely" to describe the probability or chance of landing on one extinct or endangered species section in relation to another.

5. a) Spin your spinner 10 times and record the number of times you land on each section.

   b) Describe as a number the probability or chance of landing on each section.

Design a Map

1. Label a grid with letters from A to N on the horizontal axis and numbers from 0 to 11 on the vertical axis to design a map of endangered species. Place on the map each animal or plant species from the chart and record its locations. Be sure to add directions (north, south, east, west) and a legend.

2. A wildlife worker is visiting all endangered species on your map in order to improve each species' natural habitat to help the species survive. How would the wildlife worker get from one species on your map to another? Plan a path for the wildlife worker to follow from one species to another, and record the path on a piece of paper.

Now you are ready to present your information to the class. Have fun!

Problems to Solve

Here are some more fun problems for you to solve. In these problems, the problem-solving strategy that you use is up to you. Look back at all the problem-solving strategies that you have learned so far, and pick the one that works the best to solve each problem.

Problem 17

Making Change

STRATEGY: YOUR CHOICE

Problem

You Will Need
• play money (loonies, toonies, quarters, dimes, nickels, and pennies)

Imagine you have a toonie. Figure out as many ways as you can to receive change if you bought a box of raisins for $0.89.

Reflection

1. Create a chart to show the different combinations of change you can receive. How many different combinations are there?

2. Is there a pattern to the change you receive? Describe the pattern.

3. What strategy or strategies did you use to find all the different combinations of change? Explain.

Extension

Try this problem with other products of different prices and with different groups of money. Figure out as many different combinations of change as you can and share your solution with a classmate.

Problem 18

Arranging Numbers

STRATEGY: YOUR CHOICE

Problem

You Will Need
- egg cartoons with lids and bottoms separated
- dry beans or other materials to use as counters

Your school is going on a field trip to a farm and your principal needs to know how many school buses are needed.

Grade	Kindergarten	1	2	3	4	5	6
Number of Students	22	25	27	23	26	24	28

One adult supervisor must accompany every ten students. If a bus can hold 72 people, figure out many buses your principal needs to have for the trip. To help you, use the egg cartons as pretend buses.

Reflection

1. How many supervisors were needed? How many buses were needed? How did you figure it out?

2. Use pictures, numbers, and words to show how you arranged the people on the buses.

Extension

Imagine that on the way back from the farm one of the buses broke down. The replacement bus holds 50 people. How can all of the people get back to school? Use pictures, numbers, and words. Explain your solution to a classmate.

Problem 19

Creating a Schedule

STRATEGY: YOUR CHOICE

Problem

You Will Need
• several different colours of cubes
• number cubes

You and a friend are helping to plan a softball tournament. Six teams have entered and each team has to play each other team one time. There are two softball diamonds.

1. Work with a partner to organize the tournament.

2. On chart paper create a schedule for the tournament.

3. Play the games by rolling a number cube. Each roll represents one team's score.

Reflection

1. What challenges did you face when creating a schedule for the tournament?

2. What strategy or strategies did you use to create your schedule?

3. How did you keep track of the results of the games?

4. Which team won the tournament? Was the tournament fair? How do you know?

Extension

With your partner, design the playoffs for the tournament. How will you decide which teams play in the playoffs? Compare your playoff system with another set of partners. Discuss and compare how you designed the system and the results.

Problem 20

Buying Tickets

STRATEGY: YOUR CHOICE

Problem

You Will Need
• 20 tickets or 20 small pieces of paper

The Fun Fair has arrived and you and a friend want to visit all of the attractions. Imagine you have $20.00 to buy tickets with, and each ticket costs $1.00. You can visit each attraction more than once.

Figure out the different combinations of tickets you and your friend can buy with $20.00.

Attraction	Number of Tickets
Ferris Wheel	5
Roller Coaster	6
The Cups	3
Mountain Madness	7
Bumper Cars	4
Haunted House	2
House of Mirrors	1

Reflection

1. How many different combinations of tickets can you buy with $20.00?

2. How many times can you visit each attraction? How many attractions can you visit? Explain.

3. In your notebook, explain the strategies you used to solve the problem. Did you use more than one strategy? Discuss your strategies with a group.

Extension

Imagine you have $30.00 to spend. The ticket prices remain the same, but now you have to pay admission and buy food and drinks. With a partner figure how much you will pay for admission, how much you can spend on food and drinks, and how many attractions you can visit. Explain your solution to the class.

Problem 21

Comparing Prices

STRATEGY: YOUR CHOICE

Problem

You Will Need
• classified advertisements or sales flyers for bicycles
• calculator (optional)

You have outgrown your bicycle and you want to buy a new one. To you help save the money you need to buy a new bike you must first sell your old one. You decide to place an advertisement in a local newspaper. You do some research to find out what each newspaper charges for advertisements.

Newspaper	Cost per word	Cost per Colour Advertisement	Cost per Photograph
The Sun	$ 0.10	$1.00	$3.00
The Star	$ 0.11	$2.00	$1.00
The Herald	$ 0.12	$3.00	$2.00

Imagine you have $10.00 to spend. Decide what you want to appear in your ad, for example, what you want to say, or if you want colour or a photo. Figure out how much it would cost to place your advertisement in each newspaper. Show your work.

Reflection

1. How much did each advertisement cost? Which newspaper would you place your advertisement in? Explain your reasons.

2. How much money do you have left over? How can you change your advertisement to use all of the money you have? How can you change the advertisement to save money?

Imagine that the bicycle you want to buy costs $100.00 and you sold your old bicycle for $35.00. You have already saved $30.00 from doing chores around the house. How much more do you need to save and how long will it take by doing the following chores? Work with a partner to solve this problem. Show your work.

Chore	Frequency per Week	Amount Earned per Week
Drying Dishes	3	$1.00
Cleaning Room	2	$2.00
Folding Laundry	1	$3.00

Problem 22

Measuring Squares

STRATEGY: YOUR CHOICE

Problem

You Will Need
• pattern blocks
• rulers
• paper
• scissors

The grade 4 class has been asked to make a quilt for the school. There are 25 students in the class. The quilt will be one metre by two metres and will be made of many squares. Figure out the measurements of each square if each student makes one square.

Reflection

1. Show your work using pictures, numbers, and words.
   What was the hardest part of this activity?

2. Which problem-solving strategy did you use to solve this
   problem? Explain to a classmate why you chose this strategy.
   Which strategy did your classmate use? Discuss and compare
   your results.

Extension

As a class, decide on a size for a paper quilt. Determine the size
of each square piece of paper. Use pattern blocks to make an
interesting design that tessellates. Colour your tessellation and
create a bulletin board display.

Vocabulary

tessellation: A grouping of two-dimensional
figures usually of the same shape and size that
cover a surface without overlapping or leaving
gaps

Celebrating Math

Congratulations! You have learned many new things this year, and now it's time to use what you have learned to celebrate. In Celebrating Math, you will prepare for a Sports Day. There are six fun activities that let you practise the math skills you have learned.

Before you begin Celebrating Math, look through your notebook and journal. Think about all the math skills you have learned throughout the year. Think about what you liked most and what you found most challenging. Discuss your answers with a classmate.

Lesson 1

Dividing Teams

SPORTS JOURNAL

PLAN:
You will use your division skills to make teams.

FACTS:
Today you will begin preparing for Sports Day.

Get Started

During the year you have learned about division. With a partner, share what you have learned. What do you find the easiest about division? What do you find the most challenging? Why?

Build Your Understanding

Organize the Teams

You Will Need
• counters

Imagine that your school has 267 students from kindergarten to grade 8. For sports day, students have been organized into nine teams.

1. How many students are on each team if the teams must have the same number of students? Use pictures, numbers, and words.

2. You will notice that there is a remainder when you try to form teams. These remaining students were placed into teams:

   • Three of the remaining students were placed on Team 6. One fewer was placed on Team 5.

   • Half as many students were placed on Team 3, as were placed on Team 5.

   How many students are on each team now?

3. At this school, there is almost exactly an equal number of students in each grade. What is the lowest number of grade 4 students on each team if grade 4 students are divided equally among all nine teams?

What Did You Learn?

1. Explain how you figured out how many students would be on each team.

2. Explain how you figured out how many students from grade 4 would be on each team.

3. What would happen to the number of students on each team if the total number of teams increased?

4. What would happen to the number of students on each team if the total number of teams decreased?

Practice

Math Problems to Solve

Fill in the blanks to make the problem true.

1. ■ ÷ ■ = 20

2. ■ ÷ ■ = 33

3. Create more questions like the ones above, and share them with a classmate.

Lesson 2

Measuring With Fractions and Decimals

SPORTS JOURNAL

PLAN:
You will apply and practise your math skills related to fractions, decimals, and measurements to solve problems involving the standing long jump.

FACTS:
Long jump, high jump, triple jump, and hurdles are some jumping sports.

Get Started

Look at the standing long jump results in the chart to the right. Students have measured their jumps with a measuring bar that is one metre long.

1. Copy a number line like the one below into your notebook, and arrange students from the chart in order from longest to shortest standing long jump. Explain how you decided on your order.

0 0.1 0.2 0.3 0.4 0.5 0.6 0.7 0.8 0.9 1.0

2. Use your number line to figure out how many centimetres each student jumped. Record your answers.

Name	Fraction of Measuring Bar
Sri	$\frac{4}{8}$
Carlo	$\frac{1}{4}$
Ali	$\frac{7}{8}$
Henna	$\frac{3}{10}$
Bart	$\frac{1}{3}$
Dana	$\frac{9}{10}$
Ian	$\frac{3}{4}$

Build Your Understanding

Measuring With Fractions and Decimals

1. Work in groups of three or four. Pick an empty section of your classroom or gymnasium. Measure a 50 cm piece of masking tape and put it on the floor. This will be the jump line.

2. a) Each member of the group will try this. Place your feet so that your shoes do not cross the jump line.

   b) With your feet together, jump as far as you can. Stay in the spot where you land so that another person in your group can measure the distance you jumped.

   c) Each person should have three turns jumping and three turns measuring.

3. Keep a record of all the jumps in your group. When your group is finished jumping, arrange the jumps in order from shortest to longest.

4. Make a graph of the results.

What Did You Learn?

1. What unit of measurement did you use to measure each jump? Why?

2. What unit of measurement would you use to measure the high jump? What about the running long jump? Why?

3. Look at your results from the activity. Do you notice any patterns? Explain.

Practice

1. Review the jumps measured and recorded in the activity. Round each jump to the nearest decimetre.

2. What was the total distance jumped by your group? Show your work.

3. One group recorded the following long jumps in centimetres:

   55, 57, 58, 59, 59, 66, 68, 68, 74, 76, 77, 78, 85, 86, 86, 89, 91, 95, 96, 96

   Use the data to make a stem-and-leaf plot.

Lesson 3

Calculating Distances

SPORTS JOURNAL

PLAN:
You will apply your multiplication skills
to solve several math problems related
to running.

FACTS:
Running takes skill and endurance.

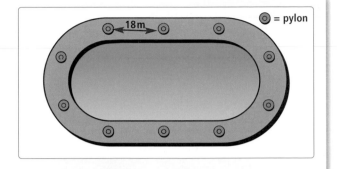

Get Started

Work on your own to figure out the total distance of each running
track listed below. Record your results in your notebook, and use
diagrams to help you, like the one shown in the Sports Journal.

1. $\frac{1}{10}$ of a track is 18 m.

2. $\frac{1}{5}$ of a track is 100 m.

3. $\frac{2}{8}$ a track is 50 m.

4. $\frac{3}{6}$ of a track is 200 m.

5. $\frac{3}{9}$ of a track is 125 m.

Build Your Understanding

Counting Steps

1. Work with a partner to investigate how many steps you run on
the spot in one minute.

One person will be the runner while the other person will
watch the clock and will time the runner for one minute.
Before you begin, estimate the total number of steps you think
you will run on the spot in one minute.

2. To figure out the actual amount, the runner will count the total number of steps during the minute of running. To do this, hold your hands out over your knees. Each time a knee taps your hand, count it as one step.

3. When the minute is over, record the total number of steps and then switch so that your partner has a turn.

4. Use your information to figure out how many steps you would run in 5 min, 10 min, 25 min, one hour, and one day. Show your work.

What Did You Learn?

1. Explain how you figured out how far you ran in 5 min, 10 min, 25 min, one hour, and one day.

2. Do you think you would really be able to run the total number of steps that you calculated for one day? Why or why not?

Practice

A Math Problem to Solve

What would be the most efficient way to run races if 267 students from your school have to run at least once? What method would you use to determine the winners? Explain your thinking using pictures, numbers, and words.

Lesson 4

Adding and Analyzing Scores

SPORTS JOURNAL

PLAN:
You will use your knowledge of big numbers, addition, measurement, and probability to solve math questions about throwing.

FACTS:
The discus, shot put, and team sports, such as football, all involve throwing an object.

Get Started

1. Imagine that kindergarten students, on average, can throw a football one metre. Now imagine that the grade 8 students, on average, can throw the football five metres. If, from kindergarten to grade 8, students' throwing improves by an equal amount each year, calculate the distance students in each grade would throw.

2. Explain how you arrived at your answer using pictures, numbers, and words.

Build Your Understanding

Hit the Target!

You Will Need
• beanbags

1. Work in a small group to design a target like the one shown below.

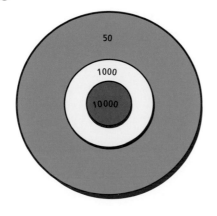

2. Tape your target to a wall.

3. Place a piece of tape on the floor that is exactly 2.5 m from the target. This will be the throwing line.

4. Which score space has the greatest probability of getting hit? Why?

5. Take turns throwing a beanbag underhand at the target. After each throw, record the person's score.

6. Repeat until everyone in your group has had three turns. Then calculate each person's total score.

1. Arrange the scores from highest to lowest.

2. Did you notice a pattern among the scores?

3. Did your results match your answer to Build Your Understanding question 4?

4. Do you think the scores on the target are fair? Why or why not?

5. How could you change the activity to make it more challenging or less challenging?

Practice

1. Repeat the activity using a new target with different scores, and a new throwing line at a different distance.

2. Look at your target and figure out the highest score possible in three throws, four throws, and five throws. Continue the pattern up to nine throws.

A Math Problem to Solve

3. Andrew, Diana, and Mario decide to repeat the activity using a new target with different scores. The smallest section on their target has a score of 1000. As each section on their target gets bigger, the score is cut in half. They take five turns each. Andrew's final score is 2500. Diana's final score is 3250 and Mario's is 2250. All three students hit each of the three sections on the target at least once.

   a) Draw a picture of their target. Explain how you decided on the scores for each section.

   b) Calculate how many times each student hit the different sections on the target. Make sure your answers match the students' final scores. Show your work using pictures, numbers, and words.

Lesson 5

Calculating Cost

SPORTS JOURNAL

PLAN:
You will use your math skills to purchase snacks for the Sports Day.

FACTS:
Many sport fans love to enjoy a special treat like popcorn.

Get Started

Imagine that you have conducted a survey of favourite snacks of some students in your school. The chart to the right shows what you found out.

1. Which snacks did students in your school like the most?

2. Which snack did students in your school like the least?

3. Think of two questions from the survey to ask one of your classmates.

Type of Snack	Number of Students
watermelon	卌 卌 卌 卌
popcorn	卌 卌 卌 卌 卌 卌 卌 卌 卌 卌 ||
oranges	卌 卌 卌 卌 卌 卌	
ice-cream bars	卌 卌 卌 卌 卌 卌 卌	

Build Your Understanding

Food Planning

You have been asked to help decide how much food is needed for students surveyed in Get Started. This chart shows how many servings there are for each type of snack.

Serving Chart	
Food	Servings
1 kg of watermelon	10 half slices
850 g bag of popcorn	30 small bags
1 kg bag of oranges	16 halves
1 box of ice cream bars	12 ice-cream bars

Use the school survey, the serving chart, and the illustration to the right to answer the following questions:

This is the cost of each type of snack:

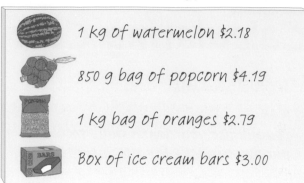

1 kg of watermelon $2.18

850 g bag of popcorn $4.19

1 kg bag of oranges $2.79

Box of ice cream bars $3.00

1. Make a shopping list of all the snacks you will need to buy for students surveyed. How much of each food will you have to buy? Would you have any food left over?

2. How much would it cost to buy all the food for the students?

3. Imagine that you paid for the snacks with a $50.00 bill. How much change would you receive? Draw the bills and coins you might receive as change.

4. Think of two other ways to show the change.

What Did You Learn?

1. How did you figure out how much of each food item you needed?

2. Explain how you determined how much money you would need to spend on each food item.

Practice

A Math Problem to Solve

Make up your own problem about Sports Day snacks. Give your problem to a classmate to solve.

Planning a Sports Day Event

You have reached the end of the Celebrating Math unit. In this unit, you have applied your skills to investigate and solve several math questions about Sports Day. You learned that math is very much a part of sports. For example, you need to know about division to put people into teams for a sporting event.

To celebrate the math you learned this year, write a plan for a Sports Day event. Here are a few questions to consider:

1. What will your fellow students do at your Sports Day event?

2. What math will be involved?

3. What are the rules for the event?

4. Will students be in teams for your event? If so, how many students will be on each team?

5. What sports equipment will you need?

6. What math equipment will you need? How will it be used?

7. How much room is needed for the event? Where will the event take place?

8. How will you record and keep track of results?

When you have answered the questions, share your written plan with your teacher. Are any modifications needed? If yes, explain why the changes were required. Then, with your teacher's permission, share your event with your class. Have fun!

Glossary

A

A.M. Before noon (from 12:00 A.M. [midnight] to 11:59 A.M.)

acute angle An angle that has a measure less than a right angle (less than 90°)

Example:

angle The figure formed by two line segments or rays that share the same endpoint

Example:

area The amount of surface inside a two-dimensional shape. Area is measured in square units: mm², cm², dm², m², km².

Example:

3 cm

3 cm

area = 9 cm²

array A grouping of numbers in rows and columns

Example:

asymmetrical Cannot be divided into parts that appear to be reflections of one another

average See *mean*.

B

bar graph A graph that uses parallel bars to show the relationship between quantities

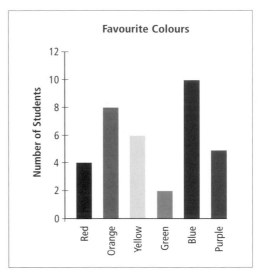

base The bottom face of a solid figure

C

capacity The amount a container can hold when it is filled

centimetre (cm) A unit of length
100 cm = 1 m

certain When something will happen

century 100 years. The year 1967 is in the twentieth century.

composite number A number that has more than two factors. The numbers 4, 6, 8, 10, 12, 14, and 15 are composite numbers.

cone A solid or hollow, pointed figure that has a flat, round base

Example:

congruent Exactly the same size and shape. Orientation does not need to be the same.

corner See *vertex*.

cube A three-dimensional solid with six congruent square faces

Example:

cylinder A solid or hollow figure that is shaped like a can. It has a circular top and bottom.

Example:

data Facts or figures about a topic. In a survey, data is information taken from people's responses to a questionnaire.

decade 10 years

decametre (dam) A unit of length

1 dam = 10 m

decimetre (dm) A unit of length

10 dm = 1 m

degree (°) A unit used to measure angles

denominator The bottom number in a fraction, which tells the number of parts in a whole

Example:

$\frac{3}{8}$ ◀— denominator

diagonal A line segment that connects one vertex in a four-sided polygon to the vertex on the opposite side of the polygon

difference The answer to a subtraction problem

Example: $10 - 7 = 3$
The difference is 3.

dividend The number to be divided

Examples: $12 \div 6$ $6\overline{)12}$
The dividend is 12.

divisor The number by which another is divided

Example: $12 \div 6$ $6\overline{)12}$
The divisor is 6.

double-line graph A line graph that uses two lines to show how two sets of related data change over a period of time. One line must be different from the other.

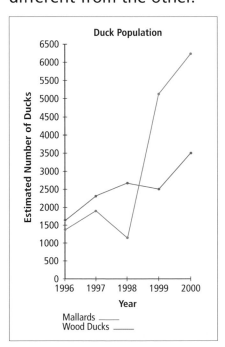

dozen A group of 12

edge The line segment where two faces of a figure meet. Edges can be straight or curved.

EXAMPLE:  edge

equilateral triangle A triangle with all sides equal in length

Example:

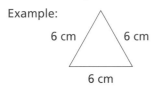

6 cm   6 cm

6 cm

equivalent Objects that are equal

estimate To find an answer that is close to the exact answer

expanded form A number written to show the value of each digit
Example: 2000 + 400 + 30 + 5 = 2435

face The flat side of a figure. A curved surface can also be considered a face.

Example: 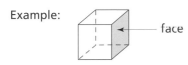 face

factor A number that is multiplied by another number to find a product

flip See *reflection*.

frequency The number of times a particular result occurs

geoboard A piece of wood or plastic that has rows of pegs or nails sticking out of it

graph A diagram that shows relationships between data. Many surveys show their results in a graph.

hexagon A polygon with six sides

Example:

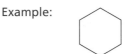

hectometre (hm) A unit of length
1 hm = 100 m
horizontal Side to side

impossible When something cannot happen

improper fraction A fraction with a numerator that is larger than the denominator
Example: $\frac{11}{3}$

intersecting lines Two lines that meet or cross at one point
Example:

irregular polygon A polygon with sides of different lengths without a pattern
Example:

isosceles triangle A triangle with two sides equal in length

Example:

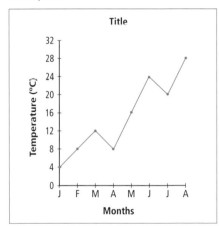
3 cm   3 cm
2 cm

K

kilometre (km) A unit of length
1 km = 1000 m

L

line A straight path in a plane made up of an infinite number of points

Example:
A   B

line graph A graph that uses a line to show how data changes over a period of time

Example:

Title

Temperature (°C)

J F M A M J J A

Months

line segment A part of a line between two points on the line

Example:
A   B

line of symmetry A line that divides a shape into two parts that are symmetrical

Example:

line of symmetry

litre (L) A unit measure of capacity. It is made up of 1000 mL.
1 L = 1000 mL

M

map legend An explanatory description or key that gives meaning to important symbols on a map

mass The amount of matter in an object

maximum The greatest number or amount reached

mean The average of a set of numbers. To calculate the mean, add up all the numbers and divide by the number of choices given.

metre (m) A unit of length
1 m = 100 cm

millennium 1000 years

millilitre (mL) A unit measure of capacity. It is one thousandth of a litre.
1000 mL = 1 L

millimetre A unit of length
1000 mm = 1 m

minimum The smallest number or amount reached

minuend The first number in a subtraction equation
Example: 10 − 7 = 3
          The minuend is 10.

Mira A small sheet of reflective but transparent plastic that reflects a drawing back, but makes it look like it's a continuation on the other side

mixed number A number that is part whole number and part proper fraction

Example: $3\frac{2}{3}$

multiple The answer given when a whole number is multiplied by another whole number

Example:

10	10	10
x 1	x 2	x 3
10	20	30

multiples of 10

N

net A two-dimensional pattern of a three-dimensional figure

Example:

numerator The top number in a fraction, which tells the number of parts referred to

Example:

$\frac{3}{8}$ ← numerator

O

obtuse angle An angle that has a measure greater than a right angle (between 90° and 180°)

Example:

octagon A polygon with eight sides

Example:

P

P.M. After noon (from 12:00 P.M. [noon] to 11:59 P.M.)

parallel lines Two lines continuously the same distance apart. They never cross.

Example:

parallelogram A shape that has four sides with opposite sides that are parallel

Example:

pentagon A polygon with five sides

Example:

percent (%) A number out of 100.

Example: 5% means 5 out of 100.

perimeter The distance around an object

perpendicular Meeting at a right angle (like one corner of a square)

Example:

pictograph A graph that uses pictures to show the relationship between quantities

Example:

How We Get to School	
Walk	★ ★ ★
Ride a Bike	★ ★ ★ ★
Ride a Bus	★ ★ ★ ★ ★ ★
Ride in a Car	★ ★

Key: Each ★ = 10 students

point A location on an object or in space

polygon A shape that has at least three straight sides

Example:

population The total number of people in a specific area

possible When something can happen

precipitation Any form of water falling from the sky or on the ground, such as rain, snow, or dew

prime number A number that has only two factors: 1 and itself. The numbers 1, 3, 5, 7, 11, 13, 17, and 19 are prime numbers.

prism A three-dimensional figure with two faces that are congruent and parallel and other faces that are parallelograms

Example:

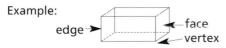

edge → face
vertex

probability The part of mathematics that looks at the chances or likelihood that an event will happen

product The answer to a multiplication problem

proper fraction A fraction with a numerator that is smaller than the denominator

Example: $\frac{3}{8}$

pyramid A solid figure with a polygon base and triangular faces that meet at a common point

Example:

Q

quadrant One of the four sections of an area that has been divided into four sections

quadrilateral A polygon that has four straight sides

Example:

quotient The result when one number is divided by another

Example: $12 \div 6 = 2$
        The quotient is 2.

R

range The difference between the maximum and minimum numbers

rectangle A polygon with opposite sides that are equal and parallel, and with four right angles

Example:

rectangular prism A three-dimensional shape in which all six faces are rectangles. A square prism is a rectangular prism with two square faces.

Example:

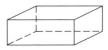

reflection (flip) The mirror image of a figure

regular polygon A polygon all sides and angles equal

remainder The amount left over when one number is divided by another
Example: For 20 counters divided into 3 groups, there would be 2 counters left over.

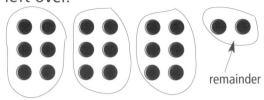

remainder

rhombus A quadrilateral figure with four equal sides and with opposite angles that are equal

Example:

right angle An angle of 90°

Example:

right triangle A triangle with one right angle

Example: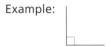

rotation (turn) To turn a figure around a centre point in one direction

rounding A rule used to make an approximation to a number. You should round up when the digit is 5 or higher, and round down when the digit is less than 5.

sample A part of a population selected to represent the population as a whole

scalene triangle A triangle with no equal sides

Example:
30 cm
13 cm
18 cm

slide See *translation*.

square A polygon with four equal sides and four right angles

Example:

standard form A number written as a numeral
Example: 2435

stem-and-leaf plot A chart used to organize a collection of data. Numbers are grouped according to their tens digits, from small to large. The stem represents the tens digits, and the leaves represent the ones digits.

Example:
Number of Birds Seen at Each Feeder

Stem (tens digit)	Leaf (ones digit)
0	3, 4, 6, 6, 8, 8, 9
1	0, 2, 4, 4, 5, 7
2	0

sum The answer to an addition problem

sunrise The time the sun first appears each day

sunset The time the sun disappears each day

surface Any of the sides of an object

survey A method of gathering information by asking questions and recording people's answers

symmetrical Can be divided into parts so that one part appears to be the reflection of the other

symmetry Parts are congruent or equal

tangram A puzzle created from a square cut into five triangles, a square, and a parallelogram

tessellation A grouping of two-dimensional figures usually of the same shape and size that cover a surface without overlapping or leaving gaps

three-dimensional Having three dimensions, for example, length, width, and height

Example: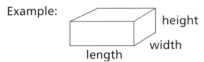

transformation The movement of a figure by a slide, flip, or turn

translation (slide) To slide a figure from one position to another position of equal distance

trapezoid A quadrilateral with only one pair of parallel sides

Example:

triangle A polygon with three sides

Example:

tripod A three-legged stand

trundle wheel A small wheel used to measure distances that are too long for a tape measure or that aren't straight

turn See *rotation.*

two-dimensional Having two dimensions, for example, length and width

Example:

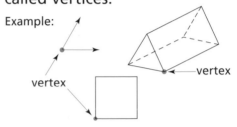

vertex The point where two lines of an angle or two edges meet in a plane figure, or where three or more sides meet in a solid figure. If there is more than one vertex, they are called vertices.

Example:

vertical Up and down

volume The amount of space inside a three-dimensional figure

Problem-Solving Strategies

Here are some helpful strategies that you can use to solve the problems that appear in *Math Everywhere*.

Problem solving is a very important part of math. Problem solving allows you to practise the math skills you have learned.

Sometimes one strategy might not help you find the solution. If that happens, try another strategy. Trying different ways to find an answer is a part of learning.

1. Act out the problem to help visualize the solution.

2. Draw a picture to help you solve the problem.

3. Use objects like counters or play money to find the solution.

4. For large numbers, you can make a guess and then check to see if your guess is correct.

5. Begin with the information from the end of the problem and work backwards to find the solution.

6. For complicated problems you can reduce large numbers to smaller numbers or reduce the number of items in the problem.

7. You can use concrete materials to build a model.

8. Looking for a pattern can help you solve many different kinds of problems.

9. You can make a table or a chart to help you organize information and find patterns in the data.

10. Making a list helps you organize information, too.

Here are some important steps to follow for all problems, no matter which strategy you use.

1. **Understand the problem:** Rewrite the problem in your own words. If you can, draw a picture of the problem. List or highlight important numbers or words.

2. **Pick a strategy:** You will be learning about many different problem-solving strategies throughout the year. For example, "Act It Out," "Draw a Picture," "Use Objects," and "Guess and Check."

3. **Solve the problem:** Use a strategy to solve the problem. Describe all steps using math words and/or symbols. Try a different strategy if you need to. Organize the results using a diagram, model, chart, table, or graph.

4. **Share and reflect:** Did the strategy you picked work? Would a different strategy also work? Does your solution make sense? Could there be more than one answer to the problem? How did other people in your class solve the problem?

Acknowledgements
Photographs

T = Top, C = Centre, B = Bottom, L = Left, R = Right

p. 3: DENNIS THE MENACE ® used by permission of Hank Ketcham Enterprises and © by North America Syndicate; 6: Fred Chartrand/CP Archive; 18: © Tim Thompson/CORBIS/MAGMA; 20: Memorial University; 23: Bill Lowry/Ivy Images; 27: Ivy Images; 31: (l) Ivy Images, (cl) © Jim Habel/Maxx Images, (c) © Angelo Hornak/CORBIS/MAGMA, (cr) © Stuart McCall/Maxx Images, (r) © Carmen Redondo/CORBIS/MAGMA; 33: © Bill Tice/Maxx Images; 36: C.I.S./ Ivy Images; 40: W. Fraser/Ivy Images; 43: © Kit Kittle/CORBIS/MAGMA; 51: COMSTOCK IMAGES/Henry Georgi; 54: Bill Lowry/Ivy Images; 55: COMSTOCK IMAGES/Stuart Cohen; 56: (b) Ivy Images; 57: (t) Bill Lowry/Ivy Images , (b) © Ero Sorila/Maxx Images; 65: (t) © Images BC/Maxx Images, (c) Bill Lowry/Ivy Images, (b) © 1999 Cameron Heryet/Maxx Images; 70: © Stuart McCall/Maxx Images; 72: Courtesy of Regina Exhibition Park; 75: Bill Lowry/Ivy Images; 80: (l) Jeff McIntosh/CP Archive, (r) Paul Chiasson/CP Archive; 83: © Bill Tice/Maxx Images; 86: Bill Lowry/Ivy Images; 89: © Altilek Images/Maxx Images; 107: (t) C.I.S./Ivy Images, (b) © Walt Anderson/Visuals Unlimited; 111: © Owen Broad/Maxx Images; 114: © Bettmann/CORBIS/MAGMA; 117: © Derrick Ditchburn/Visuals Unlimited; 120: Joe Bryksa/Winnipeg Free Press/CP Archive; 125: C.I.S./Ivy Images; 131: (tl) © Larry Wells/Maxx Images, (bl) © Thom J. Ulrich/Visuals Unlimited, (r) © Joe McDonald/Visuals Unlimited; 144: (l) Bill Lowry/Ivy Images, (c) C.I.S./Ivy Images, (r) Kevin Frayer/CP Archive; 156: © Garry Adams/Maxx Images; 167: (l) Bill Ivy, (r) Bill Ivy; 177 Michael Pasdzior/Image Bank; 179: Dick Hemingway; 185: © Hubert Stadler/CORBIS/MAGMA; 203: Visuals Unlimited; 227: SEF/Art Resource; 249: © Gerard Fuehrer/Visuals Unlimited; 268: C.I.S./Ivy Images; 269: © Gerald & Buff Corsi/Visuals Unlimited; 270: (t) © Fritz Polkin/Visuals Unlimited, (b, clockwise) © Joe McDonald/Visuals Unlimited, © Joe McDonald/Visuals Unlimited, © Warren Williams/Visuals Unlimited, Visuals Unlimited; 273: © James P. Watt/Visuals Unlimited; 277: (t) © Ken Lucas/Visuals Unlimited, (b) Art Wolfe/Image Bank; 280: © Al, Linda Bristor/Visuals Unlimited; 285: © John Gerlach/Visuals Unlimited; 287: © Walt Anderson/Visuals Unlimited; 288: (l) © Jack Milchanowski/Visuals Unlimited, (r) © Jerome Wexler/Visuals Unlimited; 291: (l) Visuals Unlimited, (r) Visuals Unlimited; 293: © Paul B. Swarmer/Visuals Unlimited; 296: © Dane S. Johnson/Visuals Unlimited; 299: © Joe McDonald/Visuals Unlimited; 303: (t) © Fritz Polking/Visuals Unlimited, (b) © Joe McDonald/Visuals Unlimited; 309: © D. Hayes/Maxx Images; 311: Tim Flach/Stone/Getty Images; 312: Bill Lowry/Ivy Images; 317: © B. Ormerod/Visuals Unlimited; 320: Bill Lowry/Ivy Images; 324: Bill Lowry/Ivy Images; 329: © Robert Pickett/CORBIS/MAGMA; 333: Bill Lowry/Ivy Images; 337: Image Bank/Getty Images; 352: Bill Lowry/Ivy Images; 345: Bill Lowry/Ivy Images; 355: Bill Ivy; 358: Bill Lowry/Ivy Images; 360: Bill Ivy; 363: Bill Ivy; 366: C.I.S./Ivy Images; 370: Bill Ivy; 373: Bill Lowry/Ivy Images; 375: Leonard Lee Rue III/Visuals Unlimited; 377: Bill Ivy; 378: Bill Lowry/Ivy Images; 379: (t) © Gary Meszaros/Visuals Unlimited, (b) Bill Lowry/Ivy Images.

Illustrations

Allen Clark: pp. 46 (bottom); Deborah Crowle: pp. 12, 19, 48, 66 (top), 92 (top), 95 (top), 106, 111, 125, 135, 212, 343, 381; Malcolm Cullen: pp. 233; Greg Douglas: pp. 3, 8, 24, 33 (top), 34, 36 (top), 37, 40, 43, 58 (bottom left and right), 62, 69 (bottom), 70, 71, 73, 76 (left), 77, 81, 83, 84, 85, 90, 92 (bottom), 93, 96, 99 (top), 104, 109, 112 (bottom), 113, 115, 120, 123, 124 (bottom), 126, 128, 129, 137, 139, 141, 158 (top), 161 (bottom), 162, 167, 176, 177, 179, 180 (top), 185, 192 (top), 196, 200, 202 (top), 236, 237, 254, 258, 358, 365 (top), 366, 371, 372, 386, 387; Stephen Hutchings: pp. 1, 11, 114, 124 (top), 145, 152, 157, 158 (bottom), 164 (top), 168, 170, 171 (bottom), 173, 182, 190, 203, 210, 234, 264, 284, 290, 360, 362, 388, 389, 394, 395, 397, 399, 401, 405; Jock MacRae: pp. 244, 340, 341, 351; Liz Milkau: pp. 16, 33 (bottom), 36 (bottom), 41, 46 (top), 51, 52, 53, 58 (top left), 66 (bottom), 67, 69 (top), 76 (right), 82, 94, 102 (bottom), 108, 112 (top), 118 (top), 122, 143, 147, 161 (top), 164 (bottom), 165, 171 (top), 175, 180 (bottom), 191, 192 (bottom), 195, 197, 198, 199, 201, 202 (bottom), 204, 207, 213, 215, 216, 219, 220, 221, 222, 225, 228, 229, 231, 232, 235, 239, 241, 243, 247, 250, 251, 252, 253, 257, 262, 324, 325, 326, 365 (bottom), 369, 383, 404; Dorothy Siemens: pp. 14; David Wysotski (Allure Illustrations): pp. 87, 89, 118 (bottom), 134, 275, 280, 293, 303, 304, 306, 313, 317, 320, 321, 355, 357, 376, 382.

Technical Illustrations: Jock MacRae
Icons: Carl Wiens

The authors and publisher gratefully acknowledge the contributions of the following educators in the development of *Math Everywhere 4:*

John Pusic
COORDINATOR—INSTRUCTIONAL SERVICES
School District 35
Langley, British Columbia

Tammy Wu
TEACHER, Caulfield School
School District 45
West Vancouver, British Columbia

Susan Brims
TEACHER, West Dalhousie Elementary School
Calgary Public Schools
Calgary, Alberta

Suzanne Prefontaine
SPECIALIST MATH TEACHER,
Holyrood Elementary School
Edmonton Public Schools
Edmonton, Alberta

Cindy Coffin
MATH & LANGUAGE ARTS CONSULTANT
Saskatoon Catholic Schools
Saskatoon, Saskatchewan

Denise McWilliams
TEACHER/CONSULTANT
formerly of River East School Division #9
Winnipeg, Manitoba

Michael Beetham
TEACHER, Westmount Public School
Waterloo District School Board
Kitchener, Ontario

June Buick
VICE PRINCIPAL, Our Lady of Fatima
York Catholic District School Board
Woodbridge, Ontario

Josephine Carnevale
TEACHER-LIBRARIAN, St. Edith Stein School
Dufferin-Peel Catholic District School Board
Mississauga, Ontario

Dana Free
TEACHER, H. W. Knight Public School
Durham District School Board
Cannington, Ontario

Wendy Gallant
VP/MATH SUBJECT LEADER, Archbishop O'Sullivan
Algonquin and Lakeshore CDSB
Kingston, Ontario

Dianne Phillips
CONSULTANT
Upper Canada District School Board
Prescott, Ontario

Theresa Spencer
SPECIAL ASSIGNMENT TEACHER
Sudbury Catholic District School Board
Sudbury, Ontario

James King
PRINCIPAL, Robert Jamison School
Halifax Regional School Board
Oyster Pond, Nova Scotia

Ruth LeBlanc
MATH MENTOR
Moncton School District 2
Riverview, New Brunswick